KU-545-265

CHATHAM HOUSE
SCHOOL RAMSGATE
LIBRARY

B.S.U.C. - LIBRARY

00280141

THE NOVELS OF
JANE AUSTEN

AN INTERPRETATION

THE NOVELS OF JANE AUSTEN

AN INTERPRETATION

Darrel Mansell

© Darrel Mansell 1973

All rights reserved. No part of this publication may be
reproduced or transmitted, in any form or by any means,
without permission

First edition 1973
Reprinted 1974, 1978

Published by
THE MACMILLAN PRESS LIMITED
London and Basingstoke
Associated companies in Delhi Dublin Hong Kong
Johannesburg Lagos Melbourne New York
Singapore Tokyo

ISBN 0 333 14661 1

Printed in Hong Kong

BATH SPA UNIVERSITY
CORSHAM COURT LIBRARY
Class No.
823 AR7   AUS M
30/10/2015

This book is sold subject
to the standard conditions
of the Net Book Agreement

TO THE MEMORY
OF MY MOTHER AND FATHER

'This is meeting quite in fairy-land! –
Such a transformation!'

Miss Bates in *Emma*

CONTENTS

PREFACE

In Kipling's story 'The Janeites' there is a mess-waiter named Humberstall who becomes so fond of Jane Austen's novels that he cannot resist writing about them. He goes around chalking remarks on the side-plates and gear-casings of his battery's artillery pieces. On their Mark Five Nine-point-two he writes 'The Reverend Collins'; on their cut-down Navy Twelve he writes 'General Tilney', and on the Skoda, 'The Lady Catherine De Bugg'.

Humberstall does not know it, but he is a critic. And he has made the battery's artillery into interpretations of Jane Austen's novels. His criticism is not very satisfactory, and tends toward a heavy-handed allegorising of the novels. He has ignored their exquisite complexity; he has produced something simple and clear, yet crude. But any other way would have had its shortcomings too. Even the most intelligent critic of Jane Austen must decide just how intelligent he wants to be. It is both impossible and undesirable to preserve anything like the complexity of art in writing about it. Thus Northrop Frye has remarked that all commentary is to some degree allegorical.

This book on Jane Austen is a little closer to Humberstall's technique than most. I have concentrated almost exclusively on a single idea: how the heroines become prepared to take their places in the world. This is the very soul of Jane Austen's art. She is intent on taking her heroines through a course of psychological reformation to which almost everything else in her novels is subsidiary. The plots, the characters other than the heroine herself, and the settings of the various scenes are constantly and relentlessly being put to use in order to further the heroine's psychological progress.

To discuss Jane Austen's novels exclusively in this way runs the risk of reducing them almost to an inert paradigm; and a paradigm she repeats, with variations, again and again. That, at times, is not very far from what I have done. But the result, I hope, has not been to make her novels somehow mean less than they have before, but more. I have lived with them long enough to be convinced that the paradigm is in Jane Austen's mind as well as mine; and that our recognising her plan helps us to appreciate her remarkable genius.

To begin with, we can appreciate Jane Austen's art for what I believe it truly is: fiction that has been slightly tempered, and thus made somewhat brittle, by a preconceived intellectual scheme. Her book, like Faust's, begins *Im Anfang war der Sinn*. She has a cool, shrewd, orderly intelligence – more so perhaps than any other of the world's great novelists. Like her own Emma, she hardly drinks tea without a stratagem. Almost always behind a scene, a detail of dress or furniture, a remark, is her carefully contrived scheme. What exists in her novels usually does so for a 'reason': a reason that seems to have come first, and that is still vaguely discernible behind the fictive texture which clothes it. She is always systematically further-ing, little by little, the psychological development of her heroine from, and toward, a definite and preconceived point.

Indeed I think Jane Austen's greatness partly lies here, in the scheme. Her efforts to fictionalise what she has planned, her efforts to find persons, places and things that will invest her scheme with a seemingly autonomous fictive life, are occasion-ally not very successful; and more important, are never of very great concern to her. She is not nearly so concerned to make her material seem 'real' as she is to use it efficiently. Often she seems merely to be using whatever minimal fictive details – a Colonel Brandon, a piano – will serve the purpose. Almost always, that is, she is briskly using her material to move the heroine along toward the psychological point Jane Austen has in mind for her.

It seems odd that Jane Austen has been so consistently celebrated for her 'realism'. Her ability to conjure up scenes, characters and details which many readers have been moved to call 'realistic' is beyond dispute. But her determination to follow an intellectual plan results also in much that is not realistic at all. Indeed, I think it is the plan which most characterises her art. And it is on this that I concentrate. Thus I have gone a short way toward considering Jane Austen's novels as a kind of allegory in which her strong, consistent intellectual purposes have usually, but not always, taken precedence over what one could conceive to be the demands of realism latent in her material.

The plan behind the novels therefore seems to me the essential feature of Jane Austen's art. All that is complex, subtle and wonderful in the novels begins with this, and never quite obliterates it. And I hope my discussion of the plan can enrich our appreciation of the novels in another, more specific way. Anyone who systematically reads the criticism knows that there are many episodes in the novels, such as Willoughby's final interview with Elinor Dashwood, the accidental meeting of Elizabeth Bennet and Darcy at Pemberley, Mrs Smith's strange narrative to Anne Elliot at Bath – episodes that are puzzling because they seem so utterly artificial, so contrived. They seem not quite an integral part of the plot, but rather to have been imposed on it from outside. Here are the cruxes in Jane Austen's novels, toward which her critics are irresistibly attracted; and about which they often make remarkably similar comments. In a recent book the author even introduces one such obligatory remark with a melancholy fatalism: 'I do not think it is frequently enough observed that. . . .'

Many of these episodes seem to me less puzzling when we understand that they have indeed been contrived without much concern for their plausibility; that they have indeed been forced into the plot because Jane Austen's overriding intellectual scheme requires them. She is intent on furthering her heroine's psychological progress toward a goal; and when she needs them she is willing to create these episodes and all sorts of other details that are far short of convincingly 'real'. We simply have to accept that events in her fiction are often not 'caused' by whatever laws of cause and effect conceivably govern our real world and fiction which aims at some kind of painstakingly realistic imitation of the world. Rather, her events often happen merely because the author, pursuing her plan to take the heroine through a carefully worked-out course of psychological reformation, *needs* the event at a given place and a given time. The plan is often uppermost; the 'realism' of the event sometimes secondary.

Thus I am always trying to get at the idea that is behind, and perhaps even 'causing', these episodes. I discuss again and again what I take to be the 'uses' to which she is putting them; I relentlessly discuss how her plan to take her heroine through a course of psychological reformation seems to require a certain event at a certain time so that the heroine's attitude will be changed. At times I have even chalked rather simple and reductive comments on the sides of objects and characters when Jane Austen's purpose in introducing them has seemed fairly clear.

This book, then, is frankly a rather single-minded interpretation of the novels; and as such it is certainly open to criticism. Indeed Humberstall was called before a court of fellow Janeites and accused of writing 'obese words' on government property:

> I told 'em that the back-side view o' the Skoda, when she was run up, put Lady De Bugg into my 'ead. They gave me right there, but they said I was wrong about General Tilney. 'Cordin' to them, our Navy twelve-inch ought to 'ave been christened Miss Bates. I said the same idea 'ad crossed my mind, till I'd seen the General's groovin'. Then I felt it had to be the General or nothin'. But they gave me full marks for the Reverend Collins. . . .

But perhaps there is one criticism that I can forestall: the criticism that I seem to be claiming at last to have cracked Jane Austen's artistic code, and to have found her 'meaning'. This criticism seems inevitably to follow from a statement like the following: 'One who advances an interpretation tacitly claims correctness for it, and thus allows the logical possibility that it may be incorrect.'[1] I do not think that Jane Austen's novels have any single correct 'meaning' – certainly not mine. I have merely tried to emphasise one of all the diverse and even contradictory meanings her great art will yield, or endure. To do so I have had to isolate what I discuss merely in order to discuss it; and if my interpretation is to have any significant

---

[1] Monroe Beardsley, 'The Limits of Critical Interpretation', Art and Philosophy, ed. Sidney Hook (New York: New York University Press, 1966) pp. 73–4.

value it will only be because readers of Jane Austen's fiction
will be able to relate my own special concerns to what we all
recognise is the great complexity of her work.

As for Jane Austen's other critics and commentators, I have
been influenced by them. In a lecture on her novels given at
Newnham College, Cambridge, and published in 1911, A. C.
Bradley said, '. . . nor . . . will you ask me whether I have
anything new to say. I do not know enough of Austen
criticism to answer the question; nor does it matter. The faithful
enjoy comparing notes; and I offer you some of mine. . . .' The
days when one could strike such a grand attitude are past, if
they were not then. I have had to reassure myself that I was
not to any significant extent going over old ground before I
was ready to write the book. Nevertheless some of my material
is bound not to be new. For instance, there is the detailed
chronological account, in my first chapter, of the composition
of *Northanger Abbey*; there may even be instances of which
I am unaware.

Almost never, however, do the critics appear in my text. If
we agree or disagree on specific points I have invited them
out into the footnotes to air their views. But in a few cases
they have had their business, I mine; and so I have merely
chronicled in the notes some other interesting opinions on the
matter under discussion, without comment. I hope this has the
effect of obscuring what I have made too clear. The footnotes
are thus a counterweight to my own rather doctrinaire concerns.
There the reader may find how realistic a certain detail is; how
very beautiful is the description of the scenery around
Portsmouth; how very much in, or out, of the tradition of Fanny
Burney is a certain turn of the plot; how very much in
character a certain remark is, and how clever; how very ex-
pressive of Jane Austen's own attitude is the attitude of her
heroine; and other matters I almost never discuss, although
there would have been some value in doing so. I find on the
other hand that the critics have far from exhausted my own
theme: Jane Austen's use of her fictional material to further
a rather brittle plan for the psychological reformation of her
heroine.

But like Tom Bertram I have my debts. The footnotes are mis-
leadingly democratic, in that a few works I found especially

important appear alongside many others which were of only
passing interest to me. Therefore I want to record here my considerable obligations to the following: O. W. Firkins, *Jane
Austen*; D. W. Harding, 'Regulated Hatred: An Aspect of the
Work of Jane Austen'; Mary Lascelles, *Jane Austen and Her
Art*; Marvin Mudrick, *Jane Austen: Irony as Defense and Discovery*; and Mark Schorer, 'The Humiliation of Emma Woodhouse'. Finally, all modern studies of Jane Austen must be based
on the fine scholarship of R. W. Chapman. We are tracked
everywhere in his snow.

As for the organisation of the book, I have taken up the
novels in the order of their composition. Indeed I pay considerable attention to Jane Austen's artistic development during
her career. But enveloped in the first three chapters is some
material that applies to all the novels together. Thus in the first
chapter there is discussion of 'active imagination' in the novels;
in the second chapter a discussion of 'facts'; in the third,
'character'.

Finally I want to acknowledge the help of people who never
appear in the text or the footnotes. The book was begun on a
Dartmouth College Faculty Fellowship. Juliet Barron checked
my references and quotations, and found more mistakes than
I care to think about. Barbara Cunningham typed the manuscript. Most important, James M. Cox, Robert Grams Hunter,
Chauncey Loomis, Noel Perrin, Martin Price, B. C. Southam, R.
C. Townsend and Thomas Vargish all gave me self-effacing and
indispensable advice.

Hanover, New Hampshire   D.M.
July 1972

I

NORTHANGER ABBEY
'Active Imagination' in the Novels

1

Northanger Abbey was not published until 1818, after Jane Austen's death; but it is probably[1] the earliest of her novels. Its history during her lifetime is obscure and puzzling. Only by tracing out the details can we get some idea of when Jane Austen's career as a novelist actually began; and of where *Northanger Abbey* belongs in the course of her development.

According to Cassandra Austen's Memorandum of her sister's writings the novel was originally written in 1798–9;[2] and it has been shown that the chronology of the events in it accords fairly well with the almanac for 1798.[3] But a reference in the novel to Maria Edgeworth's *Belinda* indicates that Jane Austen

[1] Some critics mistakenly assume that the novel follows *Sense and Sensibility* and *Pride and Prejudice* in order of composition. See for instance Harrison R. Steeves, *Before Jane Austen* (New York: Holt, 1965) p. 334; Sheila Kaye-Smith, G. B. Stern, *Speaking of Jane Austen* (New York: Harper, 1944) pp. 12–13, 26; and Margaret Kennedy, *Jane Austen* (London: Arthur Barker, 1950) Chapter iv.

[2] A facsimile of the Memorandum appears in *The Novels of Jane Austen*, ed. R. W. Chapman, 3rd ed., 6 vols (London: Oxford University Press, 1965) VI, facing p. 242. Hereafter this edition is cited in the footnotes as *Novels*, and in my text simply by page number within parentheses.

[3] *Novels*, V 277–8. But C. S. Emden, 'Northanger Abbey Re-dated?', *Notes and Queries*, CXCV (16 Sep 1950), says that the calendar for 1795 will fit equally well (p. 409). He thinks part of the novel was composed in 1794 (p. 408).

was still working on her manuscript, or was revising it, in 1801 or later.[4] The 'Advertisement, By the Authoress' which prefaces the published novel states that the work was finally finished in 1803, that it was sold to a publisher in that year, and was even advertised by him (p. 12).

On 5 April 1809, Jane Austen (or someone on her behalf) wrote to the publisher Crosby in an attempt to induce him to publish a novel he had now had in his possession for six years. The novel is almost certainly *Northanger Abbey*.[5] In his reply Crosby points out that his purchasing the manuscript did not oblige him to publish it; and he offers to return it for £10, 'the same as we paid for it' (*Life and Letters*, p. 231). Curiously, Jane Austen let the matter drop. James Edward Austen-Leigh's *Memoir* of his aunt tells us that years later, in 1816, 'when four novels of steadily increasing success had given the writer some confidence in herself',[6] she then went ahead and repurchased the copyright.

The 'Advertisement' was written in 1816, since it mentions that the novel had been finished in 1803 and 'made comparatively obsolete' by the lapse of 'thirteen years' (p. 12); and so Jane Austen obviously had in mind publishing it at that time. But, curiously again, she never did; and the novel is last heard of during her life in a letter of 13 March 1817, when, under the title 'Miss Catherine', it is 'put upon the Shelve for the present. . . .'[7] There is no evidence that Jane Austen ever gave the novel its present title.

Obviously, then, the question of when *Northanger Abbey* was 'written' does not have a simple answer. Apparently by 1803 Jane Austen had written and had tried to publish some form of the novel we now have; and there is good reason to

---

[4] *Novels*, v xiii.
[5] For the letter see William Austen-Leigh, Richard Arthur Austen-Leigh, *Jane Austen: Her Life and Letters* (London: John Murray, 1913) p. 230. Hereafter cited as *Life and Letters*. The novel was then entitled *Susan*. See *Novels*, VI (*Minor Works*) 243; and R. W. Chapman, *Facts and Problems* (Oxford: Clarendon, 1963) pp. 51–2. The latter is hereafter cited as *Facts and Problems*.
[6] *Memoir of Jane Austen* (1871), ed. R. W. Chapman (Oxford: Clarendon, 1963) p. 138. Cited hereafter as *Memoir* (1871).
[7] *Jane Austen's Letters*, ed. R. W. Chapman, 2nd ed. (London: Oxford University Press, 1967) p. 484. Hereafter cited as *Letters*.

suppose that she revised it sometime after 1803. It was not unusual for her to revise her work over a long period. Henry
Austen's 'Biographical Notice' to the posthumous volume containing *Northanger Abbey* and *Persuasion* says that some of
her novels

> had been the gradual performances of her previous life. For
> though in composition she was equally rapid and correct,
> yet an invincible distrust of her own judgement induced her
> to withhold her works from the public, till time and many
> perusals had satisfied her that the charm of recent compo-
> sition was dissolved (*Novels*, V 4).

Northanger Abbey is clearly one of these works. The date of
which the novel actually underwent whatever revision took
place after 1803 is almost certainly 1809, the year of the letter
to Crosby, or a little later.[8] But it is impossible to tell for certain
just how extensive the revision was; and we are left with the
evidence in Jane Austen's own 1816 'Advertisement' to the
novel that after 1803 any revisions of it were not very
significant. In the *Life and Letters* the Austen-Leighs point out
that

> . . . in *Northanger Abbey*, while there is good evidence from
> the author's preface of a careful preparation for the press
> before she sold it in 1803, there is no mention of any radical
> alteration at a subsequent date. On the contrary, she
> apologises for what may seem old-fashioned in the social
> arrangements of the story by alleging the length of time that
> had elapsed since its completion (p. 96).

Northanger Abbey as we have it is therefore a very early
product. It stands somewhere between Jane Austen's juvenile
writings and the sequence of novels she published during her
lifetime, beginning with *Sense and Sensibility* in 1811.[9] It is

---

[8] There are some slight borrowings in the novel from a work of
William Gilpin's published in 1809. See my article, 'The Date of
Jane Austen's Revision of *Northanger Abbey*', *English Language
Notes*, VII (Sep 1969) 40–1.
[9] For discussion of the composition of *Sense and Sensibility*, see
p. 46.

an amphibious novel, having been preserved in a state that combines something of the girlish Jane Austen of the juvenile pieces and something of a later period when the novelist of *Sense and Sensibility* was emerging. One ought to make allowances for all this in considering it.

The *Memoir* notes that Jane Austen's juvenilia 'were generally burlesques, ridiculing the improbable events and exaggerated sentiments which she had met with in sundry silly romances', and adds that 'Something of this fancy is to be found in "Northanger Abbey"' (p. 48). Jane Austen was of course well read in the fiction of her day. She says that her family were 'great Novel-readers & not ashamed of being so . . .';[10] and much of the burlesque in *Northanger Abbey* comes to focus on two more or less distinct strains of fiction with which she was familiar: the sentimental and the Gothic. These two often appear blended even in the same novel, but they are usually distinguishable enough. The most obvious characteristic of novels that are predominantly sentimental is what the *Memoir* calls the 'exaggerated sentiments' of the characters. In the following passage from Henry Mackenzie's *Julia de Roubigné* (1777) a young man looks into the room where he and his love had said farewell the night before, and says:

> The chairs we had occupied were still in their places; you know not . . . what I felt at the sight: there was something in the silent attitude of those very chairs, that wrung my heart beyond the power of language.[11]

There are two strands in the plot of *Northanger Abbey*, and most of Jane Austen's burlesque of sentiment occurs in the first strand. In it, the heroine goes to Bath and forms a friendship with Isabella Thorpe, a young lady of tumultuous emotions who seems indeed to have come straight out of a sentimental novel.

Gothic novels deal in what the *Memoir* calls 'improbable events', although there are of course improbable events in all kinds of fiction. One of the most famous of the Gothic novels,

---

[10] *Letters*, p. 38.

[11] This passage is cited by J. M. S. Tompkins, *The Popular Novel in England: 1770–1800* (Lincoln: University of Nebraska Press, 1961) as 'characteristic' of the genre (pp. 96–7).

Ann Radcliffe's The Mysteries of Udolpho, a Romance (1794), figures in Northanger Abbey on several occasions; and Jane Austen has even fabricated a characteristic Gothic passage of her own in Volume II, Chapter v. Most of her Gothic burlesque occurs in the second strand of the plot, in which the heroine is taken to an abbey that she hopes is going to be furnished with a respectable array of long damp passages, ruined chapels, and ill-fated nuns.

It is impossible to make any clean separation between the sentimental and Gothic novels of the late eighteenth and early nineteenth centuries;[12] and in Northanger Abbey Jane Austen is often glancing more or less indiscriminately at 'romances' in general. She simply says for instance that Henry Tilney's affection would be a 'new circumstance in romance' (p. 243); that Catherine Morland's way of returning home is broadly and generally 'a blow upon sentiment' (p. 232; for other examples see pp. 34, 131). And even her more specific burlesque concentrates not on what distinguishes the sentimental or the Gothic, but what they have in common, what all 'romance' has in common: the improbability, the exaggeration that sets it off from real life.

The main difficulty with Northanger Abbey is that the two strands of burlesque never seem quite to fuse; and thus the novel remains two halves rather than a whole. This is indeed a fault, but not so grave a one as many readers seem to think.[13] For Jane Austen is not so interested in ridiculing sentiment and Gothicism as what they have in common. What they have in common thus

---

[12] The best general discussion of sentimental and Gothic novels is J. M. S. Tompkins's book cited above. For the coalescing of the two kinds see Walter Francis Wright, Sensibility in English Prose Fiction: 1760–1814, in Illinois Studies in Language and Literature, XXII, nos. 3–4 (1937) chapters vii–ix. And also Ernest Baker, The History of the English Novel, 10 vols (London: Witherby, 1924–39) V 203.

[13] For discussion of the problem of unity in Northanger Abbey, see C. S. Emden, 'The Composition of NA', Review of English Studies, N.S., XIX 75 (Aug 1968) 279–87; and his 'NA Re-dated?', cited above n. 3; also Frank J. Kearful, 'Satire and the Form of the Novel: the Problem of Aesthetic Unity in NA', ELH, XXXII (1965), 511–27. But then there is Sheila Kaye-Smith in Speaking of Jane Austen (cited above). She thinks 'Northanger Abbey is technically the most "perfect" of the early novels . . .' (p. 273).

unites the two strands of the plot; and this indeed has the effect of giving the novel one plot with two strands rather than simply two plots. In the strand of sentimental burlesque, which runs up to Volume II Chapter v, Catherine Morland meets what seems to be a genuine sentimental heroine; and eventually discovers that she is no such thing. In the Gothic strand which then takes over, Catherine is introduced in turn to what seems to be a Gothic abbey, and discovers that it is no such thing either. Jane Austen has made a perfunctory effort to intertwine the strands so that the plot will make one continuous thread. John Thorpe of the first strand, for instance, makes the heroine known to General Tilney of the second; and Isabella Thorpe of the first has an affair with Captain Tilney of the second. But the truly significant unity between the two halves of the novel is merely a thematic unity which is generated by Jane Austen's very reluctance to make the halves come intimately together in any other way than by the striking similarity of what the heroine discovers in each case. This is important, and needs more emphasis than it usually receives. In both halves Catherine's final discovery is that romance is an illusion, and that real life is something else.

To Jane Austen's contemporaries *Northanger Abbey* would have been pointedly anti-romantic. One of its early reviewers writes that 'We have been spoiled for the tranquil enjoyment of common interests, and nothing will now satisfy us in fiction . . . but grand movements and striking characters'; but Jane Austen, he goes on, 'never operates among . . . uncommon characters, or vehement passions.'[14] Popular novels of Jane Austen's time that are only vaguely familiar to us today figure in the meaning of this early work to a greater extent than they ever do later on. The sentimental and the Gothic come together in it to make an aesthetic value that the novel itself is reacting against. It is as if *Northanger Abbey* were drawing nourishment from its late eighteenth- and early nineteenth-

---

[14] An anonymous review of the volume '*Northanger Abbey*' *and* '*Persuasion*'. The review appeared in *Scots Magazine* . . ., LXXXI, pt 1 (May 1818) 453–5. Unless otherwise noted I have always cited the original text of Jane Austen's early reviews. This one is reprinted in *Jane Austen: The Critical Heritage*, ed. B. C. Southam (London: Routledge, 1968). Hereafter cited as *Critical Heritage*.

century provenance to give it energy to free itself so that it can move into a fresh, new environment: an environment of 'common interests'.

Jane Austen concentrates relentlessly on this point, that the sentimental, the Gothic, must give way in her novel to the unromantic, the common, the real. Henry Tilney's humdrum affections may be a 'new circumstance in romance,' but not so new, Jane Austen says, in 'common life' (p. 243); and Northanger Abbey aggressively sets itself up as a novel of common life. The heroine comes from 'plain matter-of-fact' stock; and 'feelings rather natural than heroic' possess her. She is guided only by what she takes to be 'simple and probable' (pp. 65-6, 93, 53). She falls 'miserably short of the true heroic height' in not being able to sketch her lover's profile so that she can be caught in the act, for alas she cannot draw, and has no lover anyway (p. 16). And when she leaves for Bath on her first journey out into the world, her feelings seem 'rather consistent with the common feelings of common life, than with the refined susceptibilities . . . which the first separation of a heroine from her family ought always to excite' (p. 19).

2

Northanger Abbey thus reacts against the exaggerations and improbabilities of romance, and self-consciously marks out as its own province the common feelings of common life, life in the real world. But the result is far from 'realism' in any ordinary sense. Jane Austen's is a precisely ordered world; one which has been purified of almost everything that does not contribute to the author's strong, purposeful design. It is a stylised world, that presents itself immediately as art, not as life. This is a fundamental truth concerning Jane Austen's fiction – although many readers seem to disagree.

There is the seed of a paradox here. Again and again her heroines are pulled down into a 'real' world; but her depiction of that world in the novels is so stylised, so much the product of a very selective, efficient and determined artistic consciousness, that the result does not very often even approximate the rich complexity of the world as we know it. One of Jane Austen's nieces reports that when she was young her aunt would tell us the most delightful stories chiefly of Fairyland. . . .'[15] The environment in which her heroines move is very often close to that. If Miss Bates were ever to open one of the novels, she might exclaim, as she does when she enters the ballroom at the Crown, 'This is meeting quite in fairy-land!—Such a transformation!' (*Emma*, p. 323). Hence in the following pages the references to Jane Austen's 'real world' refer of course to whatever carefully contrived and scant particulars she has used to symbolise such a world.

Jane Austen often sets her scene in a ballroom like the one at the Crown. In the third chapter of this first novel Henry Tilney leads the heroine out to dance in the Lower Rooms at Bath; and this seems an appropriate introduction to Jane Austen's tight little fictional world. Her novels are more like ballroom dances than like anyone's conception of life in the raw. They present the relationship between the sexes in a graceful, restrained and highly stylised form of art that has developed in polite society. Henry Tilney even considers dancing an emblem of marriage (p. 76). In dancing the sexual passions are celebrated in a ceremony that hints at their power while keeping them safely contained in art. The order of social precedence is celebrated, and carefully preserved.[16] There is room for slight innovation and the cautious expression of one's individuality, but again the conventional form of the art is always preserved.[17] There is nothing that could be called 'suspense' concerning the final disposition of the couples who began; only a gentle tension as they threaten to deviate from traditional patterns, but finally

---

[15] Caroline Austen, *My Aunt Jane Austen* (London: Jane Austen Society, Alton, Hants, 1952) p. 5.

[16] 'Balls in the days of Miss Austen consisted mainly of country dances. . . . We must picture to ourselves the ladies and gentlemen ranged in two long rows facing one another, whilst the couples at the extreme ends danced down the set; the most important lady present having been privileged to "call" or lead off the dance', Constance Hill, *Jane Austen: Her Homes and Her Friends*, 3rd ed. (Bungay: John Lane, 1923) p. 58. For 'Precedence' at balls see Thomas Wilson's charming *A Companion to the Ball Room* (London: Sherwood, 1816) p. 219. In *Novels*, IV (*Emma*), pp. 507–8, Chapman briefly discusses dancing in Jane Austen's time.

[17] '. . . persons so using them ["Hornpipe Steps"] must be ever considered, as being unaccustomed to good Company and of very vulgar habits', Thomas Wilson (cited in above note), p. 205.

do not. The destined couples thread their way through an intricate design, to be united at the close.

Here then is a kind of emblem of the fiction we are going to examine. In the Lower Rooms at Bath, in the gardens at Sotherton,[18] on Box Hill, on the shore at Lyme, Jane Austen's characters come together into couples and little societies that then dissolve away. There are few sudden physical movements[19] like Louisa's fall in *Persuasion*. In *Mansfield Park* when Edmund moves toward the harp Mary Crawford is playing, he is described as 'moving forward by gentle degrees'. This is characteristic of Jane Austen's art. In the country dancing she seemed to love so much,[20] all is harmony and regularity and symmetry;[21] and these words seem to apply easily to her novels, in spite of all the qualifications that take wing at such a thunder of abstractions.

Her novels thus exhibit an elaborate and artificial design. That design is the very soul of her art. What she considers 'common' or real in her fiction does not seem to have found a place there primarily because she felt such realistic touches to be intrinsically interesting, although she undoubtedly did. The particulars in her novels are there primarily to serve some definite symbolic purpose; and by far the most common purpose is to provide whatever minimal physical environment is necessary to alter the heroine's psychology in some specific way

---

[18] Robert Liddell notes that this scene 'takes on something of the character of a ballet', *The Novels of Jane Austen* (London: Longmans, 1963) p. 75.

[19] David Daiches mentions the 'ballet movement' in some of Jane Austen's novels, in *A Study of Literature* (Ithaca: Cornell University Press, 1948) pp. 114–15. And Mary Lascelles observes of the principal characters in *Sense and Sensibility*, 'there they all stand, formally grouped as for a dance', *Jane Austen and Her Art* (London: Oxford University Press, 1965) p. 158.

[20] For some indication of how frequently Jane Austen attended them see 'Balls' in the index to *Letters*.

[21] For the 'Harmony' and 'Regularity' of country dancing, see Wilson (n. 16 above) p. 193. O. W. Firkins says of the plot of *Pride and Prejudice* that it represents the 'imposition on life of a symmetrical elegance to which life itself is uncompromisingly hostile', *Jane Austen* (New York: Russell & Russell, 1965) pp. 26–7. Yasmine Gooneratne makes much the same point in *Jane Austen* (Cambridge: Cambridge University Press, 1970) pp. 10–11.

Jane Austen has in mind at that particular moment. It may be that in varying degrees this is true of all novelists, but of Jane Austen it is truer than most.

The world Jane Austen creates in *Northanger Abbey* is remarkably functional in this respect. Persons, places and events seem often to be written into the novel primarily, and often exclusively, for the specific effects they can have on Catherine Morland's mind. Bath, for instance, is far from a richly described geographical place in the novel. It is much more a convenient fictional setting for a great moral drama taking place within the heroine. The city has a compact, neat geography that Jane Austen can lay out into moral districts; and she seems scarcely interested in creating more of the setting than is necessary to further the psychological development of her heroine.

The result is that the provisional status which the reality of persons, places, events, and things must endure at least to some degree in all art becomes very pronounced in *Northanger Abbey*. Jane Austen's subject is the mental events in the single, central, controlling consciousness of her heroine; and almost everything outside this consciousness is allowed to exist primarily for the purpose of creating it. The particularities that are allowed to exist in the novel are almost always being purposefully referred inward to this consciousness; and the novel is thus like a wheel, in which the rim and the particular spokes are all organised around and supported by the central hub to which they lead.

Jane Austen always uses her material purposefully and efficiently to create mental events – although not always so heavy-handedly as in *Northanger Abbey*. Such an early novel is typical of her work all the same; it merely exhibits in an early form what she later learned to do very subtly. Throughout her career she is, to a remarkable degree, a novelist of the spirit rather than the flesh; a novelist faced always with the artistic problem of having to find some suitable fictive material to occasion her heroine's disembodied processes of thought; a novelist who seems much more at home in the mind than in the world. In *Emma*, Mr Woodhouse lives sequestered in his Hartfield, warmed by a fire; and when he hears that young people at dances sometimes open windows he exclaims '. . . I live out of the world, and am often astonished at what I hear.'

He is threatened with a solipsism that would leave him cut off from the outer world entirely, living an imaginative life aloof from it; and in this he is the extreme which his daughter Emma, Jane Austen's other heroines, and Jane Austen herself all approach to some degree. She too liked her fire (see Letters, pp. 84, 333).

As a novelist she makes shy, reluctant forays out into the world to bring back scraps that she can treasure up, fondle, and invest with imaginative meaning, like Harriet Smith with her box of 'Most precious treasures'. The amount of material reality Jane Austen actually takes into her novels is remarkably small: a bit of court plaister, a pencil-end to invest with great meaning. There is very little particular detail, and usually even that is rigorously functional. How obvious this all seems! Furthermore, the 'character' she gives the people in her novels other than the heroine is for the most part devoid of characteristics that do not have a direct effect on the consciousness of the heroine herself (see below, pp. 16–17; and Chapter III, pp. 53–60). Even the very plots of her novels seem, at points, to be only half-hearted, perfunctory makeshifts that will help along a heroine's psychological drama which has all but retired inward.

And there are moments when these plots simply leave 'probability' behind. In any literature that follows a narrative plot there must always be a tension between events as they are caused by whatever laws of probability seem to govern the real world, and those same events as they seem to be caused by the author, pursuing whatever we can divine of his own thematic purposes. Biography may be at the extreme where the tension has almost relaxed in favour of the logic of the world; and perhaps allegory is at the other extreme where the author's own purposes have almost triumphed, and where reference to the mundane laws of cause and effect would turn almost everything into 'coincidence'. Novels of course fall somewhere in between; but Jane Austen's fall much closer to the latter extreme than most of her critics seem to think.

There are many important events in them that simply do not follow the same laws of cause and effect that such events would follow in real life or in novels that aim conscientiously to represent real life. Jane Austen's strongest concern is always to put her heroine through a carefully worked-out course of spiritual development, to which any other kind of 'plot' is going to be subservient. She does not hesitate to violate 'probability' if her own thematic purposes require it; although, because she is Jane Austen and not John Bunyan, she prefers of course to maintain the illusion of thoroughgoing reality in so far as it does not conflict with those purposes. But what characterises Jane Austen's art is that the higher purposes are always there; and as her art progresses she seems even less concerned with the semblance of realism in her plots. Her true plot appears closer and closer to that ideal state of disembodied spirituality where the makeshifts of art would have disappeared completely.

3

In *Northanger Abbey* Jane Austen is using her material to express what is essentially an inner drama. The plot is concerned with the first entrance of a young lady into the world. This is of course a common plot during the period. The sub-title of Fanny Burney's *Evelina* (1778), with which Jane Austen was familiar,[22] is 'The History of a Young Lady's Entrance into the World'.[23] For Jane Austen the plot becomes the fictional expression of the one psychological 'action' that is common to all her novels: a young lady who is headstrong enough to have created an imaginative world that conforms to her own aesthetic ideals is introduced to whatever in the novel represents the 'real' one; she is then slowly forced to surrender her aesthetic world to the real one; and the final, physical ceremony of surrender is her acceptance of a man from the real world as her husband.

Most of the later novels begin with the heroine already in possession of the aesthetic illusions that the world is going to invade. There may be a good reason for this: when Jane Austen's niece Anna was writing a novel her aunt gave her the advice, 'One does not care for girls till they are grown up'.[24] But *Northanger Abbey* is Jane Austen's one novel that begins with

---

[22] *Letters*, p. 64.
[23] For a discussion of Fanny Burney's phrase as it applies to *Northanger Abbey* see Kenneth L. Moler, *Jane Austen's Art of Allusion* (Lincoln: University of Nebraska Press, 1968) pp. 21–37.
[24] *Letters*, p. 402.

a brief account of the young heroine in the process of acquiring her illusions. Catherine is shown undergoing her 'training for a heroine; she read all such works as heroines must read to supply their memories with those quotations which are so serviceable and so soothing in the vicissitudes of their eventful lives' (p. 15). The heroine of Charlotte Lennox's The Female Quixote (1752) has likewise read novels until she has become possessed by ideas of a 'romantic Turn; and, supposing Romances were real Pictures of Life, from them she drew all her Notions . . .'.[25] Catherine is now aesthetically prepared to find a lover who will 'call forth her sensibility'. She is now prepared, and determined, to go out and be a 'heroine' (p. 16); and the first chapter ends with the invitation to Bath that will be her entrance into the world.

At the moment Catherine enters the world she seems to be under two different kinds of illusion. She has read enough of the books Jane Austen is burlesquing to have become positively charged with sensibility, with the result that she suffers from what Jane Austen's contemporary, Richard Payne Knight, describes as 'a sort of sickly sensibility of mind,' a 'trembling irritability of habit, which cannot stoop to the tameness of reality . . .'.[26] This of course is the stock in trade of romantic novels. On the other hand Jane Austen's heroine is also simply ignorant. Because she knows nothing of the world she believes it better than it is. She is later described as 'superior in good-nature . . . to all the rest of the world'. Who else could think that Captain Tilney's flirting with an engaged woman is simply 'good-nature', or that General Tilney is really 'generous and disinterested' and sadly 'misunderstood by his children' (pp. 133, 208)?

When her colourful behaviour can be ascribed to her own headstrong illusions she becomes the first of a long line of heroines in the novels: Elinor Dashwood, Elizabeth Bennet, Fanny Price (with some reservations to be discussed later) and Emma Woodhouse. But when Catherine seems merely naïve or ignorant she stands alone – although there is some resemblance

---

[25] (London: Oxford University Press, 1970) I i 7. Jane Austen mentions the novel in Letters, p. 173.
[26] An Analytical Inquiry into the Principles of Taste (London: T. Payne, 1805) pp. 446-7.

to the last of all Jane Austen's creations, Charlotte Heywood of 'Sanditon'. In *Northanger Abbey* there is some unfortunate confusion caused by these two apparent sources of Catherine's behaviour;[27] but for Jane Austen they seem to amount to the same thing: her heroine merely has illusions which are going to have to meet the common feelings of common life.

Bath in the novel is Jane Austen's stylised version of the real world, and she first presents it to her heroine as a panorama spread out at Catherine's feet. Catherine, having arrived there, moves up and up until, like Adam on the hill from which he can survey all Earth's kingdoms, she has a 'comprehensive view of all the company beneath her' (p. 21). Here is the world in its variety; and she later exclaims, 'Oh! who can ever be tired of Bath?' (p. 79). As she looks down she longs to dance. She longs to enter into the conventional, patterned, restrained movements of Jane Austen's world; as Elizabeth Bennet finally does with Darcy at the Netherfield ball, as Emma finally does with Mr Knightley at Mr Weston's.

Catherine is introduced into the dance; and one of her first partners in the delicate social movements that now begin is Isabella Thorpe, whose arm she is invited to accept. Isabella likes to pose as a young lady of sensibility, and she declares that her 'attachments are always excessively strong' (p. 40). To Catherine all this sounds familiar. She has been primed by her reading to have her own sensibility called forth, and soon the two are arm in arm.

The sensibility of these two takes the form of 'friendship', a word that has a special meaning for any devotee of romantic fiction. In the novels of sensibility it is just short of obligatory for young ladies to meet and fall into sudden, apocalyptic friendships. There is a fine example in Jane Austen's own burlesque 'Love and Friendship'. Laura, a young lady of sensibility, meets Sophia, 'all Sensibility and Feeling'; and Laura says that the two merely 'flew into each others arms & after having exchanged vows of mutual Freindship for the rest of our Lives, instantly unfolded to each other the most inward Secrets

---

[27] The confusion, if it is such, is noted by Firkins, p. 51; and by Andrew H. Wright, *Jane Austen's Novels* (London: Chatto & Windus, 1961) p. 97.

of our Hearts –'.[28] If such things happen in books they certainly ought to happen in life; and so, when Isabella declares that 'I carry my notions of friendship pretty high', and that she is determined to disprove the masculine idea that ladies are 'incapable of real friendship', Catherine knows just what she ought to feel. How marvellous that chance has 'procured her such a friend' (pp. 146, 40, 34)!

Jane Austen concentrates hard on the sudden intimacy of the two. They are united in 'sisterly happiness'. Isabella tells her, 'I am determined at all events to be dressed exactly like you'; and 'I know you better than you know yourself' (pp. 120, 42, 71). Soon these well-read young ladies have coalesced to the extent that when Isabella tells her little protégée that she has seen her alone in the parlour with John Thorpe, Catherine can only answer lamely, 'Well, if you say it, it was so, I dare say – but for the life of me, I cannot recollect it' (p. 145).

Catherine can make a spiritual sister out of such unpromising material because she is not yet ready to see Isabella as she really is. Jane Austen's heroines, when they first enter the world, are never truly receptive to it. They remake it, or create enough of it, to suit their own aesthetic preconceptions of how it ought to be – preconceptions which for Catherine at the beginning are of course those of romantic novels. Cowper's phrase, 'Myself creating what I saw', which appears in *Emma* (p. 344), is a fundamental law of epistemology in all the novels; and thus Catherine later will discover her 'self-created delusion' at the Abbey (p. 199). But she is not ready for that yet. She is still in the process of 'creating' Isabella, in the sense that she sees in her new friend what she wants to; and what she wants to see is of course the heroine she herself wants to be. She has entered the world in a mental state something like Sir Walter Elliot's dressing-room at Kellynch Hall, surrounded by mirrors, and not so much receiving her surroundings as projecting them. In the course of the novel this self-created world must give way reluctantly and painfully to the real one. The Isabella of sensibility must give way to the real one.

---

[28] *Volume the Second*, ed. B. C. Southam (Oxford: Clarendon, 1963) p. 20. For another sample of precocious friendship in Jane Austen's juvenilia, see 'The Watsons', *Novels*, VI (*Minor Works*) p. 349.

Catherine has now to develop still another literary relationship. In the vocabulary of sensibility 'love' and 'friendship' often appear together in a couplet. In *Northanger Abbey* Jane Austen writes that Catherine is not experienced in the 'finesse of love, or the duties of friendship'; and that 'Friendship is certainly the finest balm for the pangs of disappointed love' (pp. 36, 33).[29] 'Love' in these cases is the heterosexual manifestation of 'friendship', the two together making up the sum total of sensibility. This formula has great significance in *Northanger Abbey*: it is the basis of the precisely symmetrical structure of the novel. Isabella Thorpe and Catherine are now united in false 'friendship,' Isabella and Catherine's brother James in false 'love'; and now Catherine is being pushed by her new friend toward what would be a false 'love' for John Thorpe.

John Thorpe is thus the other half of an idea. He is sensibility in its other conventional manifestation, and his very existence in the novel is an indication of Jane Austen's purposeful use of characters and social situations as some sort of makeshift embodiment of ideas that exist primarily for the effect they have on the heroine's psychology. Indeed the Thorpes as 'characters' are almost buried beneath their obvious function as a means of developing Catherine's sense. Isabella, for instance, says her attachments are always 'excessively strong'; and so the same automatically has to be true of her brother (p. 90). Isabella's exaggeration of her own sentiments is likewise echoed in John's exaggeration of how fast his horse can go (pp. 45-6). The two thus come together as a kind of mutual definition of an attitude of mind that Catherine must learn is wrong: the attitude that the imagination is at liberty to exaggerate, to heighten reality in any way it wants. Catherine is destined to discover this error inductively as she sees through the brother and sister's 'love' and 'friendship': the two do have a 'family' resemblance.

With her love of precise symmetry, Jane Austen has opposed the Thorpes themselves to another brother-and-sister pair, the Tilneys. The false love and friendship of the former are to give way eventually to Catherine and Henry's true love, and to

---

[29] Mary Russell Mitford makes an interesting distinction between 'Love' and 'Friendship' in *The Life of Mary Russell Mitford*, ed. A. G. K. L'Estrange, 3 vols (London: R. Bentley, 1870) I 71 (17 Feb 1809).

Catherine and Eleanor's sisterly 'friendship' (p. 226). Henry Tilney is made to embody an attitude toward reality that is directly opposed to the Thorpes'. But when Catherine first meets him at Bath he hardly seems to; he seems indeed another version of Isabella herself. He even encourages Catherine to keep a journal, as a lady of sensibility should. He therefore seems to pick up where Isabella left off as her tutor in the wild, extravagant and improbable.

And his specialty is the Gothic. Isabella has already introduced Catherine to *The Mysteries of Udolpho*; and how gratifying to know that the Tilneys too have read and liked it. Now she can confidently say 'I shall never be ashamed of liking Udolpho myself' (p. 107). Henry now begins to encourage the 'raised, restless, and frightened imagination' (p. 51) that Mrs Radcliffe's novel inspires in her. He feeds her imagination with details of what to expect at his father's own Northanger Abbey. Indeed her illusions concerning the abbey are 'in a great measure his own doing' (p. 173). As for Henry himself, she has entered the world with a heightened sensibility, ready for a romantic hero to be thrown in her way (p. 17). Clearly Henry is the man. He is her Gothic hero – a kind of walking abbey. 'Her passion for ancient edifices' is merely 'next in degree to her passion' for Henry (p. 141).

He also encourages Catherine to have an eye for the 'picturesque'. This comes in handy for the appreciation of Gothic abbeys (p. 177). Henry therefore gives her a 'lecture on the picturesque,' the theme of which is that the beauty of nature consists in 'its capability of being formed into pictures' rather than in any beauty it has in itself. A clear blue sky, it seems, is not really proof of a fine day, for blue skies are not picturesque; and a landscape must be sorted out and rearranged according to picturesque strictures concerning 'fore-grounds, distances, and second distances – side-screens and perspectives' (pp. 110–11).[30]

---

[30] For William Gilpin's use of picturesque terminology like that in *Northanger Abbey*, see, for instance, his *Three Essays . . .* (London: R. Blamire, 1792) p. 42, where he mentions the 'ingredients of landscape'; also his *Observations, on several Parts of England . . . relative chiefly to Picturesque Beauty*, 2 vols, 3rd ed. (London: T. Cadell & W. Davies, 1808) I 20, 62 ('*first distances*', 'foregrounds'). For Jane Austen's knowledge of Gilpin's works see

Henry also introduces Catherine to 'wit.' The Morlands are plain people 'who seldom aimed at wit of any kind' (p. 66); and Henry is a farrago of smart sayings, on history, on the state of the nation, on the understanding of women (pp. 107-14). During her walk with the Tilneys to the top of Beechen Cliff, Catherine is confronted with the dazzling variety of wit in Henry Tilney, just as earlier she had looked down into the ballroom at Bath, and just as later she will be dazzled by the 'variety' on General Tilney's breakfast table.

Jane Austen has therefore made Henry the apparent patron of sensibility, of Gothicism and the allied 'picturesque,' and of 'wit'. All these seem to come together in him; he is what is common to them all. He thus becomes an even more general definition of an attitude toward reality than were the Thorpes taken together: the attitude that mind is supreme over matter. Sensibility, Gothicism, the picturesque are all aesthetic filters[31] through which to view the real world, a viewing of the real through a raised and restless imagination.

And the same is true of 'wit'. One of the most important and

---

the index to *Novels*, v (*Northanger Abbey and Persuasion*). Henrietta Ten Harmsel is simply mistaken when she says, in *Jane Austen: A Study in Fictional Conventions* (London: Mouton, 1964), that 'In *Northanger Abbey* the author's attitude is definitely in sympathy with admirers of the Picturesque . . .' (p. 64). Jane Austen is plainly having some fun at the expense of Gilpin and others. Gilpin, for instance, is hardly in sympathy with the common interests of everyday life. He is not one for taking nature as it comes; he thinks it usually must be rearranged to make it suitably picturesque: '. . . he who works *from imagination* – that is, he who culls from nature the most beautiful parts of her productions . . . combines them artificially; and removing every thing offensive, admits only such parts, as are *congruous*, and *beautiful*; will in all probability, make a much better landscape, than he who takes it all as it comes . . .' (*Observations*, I xxv–xxvi). In *The Improvement of the Estate* (Baltimore: Johns Hopkins Press, 1971) Alistair Duckworth makes the following good comment: 'However "enamoured of Gilpin on the Picturesque" she may have been, Jane Austen commonly treats an enthusiasm for this style with some irony . . .' (p. 42).

[31] Thus Gilpin observes of '*haziness*' that it 'throws over the face of landscape that harmonizing tint, which blends the whole into unity, and repose', *Observations* I 12.

unnoticed aspects of this early novel is that 'wit' in it is conceived as yet another aesthetic pose: the wilful sacrifice of the complete and real truth to nice artistry, to cleverness. When Henry displays his wit on the Cliff, his sister tells him, 'You are more nice than wise'; she advises him to be more 'serious' (pp. 108, 114). As she makes these comments, is she looking over Henry's shoulder at his author, who is already uneasy that her own wit in the novel is but a silly, unreal aesthetic posture like Isabella's sensibility? 'Wit' in this novel seems conceived as a posture that Catherine and Jane Austen herself must eventually give up if they are ever to see the world as it really is. 'Wisdom', Jane Austen wrote with apparent seriousness in a letter, 'is better than Wit' (*Letters*, p. 410; she also juxtaposes these two words in *Sense and Sensibility*, p. 298); and her career, like those of her heroines, is a slow giving over of this, an early, rather girlishly giggling aesthetic pose, to a less raised and restlessly imaginative acceptance of the common place (see Chapter V, pp. 112–24).

The sensibility, the Gothicism and the picturesqueness that Henry Tilney encourages in the young Catherine are all standard literary dispositions of mind that Jane Austen has appropriated from the literature of her day. Her genius is already evident in her attempt, which is perhaps not very successful, to embody them all, and thus to unify them, in the single character Henry Tilney. In attempting to do so Jane Austen is already moving beyond those ready-made postures struck by countless romantic heroines, toward her own general conception of what all such postures have in common. Sensibility, the Gothic and the picturesque all reveal a disposition to see the world in whatever way conforms best to one's personal aesthetic illusions about it. Thus Jane Austen has tried to bring all these illusions together under the general head of the Henry Tilney who draws Catherine into the dance at Bath.

In the Marianne Dashwood of the next novel, *Sense and Sensibility*, there are still some traces left of the standard literary expressions of this general state of mind. Like any stock heroine from a novel of sensibility, Marianne scours the countryside in search of picturesque beauty (p. 160); and the conventional 'sickly sensibility of mind,' the 'trembling irritability of habit, which cannot stoop to the tameness of reality,' show up as her 'irritable refinement of . . . mind, and the too great importance placed . . . on the delicacies of a strong sensibility . . . ' (p. 201). But in this second novel Jane Austen is already shifting the emphasis onto that more general formulation toward which Henry Tilney himself is pointing. This general formulation begins to employ the terms 'imagination' or 'fancy' in opposition to 'reason' or 'understanding'. Thus the source of Marianne's illusions is no longer novels of sensibility, specific Gothic novels or formal tutelage in the picturesque, but simply an 'active imagination' (p. 57) in general. Still later, Lydia Bennet looks at the world through what Jane Austen simply calls the 'creative eye of fancy' (*Pride and Prejudice*, p. 232); Edmund Bertram confesses to an over-active 'imagination' (*Mansfield Park*, p. 458); Emma will not submit to a 'subjection of the fancy to the understanding' (*Emma*, p. 37) and is declared guilty of 'errors of imagination' (p. 343); and Anne Elliot exclaims, 'What wild imaginations one forms, where dear self is concerned!' (*Persuasion*, p. 201).

We see this general state of mind taking shape in *Northanger Abbey*; and it will be Jane Austen's theme in all her novels. She conceives an active imagination to be a projecting of the mind outward rather than a taking of reality inward: a creative blindness. Catherine's imagination has been encouraged by her reading and by Henry Tilney to project a kind of Gothicism onto the world; and since, for instance, it is aesthetically appropriate that General Tilney's wife must have endured some fascinating Gothic captivity or murder in his abbey, Catherine is absurdly blind to the cold, marmoreal reality of her monument which declares otherwise: 'The erection of the monument itself could not in the smallest degree affect her doubts of Mrs Tilney's actual decease' (p. 190). Catherine's imagination forces everything 'to bend to one purpose' (p. 200); just as Emma, in that later development of Jane Austen's art when the heroine's active imagination is no longer translated into the specific terms of the sensible, the Gothic or the picturesque, has 'taken up' an 'idea' and 'made everything bend to it' (*Emma*, p. 134).

Catherine and Jane Austen's heroines after her thus enter the world more or less impervious to it, attempting to preserve themselves from its adulteration, tending to admit it into themselves only when it suits, or can be changed to suit, their private aesthetic purposes. We hear and overhear their tiny voices from inside their shells as her heroines filter and refine that rich and chaotic reality somewhere 'outside' the novel until everything seems acceptable for internal consumption. As they enter the world they can all, at least to some degree, understand Mrs John Dashwood's sentiment when she says 'I am convinced within myself' (*Sense and Sensibility*, p. 12). The world will now begin to penetrate Catherine from without. She will have to surrender her aesthetic preferences to the world's; and that is the subject of the next chapter.

II

NORTHANGER ABBEY
'Facts' in the Novels

1

We have seen how Catherine Morland's 'active imagination' has been encouraged by her reading, and by the company she meets at Bath; she displays that general habit of mind which remakes the real world to suit one's aesthetic preconceptions about it. Eventually in Volume II she will be confronted with a few 'facts' that will destroy her illusions and bring her down into the real world.

The imaginations of Jane Austen's characters are always threatened by 'facts'. When Reginald in 'Lady Susan' has finally discovered the truth, Mrs Johnson exclaims, 'Facts are such horrid things!' (*Minor Works*, p. 303); and Emma discourages Harriet from wasting her mental powers on 'sober facts' (*Emma*, p. 69). 'Facts' are anything that has achieved the status of what passes in fiction for objective truth rather than personal opinion. Thus in *Emma* it does eventually become a fact that Frank Churchill gave Jane Fairfax a piano. Such facts of course are always a threat to personal illusions. They make up the solid furniture of the novels against which the heroines bark their shins; and it is a distinctive feature of Jane Austen's art that her novels are sparsely furnished, which is to say comfortably furnished for the maintenance of personal illusions.

She has furnished her novels with relatively few verified objects like pianos, pencil-ends, stone monuments and abbeys; and also a few verified truths which emerge from the galaxies of conjecture that cluster and drift around these objects. These

bits of specified 'reality' that she sprinkles into the novels therefore take on great symbolic significance. From a full, rich reality
that might exist but is not allowed to, they are a carefully selected sampling which the fluid processes of thought can swirl
around in the patterns that make up the real business of the
novels.

Out of that potential fund of reality the bits that are actually
allowed to exist are remarkably few and far between. Her
heroines seize on them and retire into their solitude to turn them
every which way and invest them with great imaginative meaning. Elizabeth Bennet goes to meditate 'in the solitude of her
chamber'; she takes 'refuge in her own room, that she might
think with freedom'; she is 'eager to be alone' (*Pride and Prejudice*, pp. 157, 307, 264); Emma seeks the 'relief of quiet reflection'; she encounters a 'circumstance which I must think of at
least half a day . . .' (*Emma*, pp. 133, 395); Anne Elliot is 'in
need of a little interval for recollection'; she retires for an
'interval of meditation' in her room (*Persuasion*, pp. 185, 245).

2

One of the remarkable commonplaces of Jane Austen criticism is
that she is in some way a 'realist'. Sir Walter Scott declared in
1816 that a 'style of novel has arisen' which aims at the 'art of
copying from nature as she really exists in the common walks
of life'; and it is his opinion that *Emma* belongs to this style. Jane
Austen's technique in the novel reminds him of the 'merits of
the Flemish school of painting'.[1] Elsewhere he admires the
'exquisite touch' in her novels which 'renders ordinary commonplace things and characters interesting from the truth of
the description. . . .'[2] Bishop Whately likewise wrote that 'no
author has ever conformed more closely to real life'.[3] George

---

[1] An unsigned review of *Emma* which appeared in the *Quarterly
Review*, XIV (Oct 1815) 188–201. Reprinted in *Critical Heritage*.
Jane Austen eventually read the review (*Letters*, p. 453, 1 Apr 1816).

[2] *The Journal of Sir Walter Scott*, eds. J. G. Tait, W. M. Parker
(London: Oliver & Boyd, 1950) p. 135 (14 Mar 1826). Reprinted
in *Critical Heritage*.

[3] An unsigned review of '*Northanger Abbey*' and '*Persuasion*'
which appeared in the *Quarterly Review*, XXIV (Jan 1821) 352–76.
Reprinted in *Critical Heritage*.

Henry Lewes placed her among the authors who aim at a
'correct representation of life'.[4] And Charlotte Brontë found in
the novels a 'Chinese fidelity'.[5]

It is of course possible to find painstakingly detailed description of the physical world in the novels: description that might
be called 'realistic'. But what seems truly typical of her art is the
following, from the famous description of Pemberley: the 'rooms
were lofty and handsome, and their furniture suitable to the
fortune of their proprietor' (*Pride and Prejudice*, p. 246). This is
generalised description that has purposefully avoided the sharp
edges of particularity, any numbering of the streaks of the
tulip;[6] description that has furnished just a little factual detail
for Elizabeth Bennet's active imagination to work on in solitude.

We see this Cartesian impulse in Jane Austen as well. She
seems always to be striving for art that will produce intense

---

[4] 'Recent Novels . . .,' *Fraser's Magazine*, XXXVI (Dec 1847)
685–95. Reprinted in *Critical Heritage*.

[5] *The Brontës: Life and Letters*, ed. Clement Shorter, 2 vols
(London: Hodder & Stoughton, 1908) II 127 (12 Apr 1850). Reprinted in *Critical Heritage*. Comments on Jane Austen's 'realism'
in modern criticism are of course commonplace. Two of the starker
examples are Elizabeth Jenkins's mention of the 'photographic
realism' of Jane Austen's characters, *Jane Austen: A Biography*
(London: Gollancz, 1948) p. 240; and R. Brimley Johnson's reference
to Jane Austen's 'absolute truth to nature', *Jane Austen: Her
Life . . .* (London: J. M. Dent, 1930) p. 162. The following fine
passage in the same vein appears in H. W. Garrod's 'Jane Austen:
A Depreciation': '. . . if she had lived to be as old as Theophrastus,
she might, as he did, have exercised her close analytic powers by
writing a treatise on the nature of plants', *Essays by Divers Hands*
(*Transactions of the Royal Society of Literature*) N.S. VIII (1928)
40.

[6] Indeed the similarity between the very generalised descriptions
of Pemberley and the palace of Rasselas is remarkable: 'The palace
stood on an eminence raised about thirty paces above the surface
of the lake. It was divided into many squares or courts, built with
greater or less magnificence according to the rank of those for whom
they were designed' (*The History of Rasselas . . .*, i). Howard S. Babb
discusses the general influence of eighteenth-century aesthetics on
Jane Austen, in *Jane Austen's Novels* (Columbus, Ohio: Ohio State
University Press, 1962) chapter I ii. For her use of abstractions and
'conceptual terms' see especially his p. 11. In *Jane Austen's English*
(London: Deutsch, 1970) K. C. Phillipps also discusses her reliance
on eighteenth-century abstractions, p. 15.

thought on a minimum of particular detail. One of her criticisms of her niece Anna Austen's novel is that the 'descriptions are often more minute than will be liked';[7] and we can see Jane Austen herself revising her own description of the Edwards's house in 'The Watsons' so that in some passages the final version actually has less specific detail than the original.[8] Thus, like the painter David, who drew in the anatomy of his figures before clothing them,[9] she seems at some phase in the process of composition to have needed a body of thoroughgoing particular detail that she was later able to eliminate; and it is possible that she used consistently worked-out almanacs of the events, perhaps even road maps.[10] She 'knows all the details, and gives us very few of them'.[11]

The result is a tension in the novels between the relatively few specific details that are allowed to exist and the rich specificity that seems always possible but that the author has held back in order to draw out the active imaginations of her heroines, and of her readers; a tension therefore between the relatively little objective truth that such detail represents and occasions, and on

---

[7] See *Letters*, p. 401. Elizabeth Bowen makes an interesting observation in 'Notes on Writing a Novel', *Collected Impressions* (London: Longmans Green, 1950): 'Jane Austen's economy of scene-painting, and her abstentions from it in what might be expected contexts, could in itself be proof of her mastery of the novel' (p. 254).

[8] See B. C. Southam, *Jane Austen's Literary Manuscripts* (London: Oxford University Press, 1964) pp. 72-3. Southam quotes the passage above from the *Letters*. The anonymous reviewer of 'Northanger Abbey' and 'Persuasion' for the *British Critic*, N.S., IX (Mar 1818), 293-301 (reprinted in *Critical Heritage*) says of Jane Austen that 'At description she seldom aims. . . .' Walter Herries Pollock notes that in the novels there is 'no Balzac-like overloading of detail', *Jane Austen, Her Contemporaries . . .* (London: Longmans, 1899) p. 30.

[9] See Helen Rosenau, *The Painter Jacques-Louis David* (London: Nicholson & Watson, 1948) p. 42.

[10] See Chapman's comment in *Novels*, V (*Northanger Abbey, Persuasion*) 277. In 'Topography and Travel in Jane Austen's Novels' (*Cornhill Magazine*, N.S. LIX (1925), 184-99), F. D. Mackinnon conjectures that she even used 'road-books' when composing her novels (p. 184).

[11] [R. W. Chapman], 'Jane Austen's Methods', *Times Literary Supplement* (9 Feb 1922) 82a.

the other hand the rich activity of imagination that results from
it in the mind. There is always a tension, that is, between the
little truth that is allowed to exist and the rich fund of truth
that the narrator could easily create if she wanted to. This conspicuous scarcity of objectively founded truths is at the very
heart of Jane Austen's technique as a novelist; and that is a
long way from what we commonly understand 'realism' to be.

We can already see this technique developing in her juvenile
writing. Many of the early pieces are epistolary fiction;[12] and
in them the meagreness of objective truth is the result of the form
itself. There is no omniscient narrator to provide such truth
directly. It must be established, to the extent that it ever is, by a
process of triangulation from various epistolary points of view.
The series of letters entitled 'Lady Susan', which may have been
composed sometime between 1793 and 1805,[13] exploits this limi-
tation again and again. The correspondents, each sealed in his
own little world, are busy as ants establishing versions of some
hypothetical 'truth' that never actually exists in the work.
Reginald writes that he has found the 'true motive of Lady
Susan's conduct'; he assures his father, 'You will, I am
sure . . ., feel the truth of this reasoning' (*Minor Works*, pp. 264,
265); Mrs Vernon writes that 'Mr Smith's account . . . which
Reginald firmly beleived [sic] . . . is now he is persuaded only
a scandalous invention'; she herself has discovered 'some particulars . . . which, if true . . .'; she is certain that 'I will discover
the real Truth . . .' (pp. 259, 255, 278).

Toward the end (Letters pp. 23, 24) the letter form collapses
into one long narration from Mrs Vernon to her mother. Jane
Austen then abandons the form entirely to give her own narrated 'Conclusion'. Here we get an interesting glimpse of the
technique that is so characteristic of the later novels after she has
turned away from the epistolary form entirely. She impishly

---

[12] Jane Austen's juvenilia run heavily to short fictional pieces in
letter form. The longest of these are 'Love and Friendship, a novel
in a series of Letters' (in *Volume the Second*, ed. Southam); and the
later 'Lady Susan' (in *Novels*, vi (*Minor Works*)). According to *Life
and Letters*, *Sense and Sensibility* was originally a novel in letters
(p. 80); and B. C. Southam thinks the same may be true of *Pride
and Prejudice* (*Literary Manuscripts*, pp. 58–9).

[13] Southam, *Literary Manuscripts*, pp. 45–6; Chapman, *Facts and
Problems*, p. 52.

refuses in the 'Conclusion' to dispense any truth of her own: 'Whether Lady Susan was, or was not happy ... – I do not see how it can ever be ascertained ...' (p. 313). The effect is that the conclusion is merely a last covering letter, sent outward to the reader with no more benefit of 'facts' than any of the others.

In her later, narrated fiction the effect is often the same; for she often refuses to take on the burden of omniscience the new form offers her. Sometimes in the early novels she does, it is true, consent to give, in the narrator's voice, a necessary fact the characters have made an issue of. In *Sense and Sensibility*, for instance, Mrs Jennings sees and overhears Elinor in intimate conversation with Colonel Brandon, and concludes that the two are in love; the narrator then breaks in with the gratifying statement, 'What had really passed between them was to this effect' (p. 282). But Jane Austen is already developing techniques that allow her to avoid such statements. Already the emphasis is not on the objective truth of what 'happened', the 'outer' events of the plot; it is rather on the illusions generated in the characters by the very absence of whatever facts would stultify their illusions. It eventually becomes a fact in *Sense and Sensibility*, for instance, that Edward Ferrars is engaged to Lucy Steele. But Jane Austen never makes a narrator's authoritative declaration of the fact; she concentrates on Elinor's surrendering an illusion before a mounting 'body of evidence' (p. 139) that leaches into her consciousness from outside it during the course of the novel.

This puckish withholding on the narrator's part of some conspicuously absent fact creates a faint comedy between Jane Austen and her own characters that runs through the novels. She is wise, but silent; and they – Lord, what fools these mortals be. She lets the ladies debate after dinner for six paragraphs on the comparative heights of young Harry Dashwood and William Middleton, yet 'had both the children been there, the affair might have been determined too easily by measuring them at once ...' (*Sense and Sensibility*, pp. 233–4). Again and again she lets her characters solemnly debate about heights (see 'Lesley Castle', pp. 95–116;[14] *Emma*, p. 174), reckon distances (*Mansfield Park*, pp. 94–5), and pace off footages (*Emma*, pp. 247–9)

---

[14] In *Volume the Second*, ed. Southam.

to establish their own personal versions of a 'fact' that she, like the narrator of the conclusion of 'Lady Susan', is slyly holding clutched behind her back in a state of fictional non-existence.

3

The few isolated facts in the novels are the hard, angular challenges to the illusions of her characters, like outcroppings of rock in the sea. Jane Austen takes great pains to found them on some base that will stand firm amid the swirl of imagination that surrounds them; and her two most common practices are to found the fact in a letter or in a will.

Letters in her fiction are a kind of evidence sharply distinct from the thought and talk that surround them. Indeed they are treated with the respect due to legal documents. The letter from Darcy which is the single most important source of objective truth about his character, slipped under the door into the novel when it is time for Elizabeth to know the truth, reads like Blackstone: 'Two offences ... you ... laid to my charge'; 'the following account of my actions and their motives'; 'These causes must be stated ...' (*Pride and Prejudice*, pp. 196,198). The same is true of Frank Churchill's letter, which is slipped into the novel at the last to give some final indication of his real character. In the course of giving 'this history of my conduct' it refers to 'the event of the 26th ult.' (*Emma*, pp. 439, 440).

Again and again her characters are faced with letters and other documents when it is time for them to founder on a fact. A letter from Catherine Morland's brother gives her the truth concerning Isabella Thorpe. The fact that Lucy Steele is engaged to Edward Ferrars is partly established by a conventional recognition symbol, a keepsake portrait which Lucy produces; but before Jane Austen is ready to have Elinor admit 'she could doubt no longer', she has Lucy produce a letter (*Sense and Sensibility*, p. 134). The fact of Willoughby's engagement comes to Marianne in a letter (p. 183). Darcy's letter about himself is backed by the highly credited testimony of Mrs Gardiner, in a letter (*Pride and Prejudice*, pp. 321–5). Fanny Price finds out the 'truth' concerning the affair between Henry Crawford and Mrs Rushworth in a newspaper article (*Mansfield Park*, p. 440); she finds out the truth concerning Mr Yates and Julia in a letter (p. 442); and when she is psychologically ready to marry Edmund she gets a 'faithful picture' of his mind, again in a letter (p. 422). After Anne Elliot has been told the 'truth', the 'facts' concerning Mr Elliot, her informant says, 'And yet you ought to have proof; for what is all this but assertion?'; and from a small inlaid box she produces a letter (*Persuasion*, pp. 199–204) which she and her author are remarkably embarrassed to have to account for ('. . . happened to be saved; why, one can hardly imagine'). And when the psychological time has come for Captain Wentworth to divulge his true feelings to Anne, he writes her a letter while she is in the same room with him, probably not more than five feet away (p. 236).

But the most profoundly established facts are wills. Unlike most of the letters they are not drafted in the novels at all, but have dropped into them from some absolutely fixed point outside. They are the *données*: the ultimate facts which, having come from outside the context of the novel, it is irrelevant to question. The characters who do are so absorbed in their illusions that they are committing the ultimate heresy in Jane Austen's fiction: the heresy of questioning the very existence of facts, of a truth outside themselves. Mrs Bennet does so when she questions the entailing of Longbourn to Mr Collins; so does Wickham when he tries to interpret the fact of old Mr Darcy's will – a will which is scrupulously respected by Darcy himself.

The absolute factuality of wills is seen most clearly in *Sense and Sensibility*. The novel begins with Henry Dashwood's verbal deathbed will that his son John should look after his own step-mother and sisters. This is the unquestionable given fact around which the novel crystallizes; and in one of Jane Austen's most famous dialogues the imaginations of two of her typical characters, John and his wife, go to work on the fact until they have destroyed it and the two have enveloped themselves in the perfect state of illusion: an impervious shell of egotism. If their relatives are given nothing, 'They will live so cheap! . . . They will keep no company, and can have no expences of any kind!' (p. 12). That is, if they have no money they will not be able to afford anything, and will need no money anyway. Here is perfect circular logic that is safe from troublesome 'fact'. John Dashwood and his wife have retired into a state that all Jane Austen's heroines share with them at least to some degree at the beginnings of the novels. John can say concerning the 'fact', concerning reality itself, 'I clearly understand it now' (p. 12) – a sentiment he shares with Emma Woodhouse.

If the heroines can only steer clear of the few hard facts in the novels they are free to navigate in a world ideally suited for the maintenance of personal illusions; a world in which the working of the heroine's imaginative mind has almost crowded out external things. And very often Jane Austen does this by moving into the heroine's mind and looking outward from there, with the result that the potential external world which would be a threat to the heroine's personal illusions appears to a considerable extent as it has already been re-formed in the heroine's own consciousness.

The potentiality of a narrated, objective exposition of people, places and events has thus to some extent given way in the novels to fragmented and highly coloured versions of them. Both we and the characters themselves are in the situation of the pathetic old Mrs Bates: her eyes are bad, she is deaf, and she receives only little bits of the world outside, mostly in letters read to her – after they have been revised and censored by her daughter.

This ducking into the consciousness of a character so that facts are seldom met face to face pervades even what appears to be Jane Austen's objective narration. James Edward Austen-Leigh's opinion that in his aunt's novels 'all is the unadorned reflection of the natural object'[15] simply is not true. For instance, the narrated statement, 'Willoughby was a young man of good abilities . . . and open, affectionate manners' (*Sense and Sensibility*, p. 48) appears to be just such unadorned, objective description. But it is not. The particulars have been selected with such rigid purposefulness that the description has taken on a taint of subjectivity. It is not quite a description of Willoughby, as Marianne must learn; it is partly a description of the hero Marianne wants to see, and therefore partly a description of Marianne herself. It takes a middle ground that is a peculiarity of Jane Austen's style:[16] description that has slid part of the way into

---

[15] *Memoir* (1871), p. 153.
[16] Mary Lascelles writes that 'Jane Austen's narrative style seems to me to show . . . a curiously chameleon-like faculty; it varies in colour as the habits of expression of the several characters impress

the selecting, distorting consciousness of a character, but that is still slyly fobbing itself off as unimpeachably objective.

This point is so little obvious that it needs some emphasis. One must be very careful when quoting what Jane Austen 'says'. The well-known first sentence of Pride and Prejudice, for instance, is spoken by her[17] – but not quite. It sounds suspiciously like Mrs Bennet. The sentence is not quite 'in' that lady's mind, but has been subtly tainted by it. The phrase 'a single man in possession of a good fortune' is like the words she directs at her husband later in the chapter ('a young man of large fortune', a 'single man of large fortune', pp. 3, 4). And the first sentence of Emma, which can be solemnly referred to by critics as if it were the objective truth about Emma from the Surrey census,[18] is likewise faintly coloured by Emma's own opinion of herself.

This relentless obliquity, this relentless deflection of the potential, narrated, objective fact into someone's version of it, this relentless withdrawing into her character's consciousness from an outer world she allows to exist only barely, pervades Jane Austen's art from start to finish. It is the most general expression of her irony, her habitual but far from complete avoidance of direct statements of truth. The truth of whatever is narrated is the heavy responsibility of the narrator, but the 'truth' as seen by a character is his own responsibility. For the 'truth universally acknowledged' that begins Pride and Prejudice Mrs Bennet will have to take part of the credit.

In Ulysses Mr Deasy advised Stephen that Shakespeare says 'Put but money in thy purse', and Stephen murmurs 'Iago'. Dramatists do not 'say' anything, and Jane Austen's fiction approaches the form of drama in this respect. Much of the burden of 'truth' that a narrator has the opportunity of assuming she has purposely avoided. She condemned Egerton Brydges's

---

themselves on the relation of the episodes in which they are involved . . .', p. 102. For an interesting discussion of this peculiarity of style in Emma, see R. W. Chapman, 'Jane Austen's Methods', p. 82b.

[17] See Dorothy Van Ghent, The English Novel (New York: Harper, 1961) p. 100, for a discussion of this sentence.

[18] At any rate Wayne Booth, in The Rhetoric of Fiction (Chicago: University of Chicago Press, 1966), apparently takes the sentence as a statement of pure fact (p. 257).

Arthur Fitz-Albini because 'Never did any book carry more internal evidence of its author. Every sentiment is completely Egerton's' (*Letters*, p. 32); and in her own novels the sentiments are usually pushed away from herself and toward her characters. It is true that there are characters like Colonel Brandon and Mr Knightley who come fairly close to having the unqualified endorsement of their author, or sponsor; and just as true that her own moral values are more or less apprehensible in her work – as are Shakespeare's in his. Nevertheless her tendency to let characters speak for themselves does reveal a dramatic unabsolutist willingness to conceive truth often, but not always, as a subtle interplay of various individual points of view brought into suspension in her art. Eventually she comes to consider such dramatic deflection of truth, just as she comes to consider 'wit', to be a shirking of the truth-telling responsibility that the form of the novel has imposed on her; and Sir Thomas Bertram comes swooping down into her gravest novel to put to rout Jane Austen's symbol of her former dramatic art: the theatricals at Mansfield Park.

A niece commented that she could not recall 'any word or expression of Aunt Jane's that had reference to public events'; and that in her letters she 'seldom committed herself *even* to an opinion'.[19] She seems to have had that kind of high intelligence that slyly avoids being drawn, at least publicly, into profound subjects like religion and politics that demand or encourage some commitment to a pat 'truth' that one would have to deliver *in propria persona*. When one sets out on a search for what Jane Austen 'thinks' in her novels, it is well to keep in mind a little scene in 'Sanditon'. Sir Edward Denham has been grandly lecturing Charlotte on something he refers to as the 'sovereign impulses of illimitable Ardour' in romantic poetry, and she replies, 'I really know nothing of the matter. – This is a charming day. The Wind I fancy must be Southerly' (*Minor Works*, p. 398).

Jane Austen's novels therefore stand, perhaps even a little self-consciously, in a comic relation to the heavyweight propaganda novels of the late eighteenth century. A sample title is Isaac Disraeli's *Vaurien: or Sketches of the Times: exhibiting views of*

---

[19] Caroline Austen, *My Aunt Jane Austen*, p. 9.

the philosophies, religions, politics, literature, and manners of the age (1797);[20] and an unfair sample of their contents is the following: 'Melville took with one hand that of Cecilia, and with the other the New Testament, and held them alternately to his bosom.'[21] Jane Austen and her heroines would rather talk about the weather than the New Testament; from politics, for Henry Tilney, it is an easy step to silence (*Northanger Abbey*, p. 111). As one of her early readers commented, she 'never plagues you with any chemistry, mechanics, or political economy.'[22] Like Mr Bennet, she deflects most serious questions with irony, and retires back into her book.

Against the monumentalities of politics, of religion, of political economy, of illimitable Ardour, Jane Austen sets her famous 'little bit (two Inches wide) of Ivory on which I work with so fine a Brush . . .' (*Letters*, p. 469). She is a miniaturist. In a letter she writes that a Count Julien has some fine paintings, and 'among them, a Miniature . . . which exactly suited *my* capacity' (*Letters*, p. 276). In her ironic 'Plan of a Novel' she finds ludicrous the idea of a novel in which the heroine and her father are 'never above a fortnight together in one place';[23] and to her niece Anna she offers the serious advice, 'You are now collecting your People delightfully, getting them exactly into such a spot as is the delight of my life; – 3 or 4 Families in a Country Village is the very thing to work on . . .' (*Letters*, p. 401).

Jane Austen's is a tiny world where 'facts' have been severely pared away to make room for the working of the mind; where the very working of the mind has been pared of many matters which would threaten to engage doctrinal truths that could be conceived to exist in the large world outside. What has not been pared away – the pencil-ends that survive – seems to exist for the most part as a close to minimal raw material to keep the characters' minds in motion so that the motion itself can be

---

[20] Cited by Tompkins, p. 322 n.

[21] Cited by Tompkins, p. 303 n. The passage appears in Mary Hays's *The Story of Melville and Cecilia*, in *Letters and Essays* (1793).

[22] S. H. Romilly, *Letters to 'Ivy' from the first Earl of Dudley* (London: Longmans, 1905) p. 250; quoted by Charles Beecher Hogan, 'Jane Austen and Her Early Public', *Review of English Studies*, N.S., 1 (Jan 1950) 43.

[23] *Novels*, VI (*Minor Works*) 429.

recorded in some form apprehensible in fiction. That is not what we usually understand by 'realism'.

4

In *Northanger Abbey* Catherine Morland's active imagination has been encouraged by her early reading, by the Thorpes' love and friendship, and by Henry Tilney's summary sponsorship of sensibility, Gothicism, picturesqueness and wit. At the end of my first chapter we left her in that state of mind which reconstructs the real world to conform to one's aesthetic preconceptions about it. Now we will see how she is confronted (mostly in the latter part of Volume II) with a series of facts which her illusions cannot absorb and transmogrify, and which therefore eventually destroy the illusions themselves.

Jane Austen has her careful plan. She has concentrated on three 'facts'. Henry Tilney is implicated in each, and each carries a great deal of symbolic weight. First, there is the true character of Isabella Thorpe behind the mask of sensibility; then the true character of Northanger Abbey and its owner behind the mask of Gothicism; and finally the true character of Henry Tilney himself behind all those masks that define the general habit of mind which is Jane Austen's real subject.

How is Catherine going to discover these facts? She has come to Bath with only the parody of a chaperone. When she asks for moral advice, all Mrs Allen can do is deliver the unimpeachable proposition that 'Young people *will* be young people' (p. 104). Catherine is therefore on her own. She will get possession of the facts in the same way all Jane Austen's heroines do. She will be forced to go as far toward disillusioning herself as her own limited powers will allow; then the author will step in and contrive to present her with information from a source outside, and above, the heroine's own intelligence. Jane Austen has far from complete faith in the ability of her heroines to disillusion themselves without external and sometimes apocalyptic aid.

To help Catherine do as much for herself as she is able, her author has confronted her with the two antithetical brother-and-sister pairs, the Thorpes and Tilneys; and Catherine is forced to choose between them. Jane Austen uses this dialectical process over and over. Elinor Dashwood, for instance, moves from a knowledge of Willoughby's mind to the 'very different mind of a very different person' (*Sense and Sensibility*, p. 184) whom she will marry. And Emma Woodhouse, having lived her whole life in the company of Mr Knightley, cannot see him as he really is until she finally sees him in relation to Mr Weston; then her mind is at last able to move from the faults of the one to a recognition of the virtues of the other:

> ... a little less of open-heartedness would have made him a higher character. – General benevolence, but no general friendship, made a man what he ought to be. – She could fancy such a man (*Emma*, p. 320).

The author of *Northanger Abbey* is not very subtle in her treatment of the characters Catherine is forced to choose between. It is generally true that Jane Austen is wary of making personal moral pronouncements; and that she is even wary of standing four-square behind any one of her characters who does. But there are exceptions, especially in her early work. There are characters who seem to be sponsored by their author, and to be speaking for her. Henry and his sister are an example. They come to stand for a moral value their young author seems unreservedly behind; and the counterpart Thorpes are a value she is condemning. Indeed the Bath section of this early novel could have as its epigraph a busily opinionated passage from one of its author's early letters to her sister: 'It is *you* that always disliked Mr N. Toke so much, not *I*. – I do not like his wife, & I do not like Mr Brett, but as for Mr Toke, there are few people whom I like better' (*Letters*, p. 94).

Catherine is systematically made to see that each of the pairs represents a moral value; and the psychological action of the novel up to Volume II, Chapter v, when she leaves Bath, consists of her having to choose between the pairs. The clanking of the author's dialectical machinery can be heard in exclamations like: '... stop, Mr Thorpe. – I cannot go on. – I will not go on. – I must go back to Miss Tilney'; 'Let me go, Mr Thorpe; Isabella, do not hold me' (pp. 87, 101). Jane Austen's favourite moral writer in prose was Samuel Johnson,[24] and there is some-

---

[24] [Henry Austen], 'Biographical Notice . . .' (which prefaced the 1818 volume containing *Northanger Abbey* and *Persuasion*), in *Novels*, v 7.

the formal shift from the ironic Henry to what is to stand as the sincere one takes place in the first chapter of Volume II, at the moment Catherine meets his brother, Captain Tilney. At this moment he sheds his irony for the first time to don a gown and become, like Colonel Brandon, Edmund Bertram and Mr Knightley after him, something of a pedagogue.[27] His reply to Catherine's conjectures concerning the Captain takes on a new tone of voice: 'There was something . . . in his words which repaid her for the pain of confusion; and that something occupied her mind so much, that she drew back for some time, forgetting to speak or to listen . . .' (p. 133). At times he will briefly put on his ironic disguise again, but he has now become her mentor. Soon in her mind he 'must know best'; soon she is open to 'improvement by any thing he said' (pp. 153, 201).

In this chapter Catherine has just conjectured that Captain Tilney asked Isabella to dance only out of politeness, and that Isabella will surely refuse because she is engaged to be married to James Morland. Henry Tilney's reply is not a characteristic skittering across the surface of irony and wit, but a piercing down to a new level of truth in the novel: 'How very little trouble it can give you to understand the motives of other people's actions.' This is a comment that cuts through sensibility and Gothicism to lay bare the common feelings of common life, or what Henry later calls the 'probable' that Catherine's imagination must learn to be governed by (pp. 197–8). And this new truth from him is accompanied by some symbolic action which

---

[27] I am not aware of any discussion of Henry Tilney's change at this point in the novel; but certainly there is agreement that at some point he becomes Catherine's mentor: 'It is usual in a Jane Austen novel to find one character who . . . represents what is right. Henry Tilney is that character in this novel', Norman Sherry, *Jane Austen* (London: Evans, 1966) p. 53; Jane Austen 'throws a large part of her function as arbiter of good sense on to Henry Tilney . . .', W. A. Craik, *Jane Austen: the Six Novels* (London: Methuen, 1965) p. 9; Henry Tilney takes over 'a large part of what has been up till now the author's function: to provide a . . . commentary on . . . the incredibility of . . . literary conventions . . .', Marvin Mudrick, *Jane Austen: Irony as Defense and Discovery* (Princeton: Princeton University Press, 1952) p. 43; Henry Tilney 'is the agent of Catherine's gradual unillusionment . . .', Andrew H. Wright, p. 105; 'The job he undertakes is of instructing her how to form her own opinions rationally', Babb, p. 94.

shows Catherine that life does have its commonplace side – indeed its seamy side. She sees that Captain Tilney and Isabella are in the dance together; and what is more they are preparing to give Henry and Catherine 'hands across'. This is one of Jane Austen's exquisitely stylised scenes that acts as a correlative for a psychological 'action' taking place in the heroine's consciousness. These four, a general though unequal mixture of good and bad, are all in the dance together, as Henry is now going to teach her.

The truth about life that the new Henry tells Catherine is not quite like what Jane Austen's later mentor-heroes tell the later heroines. What Colonel Brandon tells Marianne in the next novel is stupefyingly pure and moral. But Henry's unironic truth is a little cynical, a little soiled, perhaps from contact with Jane Austen's juvenilia and her other early work. At the conclusion of the acidulous 'Lady Susan',[28] for instance, Mrs Vernon thinks that the wicked Lady Susan has at last been 'vanquished' (Minor Works, p. 285). But whether Jane Austen thinks so is another matter. For Lady Susan then makes a profitable marriage; and so far as the narrator of the 'Conclusion' is concerned, whether she lives happily ever after is anybody's guess: 'She had nothing against her, but her Husband, & her Conscience' (p. 313). We know next to nothing about her husband, and have just been told that she shows no evidence of having a conscience at all (p. 311).

It is as if the ironic Henry Tilney were right at home in Jane Austen's playfully naughty early writing; but that the shift to the mentor-Henry in this first novel is accompanied by a nervous, girlish giggle – or leer. When Catherine sees Isabella and the Captain flirting, and delivers the breathtaking sentiment that a 'woman in love with one man cannot flirt with another', Henry counters with the truth from the commonplace world that 'It is probable . . . she will neither love so well, nor flirt so well, as she might do either singly. The gentlemen must each give up a little' (p. 151). This is truth, but soured to heighten its effect; and administered by an early mentor capable of sharing a few sniggers with his brother over the brandy. None of the later heroes will be quite like this. Henry's assurance that the

---

[28] 'Lady Susan' was probably written between 1793 and 1805. See n. 12.

'mess-room will drink Isabella Thorpe for a fortnight, and she will laugh with your brother over poor Tilney's passion for a month' (p. 153) is not so close to what Colonel Brandon would say as it is to Pandarus.

As Henry talks to Catherine about Captain Tilney he even reveals a dark sense of brotherhood with him. He admits 'family partiality'; he turns aside Catherine's suggestion that he tell his father of the flirtation his brother is engaged in (pp. 219, 209). The relationship between these two later develops into the step-brotherly relationship of Darcy and Wickham; and it is the first significant manifestation of an idea that runs through Jane Austen's fiction: the idea of an organic, family relationship between good and evil that makes any true separation of them impossible. There is a sense in which the Captain is a part of the real Henry; and Henry's stepping forth from his ironic disguise in the rooms at Bath is inseparable from his introducing the real nature of his brother to Catherine. She says to him, 'you must know your brother's heart' (p. 151), and he does. The two are related by blood. When they come together in the dance they make with their partners a model of Jane Austen's little world: couples in formal pairings and separations that leave each at the conclusion with a fit moral partner; a partner arrived at through movements which require the mediation of moral opposites. It is one of her profound ideas that these opposites play their necessary parts in the conventional working out of the dance.

Catherine's introduction to the real Henry and his brother begins the movement away from Bath to Northanger Abbey; a movement that is going to confront her with the central symbol in the novel of all the false aesthetic attitudes that Henry Tilney has summarily displayed, and that are going to have to surrender to hard facts. The Abbey and its owner subsume, and stand for, them all. The crude sensibility of the Thorpes is in the Abbey: it is John Thorpe's exaggeration of Catherine's fortune that causes the General to invite her there (p. 244). Gothicism and the picturesque are there, for Henry has invested the Abbey with them as he and Catherine travel toward it (pp. 158–60). Perhaps even Beechen-Cliff wit as a false aesthetic pose resides there: at least Catherine learns on the way that the true unironic Henry does not (p. 157).

The entire novel leads up to and away from the Abbey. It is the Udolpho that Jane Austen is going to destroy with commonplace facts. Catherine associates Udolpho with Blaize Castle, which she is promised a sight of while she is staying at Bath (pp. 84–6); and Jane Austen has seen to it that her heroine never does, so that the Abbey can stand alone as the Gothic embodiment of all the illusions in the novel. 'Northanger Abbey! – These were thrilling words, and wound up Catherine's feelings to the highest point of extasy' (p. 140).

The crucial fact in this carefully laid-out novel is that the Abbey is not what Catherine has made it out to be; and Catherine surrenders to this realisation only gradually. Each step of surrender is followed by a solemn resolution never to make the same errors of imagination again, and each resolution by a version of the same error. Henry encourages her, for instance, to expect a secret manuscript and she finds a laundry bill instead (pp. 160–72). This causes a 'ray of commonsense' to dawn (p. 193) – and she goes forward to make the same error again. If the General's wife is not in chains, at least she was murdered; and Henry has to tell her that his mother passed away of a bilious fever (pp. 190–6).

This time the 'visions of romance were over' and Catherine can make the solemn resolution 'of always judging and acting in future with the greatest good sense . . .' (pp. 199, 201). But, like Emma Woodhouse, who makes mistakes, resolves 'to do such things no more' (*Emma*, p. 137), and then does them, Catherine is surrendering very reluctantly to the inductive method. If she could only see the principle behind a manuscript's turning into a laundry bill she would know that Isabella Thorpe is not love and friendship and is not going to marry James. But her mentor must now hand her this fact: a forlorn letter from a jilted James telling her that there have been troubles in sustaining the literary life in Bath too; a letter introduced more or less arbitrarily at this point (p. 202) to enforce the idea that what is disintegrating for Catherine is not simply Gothicism but that general attitude of mind which Henry Tilney has been pointing to.

As often happens in the later novels, an important truth is thus handed to the heroine readymade from some region beyond her own experience. Her ratiocinative powers at Bath were never

quite enough to bring her to this truth unaided. She needed
the aid of some truth-dispensing power beyond her, and the
tutelage or midwifery of a mentor to deliver it into her hands.
Later, Elizabeth Bennet can never quite gather the fact of
Wickham's wickedness unaided; she needs the knowledge concerning him that is handed to her in Darcy's letter. And Anne
Elliot needs the knowledge of Mr Elliot handed to her by Mrs
Smith. The authoritarian and other-worldly Sir Thomas Bertram,
who descends into Mansfield Park from Antigua to dispense
a profound and ironically unqualified truth when his children
and their author have hopelessly imprisoned themselves in the
ironic truthlessness of their theatricals, is always hovering over
Jane Austen's novels.

Catherine's last Gothic hope now rests on the General. Even
if he hasn't murdered his wife he may have literary talents
nevertheless. Thus the final point in Catherine's disillusionment
comes when General Tilney, having learned that she is not an
heiress, forces Eleanor to tell her she must leave his house. This
is the ultimate fact toward which the novel has been working.
Catherine is not going to be able to live in a Northanger Abbey.
She is going to have to go out into the unromantic world of
hard facts, the world of the commonplace – England.

The passage from the Abbey into the world is abrupt.
Catherine is in her room. She hears a noise in the hall, sees the
lock move (pp. 222–3). The Catherine of romance would now
imagine a monk in chains on the other side of the door. But for
this heroine the visions of romance are truly over; she resolves
not to be 'misled by a raised imagination'. Having rid herself
of romance, she is ready to see life. It is on the other side of
the door. She opens it – and Eleanor stands there, having come
to reveal to her the General's true mind.

At Bath Henry had begun his disclosure of the truth with
the words, 'How very little trouble it can give you to understand
the motive of other people's actions', and now what she learns
about the General seems to be the summary of all he meant.
Catherine soon thinks she has 'heard enough to feel, that in
suspecting General Tilney of either murdering or shutting up
his wife, she had scarcely sinned against his character . . .' (p.
247). Her attention, and her author's, is now focused on
character rather than architecture, and the visible furniture

of trapdoors and daggers begins to recede: '. . . with a mind so occupied in the contemplation of actual and natural evil . . . the darkness of her chamber, the antiquity of the building were felt . . . without the smallest emotion. . . .' What is now most real, and will continue to be so throughout Jane Austen's career, is the hidden motive of people's actions: '. . . how different now the source of her inquietude from what it had been then – how mournfully superior in reality and substance!' (p. 227).

Yet what are we to think of the real General Tilney? Among the Alps and Pyrenees, Jane Austen writes in that famous passage, there may be 'no mixed characters. There, such as were not spotless as an angel, might have the dispositions of a fiend. But in England it was not so: among the English . . . there was a general though unequal mixture of good and bad.' General Tilney might be Gothic in the Alps but not in the Cotswolds. Yet how Jane Austen conceives the General himself to be a mixed character when he throws Catherine out of the Abbey is not clear. His Gothicism may not have found aesthetic expression in murdering his wife, but it has found economic expression surely. If anyone belongs in the Alps it is he, and at first glance his creator seems to have out-Udolphoed Mrs Radcliffe.[29]

But Jane Austen may have thought it necessary to make the difference between his appearance to Catherine and his reality as great as possible. From hand to hand Catherine has been led to him: from Mrs Allen to sistership with Isabella; then Henry Tilney knew best; then finally she feels a 'deference for General Tilney's judgment' (p. 156). He seems to be the innermost place in the Abbey, the last Gothic illusion to be stripped away; and at the same time the means of passing out of the Abbey into the real world. As an illusion he was the *genius loci* of the Abbey; but as a shocking fact he belongs to the world. What he is, is in some sense what the world is in this early novel. The author of *Northanger Abbey* gives the impression of having stripped away some charming illusions only to expose a real world with which she is far from happy; a world in which the power of evil is very great indeed. A comment of Eleanor's rises

---

[29] Moler makes this point, pp. 38–9; so also does A. Walton Litz, *Jane Austen: A Study of Her Artistic Development* (London: Chatto and Windus, 1965) p. 63.

out of the Abbey to hang over the novel itself: '. . . you must have been long enough in this house to see that I am but a nominal mistress of it, that my real power is nothing' (p. 225).

Catherine now returns to Fullerton and treads again the well-known road (p. 237). Again and again in the novels we see this: the heroine makes a geographical or spiritual loop out into the world; she then returns home, and Jane Austen makes a playful attempt to begin the novel again as if nothing had happened. Thus the Bennet sisters return to Longbourn and look over their shoulders at the first chapter: 'The subject which had been so warmly canvassed between their parents, about a twelvemonth ago, was now brought forward again'; and Elizabeth thinks that 'Were the same fair prospect to arise at present, as had flattered them a year ago, every thing . . . would be hastening to the same . . . conclusion' (*Pride and Prejudice*, pp. 332, 337). Mrs Vernon thinks that when Lady Susan has been vanquished, 'we are all as we were before' ('Lady Susan', *Minor Works*, p. 285); even the same words reappear when Jane Bennet says that, Bingley once gone, 'we shall all be as we were before' (*Pride and Prejudice*, p. 134); Fanny Price thinks that 'Mr Crawford once gone . . . every thing would soon be as if no such subject had existed' (*Mansfield Park*, p. 324); and when Frank Churchill has left, Emma says, 'I shall do very well again after a little while – and then, it will be a good thing over' (*Emma*, p. 265).

But Jane Austen's heroines cannot go home again, at least to stay. Mrs Morland is mistaken when she tells her returned daughter to be contented, 'but especially at home, because there you must spend the most of your time' (p. 241). Fanny is mistaken in thinking that to be 'at home again, would heal every pain . . .' (p. 370); Emma cannot go back to the 'common course of Hartfield days' (p. 262). The retracing of the old pattern has merely brought out what has changed. The knowledge the heroine has acquired from her entrance into the world cannot come or go and leave no spot or blame. Walking again on the well-known road Catherine thinks about 'her own change of feelings'; '. . . how altered a being did she return!' (p. 237).

Catherine's family tries to welcome her back into the 'joyfulness of family love', but she no longer belongs to their family. They are where she began: 'free from the apprehension of evil

as from the knowledge of it' (pp. 233, 237). For them 'good-will'
is always going to supply the place of 'experience' (p. 249). To
her mother General Tilney's behaviour is something not worth
understanding; to her sister Sarah it is incomprehensible (p. 234).
And Catherine could never explain it. They would have to go
to the Abbey. For them life is simpler and more pure than for
Catherine it will ever be again. She has apprehended the fact
of evil; she has experience, and perhaps less goodwill. She has
entered the world.

Henry earlier said when he led Catherine into a dance that
he considered dancing an emblem of marriage. Now they have
come to the end of the dance. He comes to Fullerton to lead
her into the family that she has been prepared by the novel
to take her place in. It is a family free of Gothic and sentimental
illusions; yet at the same time a family with a stubborn strain
of nastiness that has been exposed as the illusions have been
stripped away. This is one of Jane Austen's great themes. The
family is a general though unequal mixture of good and bad.
It is Henry's family, but also the General's. And Catherine
acquires the Captain as a brother-in-law, just as Elizabeth
Bennet will hold out her hand in sistership to Wickham –
circumstances apt to elicit the common feelings of common life.
Everything that is nicely sentimental, or picturesque, or Gothic,
or even laced with pretty wit – all that has been left behind. We
are in the commonplace world now. That is Catherine's home,
a place for both good and bad. How fitting that the young
couple go to live at Woodston – within twenty miles of the
wicked General's Abbey.

III

SENSE AND SENSIBILITY
'Character' in the Novels

1

Cassandra Austen's Memorandum records, 'Sense & Sensibility begun Nov. 1797,' and adds that 'I am sure that something of the same story & characters had been written earlier & called Elinor & Marianne.'[1] The novel was not published until 1811; and so, like *Northanger Abbey*, it is one of Jane Austen's early 'gradual performances'.

Marianne Dashwood still draws on Jane Austen's waning interest in burlesque. Like Catherine Morland, she is in training to be a heroine of sensibility.[2] She knows from her reading just how such a heroine should behave. She 'would have thought herself very inexcusable had she been able to sleep at all the

[1] *Novels*, VI (*Minor Works*), facing p. 242. The Austen-Leighs think 'Elinor and Marianne' was composed between 1792 and 1796; it was apparently read aloud in the family during that period. And it may have been a novel in letters. See p. 26 above, note 12. Jane Austen seems still to have been working on it later than 1798, since the published novel mentions Scott as a popular poet. See A. C. Bradley, 'Jane Austen', *A Miscellany* (London: Macmillan, 1929) p. 34 n. According to the *Memoir* (1871) she was probably revising the novel in 1809–10, during her first year at Chawton (p. 101); and there is no reason to think she did not make revisions even slightly later. By April 1811 the novel was in the printer's hands (*Life and Letters*, p. 243); and by 25 April she was correcting proofs (*Letters*, pp. 272–3). A second edition appeared in 1813 with corrections by the author. See R. W. Chapman, *Novels*, I (*Sense and Sensibility*) xiv.
[2] B. C. Southam (*Literary Manuscripts*) notes that the word 'sensibilities' itself has in Jane Austen's fiction 'burlesque overtones', p. 48.

first night after parting from Willoughby' (*Sense and Sensibility*, p. 83). Her oration bidding farewell to 'Dear, dear Norland' (p. 27) may even be indebted to Catherine's favourite *The Mysteries of Udolpho*.[3] Marianne also has Catherine's interest in the picturesque: she scours the countryside in search of 'picturesque beauty'; and she 'would have every book that tells her how to admire an old twisted tree' (pp. 160, 92).[4] In short, her opinions 'are all romantic'; she is opposed to 'common-place' notions; she laments how deficient Elinor is in 'feelings'; and she knows how to weep profusely out of 'sensibility' (pp. 56, 53, 18, 83).[5]

Willoughby is Marianne's Northanger Abbey: the focus of aesthetic illusions that have come mainly from the books she has read. Jane Austen told us that Catherine's 'fancy' had 'portrayed' a Northanger Abbey like the one in her favourite story (*Northanger Abbey*, p. 162); and now Marianne, when she meets Willoughby, thinks much the same thing, in some of the same words: his 'person and air were equal to what her fancy had ever drawn for the hero of a favourite story . . .' (p. 43). Like the General's Abbey he seems indeed to belong to literature and not to life. Jane Austen has dissociated him from the logic of everyday occurrences at the very beginning, when he drops into the novel just in time to rescue a damsel with a sprained ankle. In this respect he resembles the too-good-to-be-true Edward Stanley in the juvenile 'Catherine'. Edward suddenly arrives from France, 'as handsome as a Prince' (*Minor Works*, p. 214), just in time to take the heroine to a ball.

---

[3] This is noted by C. Linklater Thomson, *Jane Austen: A Survey* (London: Horace Marshall, 1929) p. 78; on the passage see also Moler, p. 59.

[4] *Gilpin's Remarks on Forest Scenery* . . . (*Relative chiefly to Picturesque Beauty*), 2 vols (London: R. Blamire, 1791) discusses the picturesqueness of a 'blasted tree', I 14.

[5] In *Observations on the Western Parts of England, relative chiefly to Picturesque Beauty* . . . (London: T. Cadell and W. Davies, 1798) Gilpin quotes some lines of poetry on the shortcomings of a man 'graced with polished manners and fine sense,/Yet wanting sensibility' (p. 340 n). The lines thus testify to the intimate relation between 'sensibility' and a love of 'picturesque' beauty. Gilpin is quoting Cowper's *The Task*; and so Cowper (or Gilpin?) may indeed have inspired Jane Austen's title (see R. W. Chapman, *Facts and Problems*, p. 78 n).

Love at first sight occurs in Gothic novels of course; but it is associated especially with novels of sensibility. The giddy heroine of one of Jane Austen's juvenile pieces writes that this kind of love 'is the only kind . . . I would give a farthing for – There is some Sense in being in love at first sight'.[6] Marianne's sudden love for Willoughby is thus a manifestation of several different aesthetic poses rather than simply one. She is being sentimental, Gothic and picturesque[7] all at once – which is as much as to say that she is exhibiting that general state of mind they all have in common. Her overheated imagination has created an aesthetically pleasing world that puts up a strong resistance to any data from the real one. Like Sir Walter Elliot in his dressing-room, she is surrounded by reflections of herself. She 'expected from other people the same opinions . . . as her own . . .'; she can easily trace matters 'to whatever cause best pleased herself'; she is 'able to collect her thoughts within herself'; she finally comes to realise that Willoughby 'talked to me only of myself' (pp. 202, 243, 221, 190).

---

[6] 'A Collection of Letters', *Volume the Second*, ed. Southam, p. 182.

[7] A conventional phrase for love at first sight is 'first impressions'; and the phrase appears in one of the books on the picturesque that would have helped Catherine and Marianne admire old twisted trees and abbeys: 'There is no principle of the art [of landscape gardening] so necessary to be studied as the effects produced . . . by . . . that general disposition of the human mind, by which it is capable of strongly receiving *first impressions*. We frequently decide on the character of places, as well as of persons, with no other knowledge . . . than what is acquired by the first glance . . .; and it is with difficulty . . . that the mind is afterwards constrained to adopt a contrary opinion', Humphrey Repton, *Observations on the Theory and Practice of Landscape Gardening* (London: J. Taylor, 1803) p. 136. This seems to have escaped notice. Repton is mentioned in *Mansfield Park*. See *Novels*, III, note to p. 53.

Jane Austen would have encountered 'first impressions' in *Sir Charles Grandison*, where Mrs Shirley says, '. . . I had very high ideas of first impressions: eternal constancy: of Love raised to a pitch of idolatry' (Volume VI, Letter 42). B. C. Southam notes this in *Literary Manuscripts*, p. 11. For Jane Austen's appreciation of Richardson see the 'Biographical Notice', *Novels*, V 7. 'First impressions' occurs also in *The Mysteries of Udolpho* itself, pt I, chap. i (Southam, p. 59); and the phrase was the original title of what eventually became *Pride and Prejudice*. See Cassandra Austen's Memorandum, *Novels*, VI (*Minor Works*), facing p. 242.

She has not even met Willoughby in the respect that a real object has made much of an impression on her mind. Rather, she has gone a long way toward creating him. In her mind is a private picture of a romantic hero. Therefore when Willoughby carries her home her 'imagination' becomes 'busy' (p. 43), and he is made to answer immediately to the picture. She is now capable of gazing at a figure in the distance and exclaiming, 'It is he . . . – I know it is!' – although, as her sister gracelessly points out, it is actually somebody else (p. 86). Marianne's abbey, like Catherine's, is thus largely a 'self-created delusion'.

In the course of the novel Marianne's romantic mind is confronted by certain 'facts' that eventually force it to surrender to the supremacy of matter. Her love for Willoughby surrenders to another kind of attraction, for Colonel Brandon. This attraction grows slowly and unromantically in the novel, as Marianne gives in to the demands of the real world. In the early novels Jane Austen often attaches to such romances the damp word 'esteem', apparently to set them off from first impressions. In *Pride and Prejudice*, for instance, Elizabeth comes to feel 'esteem' for Darcy, which is the 'other less interesting mode of attachment' (p. 279); and in *Sense and Sensibility* Marianne too comes to feel 'esteem' for Colonel Brandon (p. 378).[8] True heroes, princes and knights appear very slowly in Jane Austen's novels as the heroines become receptive to the commonplace world. Thus Edmund Bertram's name comes eventually to be a 'name of heroism', of 'knights' for Fanny Price (*Mansfield Park*, p. 211);[9] and the most knightly of them all appears slowly in *Emma*.

In *Northanger Abbey* Jane Austen roughly blocked out her plan for bringing her heroines down into the world. Now she

---

[8] In his discussion of 'esteem' in the novel Joseph Wiesenfarth cites Gay's use of the word in his *Fables* (*The Errand of Form* (New York: Fordham University Press, 1967) p. 172, n. 31).

[9] The following lines appear in Crabbe's *Parish Register* (II 502–5):

Sir Edward Archer is an amorous knight,
And maidens chaste and lovely shun his sight;
His bailiff's daughter suited much his taste,
For Fanny Price was lovely and was chaste. . . .

See E. E. Duncan-Jones, 'Jane Austen and Crabbe', *Review of English Studies*, V (Apr 1954) 174.

uses it again. Marianne's discovery that Willoughby is not going to be the hero of her favourite story even comes in two stages which clearly resemble the stages of Catherine's discovery that the abbey is no Udolpho. The first is Willoughby's snubbing her in London and her receiving the letter from him which declares that he has long been engaged to someone else. These events resemble Catherine's series of disenchantments at the abbey beginning with the secret manuscript that turns into a laundry bill. In this stage of the heroine's career what appeared Gothic and romantic turns into the commonplace. Marianne is now forced to admit that no formal engagement to Willoughby ever did actually exist but was only 'implied' (p. 186) in her own romantic mind; and this is at the same time a crucial admission concerning her romantic engagement to the world in general.

There is then a second stage in which the commonplace turns into genuine evil: General Tilney forces Catherine to leave his house; Willoughby proves to have been a wicked seducer. In this second stage, Catherine's discovery of the General's viciousness is her central, symbolic discovery of the unpleasant nature of the world in which she is going to have to live; and again the same is true for Marianne. But Marianne's discovery is psychologically much more complex. Colonel Brandon, who is her spiritual mentor, tells Elinor that Willoughby is a seducer, in the hope that the information will be of 'use' in making Marianne feel less wretched (p. 210); and Elinor duly relays to her sister what he has said. It is significant in the development of Jane Austen's fiction that after hearing this news Marianne is still as wretched as before (p. 212). The Colonel's information has not been of any immediate 'use'. She can eventually feel the 'torture of penitence' it is true, but 'without the hope of amendment' (p. 270).

What is interesting here is that Jane Austen has already in this early novel qualified the efficacy of 'sense' in overcoming the anguish of 'sensibility' – a qualification that becomes stronger as her art matures. Colonel Brandon is above all a man of sense; and he has relayed to Elinor, that avatar of sense among the Dashwood sisters, what should rationally be of use in tempering Marianne's sensibility. But 'sense' has proved not quite to be the answer.

When Marianne's intellect has learned the fact of Willoughby's wickedness, the plot of this early novel has come to a resting place. It is usual in the novels for the heroine now to receive gratuitous aid in her spiritual regeneration from an unexpected quarter. In the next novel, for instance, aid comes from the Gardiners. When Elizabeth, having refused Darcy's proposal, returns to Longbourn, it 'was . . . necessary to name some other period for the commencement of actual felicity' (*Pride and Prejudice*, p. 237); and the Gardiners then move into the plot to take her to Pemberley. But Jane Austen seems to have been unable to devise any satisfactory plot business in *Sense and Sensibility* to move Marianne off the dead centre of penitence without hope of amendment, and so resorts to giving her a fever. Here is a clear case of Jane Austen's snatching at an unlikely but handy plot device to further her psychological plan. The fever, like Pip's in *Great Expectations* (lvii), serves the double purpose of punishing Marianne and of scrambling her brain so that she can begin a new and chastened life. Tom Bertram gets the same treatment, and regains 'his health, without regaining the thoughtlessness and selfishness of his previous habits' (*Mansfield Park*, p. 462). And so Marianne now returns home, launches a scheme of 'rational employment and virtuous self-control', of 'reasonable exertion', and vows that from now on her 'feelings shall be governed' (pp. 343, 342, 347).

Marianne's illusions about first impressions and heroes of favourite stories have now surrendered to facts and pathology. But before Jane Austen will give her the final approval of marriage to Colonel Brandon, Marianne must have the 'fact' (p. 347) of Willoughby's 'apology' for his misconduct delivered to her by Elinor, who has been keeping it in store. Jane Austen seems to consider Marianne's hearing this extenuating account of Willoughby's behaviour a last, crucial step in her development. Marianne herself agrees: she wants to be 'assured that he never was so *very* wicked as my fears have sometimes fancied him. . . .' She says that her 'peace of mind is doubly involved in it' (pp. 344–5).

The reasons why her peace of mind is so involved are only partly transmitted in her telegraphic prose: 'not only is it horrible to suspect a person, who has been what *he* has been to *me*, of such designs, – but what must it make me appear to myself?' The first of the reasons is obvious; and the second is a halting attempt at the idea that the revelation of Willoughby's true character is also to some extent a revelation of her own. After all, she had begun the novel thinking she 'could not be happy with a man whose taste did not in every point coincide with my own'; and Willoughby seemed indeed 'exactly formed to engage Marianne's heart'. He is '. . . Willoughby, whose heart I know so well. . . .' He answered 'her ideas of perfection' (pp. 17, 48, 189, 49). He talked to her only of herself.

Now she is faced with the fact that he is not what she thought; and this carries the implication that perhaps she too is not what she thought: that the two of them are indeed exactly formed to engage each other's heart when the truth is known. Thus there is lurking in the relationship between these two the possibility that whatever wickedness is at last discovered in the man for whom she felt such an attraction is also potentially in herself as well; and that for this reason it would be good to know that Willoughby 'never was so *very* wicked'.

The revelation of the wickedness in those illusory ideas of perfection to which Jane Austen's heroines are attracted always has this implication for the heroines themselves. In this early novel Jane Austen handles the implication very cautiously. Marianne's potential wickedness has been shunted off onto her counterpart Eliza, who has the 'same warmth of heart, the same eagerness of fancy and spirits' (p. 205). Eliza goes astray, and her own daughter Eliza is then seduced by the storybook hero that she and Marianne have shared. In these Elizas Jane Austen has indirectly revealed what may indeed lie beneath the romantic yearnings of the early Marianne. This lurid aspect of her character is frozen safely in mere potentiality, because her affair with Willoughby is already over when the Colonel tells the story comparing Eliza to her; just as the racier details of Willoughby's unsavoury character itself have been safely bottled up in the Colonel's neatly organised narrative of past events before Jane Austen will allow such details to exist in the novel.

In the next novel Jane Austen is much bolder. Elizabeth Bennet meets Wickham, and is 'convinced, that . . . he must always be her model of the amiable and pleasing' (*Pride and Prejudice*, p. 152). When the full extent of his waywardness is disclosed, the implication for the character of Elizabeth herself is shunted only as far as her own sister Lydia, a kindred spirit in that she does indeed elope with him. Here the kinship between the two young ladies has become more than metaphorical.

2

In *Sense and Sensibility* we see remarkably little of the hypothetical, 'true' Willoughby; and Marianne hardly sees him at all. Our impressions of Willoughby are so vivid that we are apt to be sceptical about this, yet it is true. The Willoughby at Barton comes to us and to Marianne for the most part as he has already been transformed in her own romantic imagination. Willoughby the seducer comes to us already entombed in the Colonel's lapidary syntax, and to Marianne in a version of the Colonel's story passed on by Elinor. We do see Willoughby once briefly at Cleveland, unmediated by any character's consciousness – while Marianne is upstairs. He is unfamiliar, restless, and leaves quickly for some other novel, to Elinor's relief and perhaps to Jane Austen's.

'Character' in Jane Austen's novels often has this ontological problem. Harriet Smith 'exists' in *Emma* partly as a projection of Emma's own imagination. The same is true of Frank Churchill. We get an unmediated glimpse of him at the conclusion in a letter, but by then whoever wrote the letter has left the novel for Windsor (he reappears briefly in Chapter xviii). Even characters who get through to us more or less 'objectively' do not very often exist as free agents in the novels. Often they seem to be in Jane Austen's employ, defining the central character in whom she is really interested, and to whom they therefore owe their opportunity for existence. The heroine's consciousness is always the organising centre of the novel; and her consciousness is the sum total of her reactions to all these subsidiary characters and other bits of reality that seem to have been placed around her primarily for the purpose of defining her.

No matter what the critics say, Jane Austen is hardly in love with 'character' for its own sake. In her 'Plan of a Novel' she ridicules the idea of a novel composed solely to 'exhibit a wide variety of Characters';[10] and in a letter she criticises Samuel Egerton Brydges's *Fitz-Albini* on the ground that 'There are many characters introduced, apparently merely to be delineated' (*Letters*, p. 32). Hers is far from an unusual attitude, but not all novelists share it. Sir Walter Scott, for instance, writes: 'When I light on such a character as Baillie Jarvie . . . my imagination brightens, and my conception becomes clearer at every step . . ., although it leads me many a weary mile away from the regular road. . . .'[11] Few characters ever took Jane Austen out of her way, although William Price in *Mansfield Park* is one of the interesting exceptions.[12]

She is always purposefully and efficiently 'using' her characters; and many of them hardly strike one as 'real' in an ordinary sense, any more than a caryatid would. But generations of readers seem to have found them so. An anonymous reviewer in 1818 says of Jane Austen's characters that 'whatever interest they excite . . . results . . . from the unaccountable pleasure . . . we derive from a simple imitation of any object;' we 'instantly recognise among some of our acquaintance, the sort of persons she intends to signify, as accurately as if we had heard their voices'.[13] Her great-nephew Edward, Lord Brabourne, refers to the 'figures which Miss Austen places upon the canvas, in such a manner as to make us all feel that they are not only real living people, but personal acquaintances of our own. . . .'[14] To George Henry Lewes, 'you know the people as if you had lived with them'.[15] And E. M. Forster uses Jane Austen's characters to make his distinction between 'flat' characters and ones, like

---

[10] *Novels*, VI (*Minor Works*) p. 429. But in *Northanger Abbey* Jane Austen does say that one feature of good novels is the 'varieties' of human nature they display (p. 38).

[11] *The Fortunes of Nigel* (1822), 'Introductory Epistle'.

[12] But then he may owe something to Jane Austen's sailor brothers Francis and Charles. See J. H. Hubback, Edith C. Hubback, *Jane Austen's Sailor Brothers* (London: John Lane, 1906) pp. 24–7. For Jane Austen's indulgence in William's naval enthusiasms see especially p. 375 of *Mansfield Park*.

[13] Cited above, p. 25 n. 8.

[14] *Letters of Jane Austen*, 2 vols (London: Richard Bentley, 1884) I 68. Cited hereafter as Brabourne.

[15] An unsigned review, 'The Lady Novelists', *Westminster Review*, LVIII (July 1852), 70–7. Reprinted (in part) in *Critical Heritage*.

many of hers, that are 'round' and 'ready for an extended life'.[16]

Who could deny that all this is true of Elizabeth Bennet and Emma? But it is hard to conceive of Mr Collins or even Jane Bennet stepping out of the novel and beginning an extended life, although Jane Austen thought she saw a portrait of the latter at an exhibition (Letters, pp. 309-10). Many of her characters come close to having the status of gears,[17] in that they have been given merely a set number of characteristics that all seem necessary to their very limited function in the novel. Mr Collins, for instance, is not far from the truth when he says of Charlotte Lucas, 'We seem to have been designed for each other' (Pride and Prejudice, p. 216). Willoughby seems at first 'exactly formed to engage Marianne's heart'; but Marianne is 'every thing but prudent', and in this respect the gear designed to engage her is a value named Colonel Brandon, a 'very prudent man' (pp. 6, 70).

The very characteristics themselves seem often to have been conceived as if they were cleanly distinct from one another like cogs, and therefore capable of being enumerated.[18] In a juvenile piece Miss Simpson's 'only fault' is ambition. 'Her second sister Sukey was Envious, Spitefull & Malicious' ('Jack and Alice, A Novel', Minor Works, p. 13). The guests at Mrs Ferrars's 'almost all laboured under one or other of these disqualifications for being agreeable – Want of sense, either natural or improved – want of elegance – want of spirits – or want of temper' (Sense and Sensibility, p. 233). When Henry Crawford speaks of Fanny Price's charms, he is nevertheless articulate enough to give them in a list (Mansfield Park, p. 294). And Mr Knightley can itemise Frank Churchill's 'faults' (Emma, p. 448).

---

[16] Aspects of the Novel, Chapter IV i.

[17] '. . . her writings are a capital picture of real life, with all the little wheels and machinery laid bare like a patent clock', Life of Henry Wadsworth Longfellow, ed. Samuel Longfellow, 2 vols (Boston: Ticknor, 1886) I 323. Quoted by Hogan (see p. 33 n. 22), pp. 53-4.

[18] 'Jane Austen believes that she understands not only the causes of character growth but also the observable details of how people behave. If anyone's conduct provides a puzzle, there is always an explanation – a single, clear explanation', Laurence Lerner, The Truth-tellers (New York: Schocken, 1967) p. 148.

Again there are exceptions, among them Darcy. At the beginning Longbourn society thinks his 'character' is 'decided' (*Pride and Prejudice*, p. 11); but the course of the novel reveals that he goes beyond first impressions. He moves from the mechanical to the organic, and his grounds at Pemberley become a correlative of his true character. The 'prospect' from his dining-parlour shows Elizabeth 'the winding of the valley, as far as she could trace it . . .' (p. 246); and Darcy thus becomes one of Jane Austen's few characters other than the heroines to have limits that are not fairly easy to define. It would take longer than Mr Gardiner can spare to walk around Darcy's grounds (p. 253). They border on the *je ne sais quoi*.

But Jane Austen seems most at home indoors, surrounded by artifacts made of parts that fit with precision. What seems easiest to imagine in her hands is not something organic, like a rose or a cat, but a pair of scissors. And her predominantly mechanistic conception of character has a profound effect on the moral nature of the novels. The people in them often discuss 'faults' as if 'character', like machinery, could not be conceived to have anything like an internal volition of its own, but instead lies inert until acted upon by specific environmental causes that have their specific, determinable effects on the mechanism. Even Darcy accounts for his bad manners by saying, 'Unfortunately an only son . . . I was spoilt by my parents . . .' (*Pride and Prejudice*, p. 369). And we are told rather snippily that Henry Crawford's behaviour is due to his being 'ruined by early independence and bad domestic example . . .' (*Mansfield Park*, p. 467).

'Faults' of character are thus generally isolable, avoidable, and sometimes even remediable. Elinor announces that '*One* observation may, I think, be fairly drawn' from Eliza's story, 'that all Willoughby's difficulties have arisen from the first offense against virtue, in his behaviour to Eliza Williams' (*Sense and Sensibility*, p. 352). The reformed, or repaired, Edward Ferrars accounts for his previous bad behaviour by saying, 'Had my mother given me some active profession . . . it would never have happened . . .' (p. 362). Likewise Edmund and Fanny generously imagine 'how excellent' Mary Crawford 'would have been had she fallen into good hands earlier' (*Mansfield Park*, p. 459).

What is equally remarkable, most of Jane Austen's characters have very few external features of any kind.[19] Let anyone who thinks he knows what her characters look like go through the text collecting details. The idea, more or less common in the eighteenth century,[20] that a character's inner nature is somehow bodièd forth in his physiognomy appears only faintly in her novels: Mrs Gardiner does say of Darcy that there is 'something of dignity in his countenance, that would not give one an unfavourable idea of his heart' (*Pride and Prejudice*, p. 258), but for the most part the inner nature of Jane Austen's people, like the inner nature of her Northanger Abbey, does not very obviously appear in whatever external features there are. First impressions are risky. Lady Susan must be Jane Austen's wickedest creation, yet Mrs Vernon can write of her that 'I never saw a face less indicative of any evil disposition than her's . . .' ('Lady Susan', *Minor Works*, p. 270).

To the extent that Jane Austen's characters are short on verifiable external detail, the heroines and the reader are of course free to create what they want to see. Elinor says of Edward Ferrars, '. . . I know him so well, that I think him really handsome; or, at least, almost so' (*Sense and Sensibility*, p. 20). And Elizabeth Bennet, having heard Wickham's sweet nothings, 'honoured him for such feelings, and thought him handsomer than ever as he expressed them' (*Pride and Prejudice*, p. 80).

The same is also true of the 'insides' of many of the characters. It is striking that the men in the novels who are most immediately attractive exhibit 'character' that will yield to almost any first impression the heroine has in mind. The early Edward Stanley 'could . . . always take either side' in an argu-

---

[19] The authors of the *Life and Letters* refer to Jane Austen's 'building up her characters [in *Emma*] almost entirely without formal description' (p. 307). According to Firkins, 'The body is not an actor in the play. After specification the features vanish' (p. 164).
[20] Thus in *Spectator* 86 (8 June 1711) Addison refers to the common belief that 'every one is in some Degree a Master of that Art which is generally distinguished by the Name of Physiognomy; and naturally forms to himself the Character or Fortune of a Stranger from the Features and Lineaments of his Face. . . . Every Passion gives a particular Cast to the Countenance, and is apt to discover itself in some Feature or other.' I am indebted to Gunnard Nelson for this reference.

ment ('Catherine', *Minor Works*, p. 231). When it comes to
card games Tom Musgrave says, 'Whatever you decide on, will
be a favourite with *me*' ('The Watsons', *Minor Works*, p. 358).
Henry Crawford is 'every thing to every body', and says he
feels 'as if I could be any thing or every thing' in the play they
are to put on. He is the best actor at Mansfield Park, and can
read any speech in Shakespeare with equal beauty. He even
gives Edmund some tips on sermon-reading; and when he courts
Fanny his attentions are shown easily 'adapting themselves' to
the 'delicacy of her character' (*Mansfield Park*, pp. 123, 165,
337, 341, 231). Emma's idea of Frank Churchill is that 'he can
adapt his conversation to the taste of every body'; and Anne
notices of Mr Elliot that, 'Various as were the tempers in her
father's house, he pleased them all' (*Persuasion*, p. 161). These
characters, like Satan and Lovelace,[21] take many shapes – except
that in Jane Austen's fiction it is the heroines who are partly
responsible for the shapes.

Even the good men the heroines marry – Edward Ferrars,
Colonel Brandon, Darcy, Edmund Bertram, Mr Knightley –
have in common a rather vague and colourless exterior that
nicely matches their inner reticence. Again Darcy is something
of an exception, although Mrs Gardiner says even of him that
he wants a 'little more liveliness . . .' (*Pride and Prejudice*, p.
325). Perhaps Jane Austen simply preferred such men, at least
in fiction. They certainly minimise the risks she takes when she
enters a man's world. Furthermore, they compel the heroines
to move beyond first impressions to an apprehension of inner
knightliness that requires studious application. If one is going
to esteem Colonel Brandon, it had better be for his soul. But
most important, the general character her heroes have to some
extent in common seems largely the result of her moving so
often into her heroines' minds and looking out at 'character'
from there. In the course of the novel the heroine comes to
'see' her spiritual mate; and very much detailed, purportedly
objective characterisation of him on Jane Austen's part would
tend to interfere with the illusion that he is being discovered
mainly from within the heroine's unobjective consciousness.

[21] The *Memoir* (1871) observes that Jane Austen's 'knowledge of
Richardson's works was such as no one is likely again to acquire . . .'
(p. 89). See also p. 48 above, n. 7.

There are of course some characters in the novels who are presented with such rigid authorial objectivity that the heroines and the reader have almost no leeway for interpretation whatever. These are generally 'humour' characters, or types.[22] Lady Denham is introduced as a type of the 'great Lady' ('Sanditon', *Minor Works*, p. 375). Mrs Bennet's humour is her 'nerves'; and her character comes close to being simply a 'mean understanding, little information, and uncertain temper' (*Pride and Prejudice*, p. 5). 'Vanity was the beginning and the end of Sir Walter Elliot's character . . .' (*Persuasion*, p. 4).

There are indeed such humour characters in Jane Austen's novels. But what is interesting is that often 'character' for her is simpler even than this. Often she confronts her heroines with people who have very little character at all in the ordinary sense, just as she confronts her heroines with a reality that is also in other respects relatively free of factual detail. The heroines are therefore free to characterise themselves, by projecting their own illusions onto their more or less neutral surroundings. Thus Harriet's last name is 'Smith'. When she is first introduced she is not even allowed to appear or to speak except as she has already registered on Emma's consciousness (*Emma*, pp. 22–3). Harriet is fairly free of verifiable detail that

---

[22] Firkins discusses a 'group of characters . . . for which the formula is the raising of a single trait to the highest power' (p. 18). Likewise Reuben Brower uses the term 'fixed characters' to describe Mr Collins, Mrs Bennet and Lady Catherine de Bourgh (*The Fields of Light* (New York: Oxford University Press, 1951) p. 174). And Margaret Kennedy distinguishes between Jane Austen's 'three-dimensional' characters and ones, like Mr Collins and Lady Catherine, who 'are not' (p. 54). It is interesting that late in Jane Austen's career she developed a special interest in these two-dimensional types. Thus in *Persuasion* Captain Benwick is presented almost as if he were merely the type of the bereaved lover. He simply 'had a pleasing face and a melancholy air, just as he ought to have' (p. 97). Jane Austen's last work, 'Sanditon', is largely populated by such types. E. M. Forster writes of the heroine: '. . . whereas Eleanor [sic] Dashwood, Fanny Price, Anne Elliot, were real people whose good sense, modesty, and detachment were personal qualities, Charlotte turns these qualities into labels, and can be seen . . . as she sits observing other labels upon the sea-front', *Abinger Harvest* (New York: Harcourt Brace, 1936) pp. 152–3. B. C. Southam discusses this feature of 'Sanditon' in *Literary Manuscripts*, pp. 112–13.

would interfere with Emma's active imagination. Her most characteristic utterances are, 'What shall I do? What would you advise me to do? Pray, dear Miss Woodhouse, tell me what I ought to do'; and 'Whatever you say is always right' (pp. 52, 74). Emma can therefore go a long way toward creating a Harriet, first in her mind, then with a brush. She is free to create a Frank Churchill, too, from the one who says, 'Oh! Miss Woodhouse, why are you always so right?' (p. 259). Sir Walter Elliot also has his own raw material for the artistic creation of character, and her name is Clay. To him, her 'character is just another mirror in Kellynch Hall, one which says, 'We are not all born to be handsome' (*Persuasion*, p. 20).

3

An impressive tradition has made Elinor, and 'sense', the heroine of *Sense and Sensibility*.[23] She is supposed to be Jane Austen's delegate at Norland, and we are to understand that she eventually brings her sister Marianne around to the right way of thinking.[24] This is a serious misreading of the novel.

---

[23] Two of many examples: 'The interest and merit of the piece depend altogether upon the behaviour of the elder sister', review of *Emma* cited above, p. 23 n. 1; 'I suppose that the former [Elinor], being "Sense", has the best claim to the heroine's niche', Brabourne, I 93.

[24] The remarkable idea that Jane Austen is in total sympathy with Elinor goes on and on. 'To Elinor Dashwood the metaphor of a well-scoured channel for the author's own comments may be appropriate', Lascelles, p. 200; Elinor 'no doubt embodies Jane Austen's youthful conception of a perfect woman', Thomson, p. 81; in Elinor, Jane Austen 'has created a character so faultless that ridicule is impossible', her 'opinions coincide with those of Jane Austen', Craik, *Jane Austen: the Six Novels*, pp. 33, 35; 'Elinor is her author's conscience; . . . and she . . . is totally shielded from her author's . . . social disapproval', Mudrick, p. 85. Mudrick's argument on this point is especially interesting. He acknowledges that Elinor yields somewhat to Willoughby's charm at Cleveland, and chooses to account for this by saying that there is an 'inconsistency' in Jane Austen's treatment of her heroine (p. 85).
The following are samples of criticism on the subject of the supposed triumph of 'sense' over 'sensibility': Elinor 'does not change or learn anything in the course of the book', Kennedy, p.

Elinor is predominantly 'sense'[25] of course, and Marianne sensibility; and it is also true that Marianne has acquired much more sense by the end. But Elinor does too acquire just a little of her sister's sensibility. Readers tend to overlook this, and thus to destroy the delicate structure of the novel. For Jane Austen has created something like a double heroine; she also does so in the next two novels. The central consciousness which looks out at the world here is not Elinor's, but hers in conjunction with Marianne's.

These two indeed shared the title of the youthful novel that eventually became Sense and Sensibility, and we have to keep in mind that they share the title of the published work also. Neither of these dispositions ever quite cancels out the other in the course of the novel. The two sisters merely converge on an imaginary point somewhere between them. This would be the ideal 'heroine' of the novel:[26] a heroine who could never exist in this, or Jane Austen's, imperfect world; and who would perfectly reconcile what neither of the Dashwood sisters alone ever quite does.

An opposition that occurs commonly in the eighteenth century pits 'sense' or 'reason'[27] against 'sensibility' or 'feeling' or 'passion'. Richard Payne Knight, the writer on the picturesque, declares for instance that the 'end of morality is to restrain . . . all the irregularities of passion . . .; and to subject

---

56; 'Elinor is a straight line of sanity ruled through the book', Elizabeth Bowen, 'Jane Austen', The English Novelists, ed. Derek Verschoyle (London: Chatto & Windus, 1936) p. 107; 'in the end . . . Jane Austen yields to the dictum that sense must win out over sensibility', Ten Harmsel, p. 43; 'Sense is justified, sensibility shown as weakness', Sherry, p. 58; '. . . meant to be a comedy in which we come to realise the superiority of Sense', Lerner, p. 160; 'a true over a false vision of life', Lascelles, p. 120.

[25] 'Elinor, as Sense . . .', Kennedy, p. 56; Elinor 'is the personification of good sense', Firkins, p. 11; Elinor 'represents common sense', George Moore, Avowals (London: Heinemann, 1936) p. 36; 'Elinor who is Sense, and Marianne who is Sensibility', John Bailey, Introduction to Jane Austen (London: Oxford University Press, 1931) p. 29.

[26] Wiesenfarth makes this point, p. 35.

[27] The French translation of the title in the nineteenth century was usually Raison et Sensibilité. See Chapman, Facts, p. 139; and Johnson, p. x.

the conduct of life to the dominion of abstract reason. . . .'[28] In spite of what some critics seem to think, this is hardly a credo to which Jane Austen would subscribe. True, some of her characters might. Mr Collins takes care that in proposing to Elizabeth he is not 'run away with by my feelings on this subject'. Mary Bennet, too, wants very much to be sensible, and no one can doubt that she is when she delivers the proposition that 'every impulse of feeling should be guided by reason'.

If this is 'sense', it is not Elinor's. She has 'good sense' it is true, but also an 'excellent heart; – her disposition was affectionate, and her feelings were strong' (p. 6);[29] just as Marianne is not simply 'sensible', but 'sensible and clever' (p. 6). Elinor thinks a better acquaintance with the world will do her sister good (p. 56), and the same of course is true of herself. In a career that parallels her sister's, Elinor's nascent sensibility is now drawn out to temper her strong good sense.[30]

Elinor's illusion at the beginning of the novel, unlike Catherine's and Marianne's, does not originate even partly in the books she has read. It is simply a faith in the sufficiency of her intelligence. She is proud of her powers of observation (p. 305). She is confident they are superior to her sister's, and so delivers to Marianne her own first impressions of Edward Ferrars with a grand 'I venture to pronounce' (p. 20). But in the course of the novel Elinor too must accept facts that penetrate her illusions. Readers sometimes overlook this. Marianne has made a Willoughby who answers her ideas of perfection, and Elinor has made an Edward.

In many respects Elinor's romance with Edward obviously echoes Marianne's with Willoughby. Jane Austen has worked hard at this. Willoughby apparently is in possession of a lock of Marianne's hair; and Edward has a ring which Elinor thinks holds a plait of her own. Willoughby suddenly leaves the neigh-

---

[28] *Analytical Inquiry*, p. 451.

[29] Among the very few critics who call attention to this is an anonymous reviewer in 1812. He refers to Elinor as 'possessing great good sense, with a *proper quantity of sensibility*', *Critical Review*, I, Fourth Series (Feb 1812) 149–57. Reprinted in *Critical Heritage*.

[30] But not according to W. A. Craik, who seems to think Elinor does not change at all. Her 'dilemma is contrived, the work of agencies outside herself, and all she has to do is to endure it', *Jane Austen: the Six Novels*, p. 50.

bourhood of Barton cottage under mysterious circumstances
that turn out to have been caused by a summons from his
guardian, Mrs Smith; Edward suddenly leaves the cottage under
equally mysterious circumstances that Elinor supposes are due
to his having been summoned by his mother. Marianne's receiving a letter that tells her Willoughby is engaged echoes
Elinor's being shown a letter that helps prove to her that Edward
too is engaged. Indeed when Marianne hears of the engagement
she thinks 'Edward seemed a second Willoughby' (p. 261).
Willoughby's break with Mrs Smith echoes Edward's with his
mother. Even the news of Willoughby's marriage seems to have
been given a deliberate echo in the false news of Edward's. And
Willoughby's final apology to Elinor (pp. 316–32) is followed
by Edward's (pp. 362–3).[31]

Jane Austen is her usual systematic self in working out her
plan for Elinor's reformation. The results of unalloyed sensibility are portrayed in Marianne's counterpart the young Eliza
Williams, who actually runs off with Willoughby; and the
results of unalloyed sense are similarly portrayed in Elinor's
counterpart Lucy Steele, to whom Edward is actually engaged.
The resemblance Colonel Brandon points out in the first case
Jane Austen points out herself in the second. She makes clear
that Lucy, like Elinor, is distinguished by a kind of 'sense' (see
Elinor's comment on her, p. 263). Lucy too makes a reference
– a sly reference – to her own powers of observation (p. 148).
And just as upon Elinor the 'whole task of telling lies when
politeness required it, always fell' (p. 122), so Lucy shows a
certain finesse in doing just the same thing. Elinor can practise
flattery ('a little of that address', p. 145) to get what she wants,
and so can Lucy ('flattery', p. 254).

Jane Austen comes down relentlessly on the similarities between these two. Elinor sensibly recommends to Edward that
'a little humility may be convenient' in reconciling him with
Mrs Ferrars so long as she holds the purse strings; and Lucy
too perseveres in her own 'humility of conduct' towards Mrs
Ferrars after she has married Edward's brother (pp. 372, 377).
The two are enough alike to Mrs Ferrars that she thinks Edward's

---

[31] W. A. Craik (above) has an excellent discussion of parallels
between Elinor's romance with Edward, and Marianne's with
Willoughby. See p. 53.

marrying Elinor rather than Lucy would merely pair him with the 'least evil of the two' (p. 297). And in the end she gets them both. One is clearly superior to the other in ways that matter, but both are versions of 'sense'. Perhaps the distinction in the novel between 'sense, either natural or improved' (p. 233) is meant to apply to these two. Lucy is indeed something not far from an unimproved Elinor – an Elinor with bad grammar. One is only wood, the other hard as steel, but they end with the same name.

Lucy even vows the conventional bosom 'friendship' for Elinor (p. 240), and soon after they meet makes a confidant of her. Lucy accounts for such instantaneous intimacy with a statement that has a significance beyond what she means, or Elinor understands: '. . . as soon as I saw you, I felt almost as if you was an old acquaintance' (p. 132). This might just hint at some dark spiritual kinship. The same is true of her question to Elinor concerning the secret engagement: 'What would you do yourself?' (p. 133). These two young ladies do indeed mirror each other in a disturbing way. They share more in common than Edward. The plait of hair Elinor thinks is her own is Lucy's.

In one of Jane Austen's most remarkable scenes, an early scene at Barton Park, the 'two fair rivals' are 'seated side by side at the same table, and with the utmost harmony engaged in forwarding the same work' (p. 145) – the real work of course not being a filigree basket but Edward. Here are these two versions of 'sense' huddled together over their close, exacting work, their shrewd, wily picking at each other covered by Marianne's undoubtedly romantic piano music; and Elinor is being almost as conniving as Lucy, if much more graceful and grammatical. She is 'careful in guarding her countenance from every expression that could give her words a suspicious tendency' (p. 147). In this room we can see sense and sensibility engaged in their indigenous handiwork; and just as Marianne takes on in the novel some of Elinor's good sense, so Elinor is going to move slightly further away from her sister-in-sense Lucy, by taking on just a little of Marianne's sensibility. Elinor's change of heart is slight, but crucial in the meaning of the novel.

She even has her moment of discovery, although Jane Austen does not put much emphasis on it. When Lucy discloses the important 'fact' (p. 139) that she is engaged to Edward. Elinor feels an 'emotion and distress beyond any thing she had ever felt before' (p. 135). She has been shown by 'sense' comparable to her own that the Edward she thought she was so intelligent in perceiving was at least partly an illusion; and this is inseparable, as it is in all Jane Austen's novels, from her discovery that she has had an illusion about herself. She has seen that whatever in her own mental constitution falls strictly under 'sense' in opposition to her sister's 'sensibility' leads nevertheless to a similar error of imagination. Her modest abbey has given way to a fact, and she resolves to 'combat her own affection for Edward and to see him as little as possible' (p. 142).

Elinor's resolution corresponds to Marianne's after she has heard the story of Willoughby and Eliza. She now feels the torture of penitence without the hope of amendment. She is not yet ready for the reformed Edward who will ask for her hand at the end, any more than Marianne's penitence made her ready for the Colonel. Elinor's sense has been touched, but not her sensibility. In the interests of neatness and symmetry she too needs to be given a fever that will disorient her, and in this case infuse into her sense a little sensibility.

The fever Jane Austen gives Elinor seems just as awkwardly contrived as the one she gives Marianne. It is the famous scene in which Willoughby comes to Cleveland and pours out his soul to Elinor. It is easy to dismiss the scene as a decorative filigree Jane Austen could have dispensed with;[32] but that is not the answer. She is ironic in her 'Plan of a Novel' about characters so 'Wicked' that there is 'hardly a resemblance of Humanity left in them' (*Minor Works*, p. 429), and Willoughby's confession gives him the semblance of humanity he certainly needs at this point. But the real significance of this interview is not the humanity it gives to him but to Elinor. She finds that his

---

[32] Many critics just do not think Willoughby's scene with Elinor at Cleveland has any significant relevance to the novel at all. It is a 'blunder that cannot be condoned', George Moore, *Avowals*, p. 38; it is 'quite inappropriate to the book', Andrew H. Wright, p. 95; it is 'parenthetical', Lascelles, p. 168; 'The situation might . . . be cleared up at once by Lucy Steele's elopement with Robert, but . . . Miss Austen delays the catastrophe by Marianne's illness and Willoughby's confession', Thomson, p. 234. But Moler rightly sees the significance of the scene; see his pp. 71-2.

influence on her is now 'heightened by circumstances which ought not in reason to have weight' (p. 333) – a sentiment Marianne would understand. Elinor's new and tender feelings thus infuse her with just a touch of febrile sensibility which runs irreconcilably counter to her constitutional sense, and which she is now going to have to endure – as do the rest of us.

Elinor had been convinced that Willoughby was 'deep in hardened villainy' (p. 184); but now, as she hears his confession, her heart is unaccountably 'softened' (p. 325). This again is a symbolic event that occurs, although sometimes unobtrusively, in every one of the novels: a softening of the heroine's heart toward the false hero. In *Mansfield Park*, for instance, Fanny Price's heart is 'softened' (p. 365) toward Henry Crawford; and if Jane Austen had worked on *Northanger Abbey* alongside or after *Sense and Sensibility*, Catherine's heart would probably have been made to soften toward Captain Tilney rather than toward that safe semblance of badness, his intentionally masked brother.

Elinor cannot live any longer isolated in her virginal world of rigid good sense. She belongs to the real one, which she enters formally when at Cleveland she takes Willoughby's hand (p. 331). No event in the novel is more important than this. Elizabeth Bennet will take Wickham's in a similar scene, and Fanny Price will take Henry Crawford's. Elinor now has in her a little of Marianne, and Eliza. At the beginning Marianne had said, 'Elinor has not my feelings' (p. 18), and now to some extent she has them.

4

Elinor and Marianne's loop out into the world, from dear Norland to the cramped Barton Cottage, from there to the spacious Barton Park, then to London, and closer home again to Cleveland, has introduced the two sisters to the same world: the world indicated in the title. Elinor now has a little of Marianne's feeling, Marianne some of Elinor's sense. The two now stand on common ground. They are ready to go home, to complete the circle and point to the common ground which is their version of the well-known road Catherine returns home to walk again. 'There, exactly there', Marianne says, 'there I fell . . .' (p. 344); and Elinor should be pointing there too.

In *Northanger Abbey* Catherine and Isabella share the sister-hood of romantic 'friendship'. In *Sense and Sensibility* Jane Austen has introduced true sisters, and their blood relationship itself becomes an expression in the novel of the common state of mind toward which the two converge. Pairs of sisters with more or less antithetical characteristics in Jane Austen's work go all the way back to juvenile pieces like 'Frederic & Elfrida', where the 'Wit & Charms' of the 'amiable Rebecca' are opposed to the 'Exterior & beautifull outside' of her sister Jezalinda (*Minor Works*, p. 6). The specific relationship of Elinor and Marianne, however, seems to be anticipated[33] in 'The Watsons'. Emma Watson, who has been raised in elegance by her aunt and uncle, returns home to her humble family, where she suffers the 'dreadful mortifications of unequal Society' (*Minor Works*, p. 361). She is reunited in her family with her giddy older sister Elizabeth, who in her absence has felt the charms of the raffish Tom Musgrave. Elizabeth thinks her sister is destined to follow suit: 'I defy you not to be delighted with him if he takes notice of you' (p. 319).

Emma, however, considers herself above such charms: 'My conduct must tell you how I have been brought up' (p. 318). Her sister is impressed by this loftiness, and exclaims on one occasion, 'My dearest Emma! – You are like nobody else in the World' (p. 342). The piece was never finished, although there are some surviving indications of how Jane Austen intended to carry it on. Emma was apparently to marry the good Mr Howard.[34] But it seems very likely that before this took place Jane Austen would have made Emma soften toward Tom Musgrave in the same way that Elinor does toward Willoughby. Elizabeth's blood is in Emma no matter how the latter was brought up. She is a Watson as much as Elinor is a Dashwood; and in what we have of the story a Mrs Edwards points toward

---

[33] 'The Watsons' is unfinished and undated. It was probably composed between 1803 and 1805. See Southam, pp. 64–5.

[34] See *Novels*, VI (*Minor Works*) pp. 362–3, where Chapman quotes from the *Memoir* (1871). For the unusually close relationship of Jane Austen to her own sister Cassandra see *Memoir* (1871) pp. 16–17; and Hill, p. 238.

the pull of consanguinity that would probably have drawn
Emma toward Elizabeth: 'Miss Emma Watson puts me very
much in mind of her eldest Sister' (p. 324).

This certainly is the case in *Sense and Sensibility*. When
Elinor and Marianne return to Norland they have arrived at
a truer sisterhood than they had at the beginning. Their bloods
have to some extent mingled.[35] It is very important nevertheless
that they are still two distinct persons: one whose predominant
character tends toward sense, the other toward sensibility. In
none of the novels do these or any other more or less antithetical
characteristics become reconciled in one person; although Jane
Austen seems to be working toward such a hybrid in Anne
Elliot, who appears in the last complete novel, *Persuasion*. In
a confectioner's shop at Bath Anne cannot decide whether she
is going to the door to see if it has stopped raining or to look
for her beloved Captain Wentworth; and she resolves that 'one
half of her should not be always so much wiser than the other
half, or always suspecting the other of being worse than it was'
(p. 175). Here is sense enough to come in out of the rain, and
yet sensibility too, both in one character – an Elinor-Marianne.
But as a rule antithetical characteristics are absolutely reconciled only at that imaginary point of convergence suggested by
the movement, for instance, of Elinor and Marianne towards
each other in the course of this novel: towards that imaginary
point where the two sisters would have become one; where they
would cease to be separate sisters and would have become that
beautiful idea which always seems to be searching in Jane
Austen's fiction for a character finally to embody it.

Jane Austen seems never to have found that character. What
she has found is the 'family'. It is here that all differences are
reconciled. At the beginning of *Sense and Sensibility* the three
Dashwood sisters and their mother were systematically introduced in terms of one another, as if they were points along a
line linking 'sense' and 'sensibility'. Again in the next novel
the Bennet family are introduced as variations of 'pride' (see
p. 82 below). A touch of nature makes them kin. The course
of both these novels brings out the family likenesses more and

---

[35] Andrew H. Wright notes that late in the novel the two sisters
'become increasingly like each other', p. 91.

more; as if the sisters on whom the novels concentrate were moving inward from their original, individual, positions toward a central pool of common family characteristics they share with each other and with the rest of the family. Marianne acquires some of her sister's sense, Elinor some of Marianne's sensibility. Lydia runs off with Wickham, toward whom her sister Elizabeth had felt attracted. Later, Anne Elliot will trade glances with the man her sister had intended to marry. The common characteristics of the family thus seem to be present in every member, if only as a faint potentiality; and the course of the novel draws out the potentiality, establishes the common kinship, as the characters surrender some of their individuality to the family.

But not all their individuality. When Elinor and Marianne return to the Park they are more closely related than they were when they left, but their individual sense and sensibility still can never completely blend in one person. What ultimately reconciles these sisters is simply their membership in the same family. In that entity, the family, Jane Austen has deployed the disparate and even irreconcilable characteristics of humankind; and it is the fact of membership in the family that must reconcile them.[36] And so it is in the novels that the characters again and again affirm the deep irrefragable unity of the family; and Henry Tilney declares his 'family partiality'.

Jane Austen says that 'pictures of perfection' make her 'sick & wicked' (*Letters*, pp. 486–7). Her irony, her unwillingness to commit herself to reductive schemes and absolutes, her retiring into the 'dramatic' form, can be seen in the irreducible relativism of her families. Elinor may in some respect be 'better' as a compromise than Marianne; but, if something must be perfect, what is perfect for Jane Austen is finally the family to which they both belong.[37] This relationship goes beyond judgements of good and evil, Lady Catherine's judgements or Jane Austen's. The Dashwoods, the Bennets, are all her *dramatis*

---

[36] Again, Wright to my knowledge is the only critic who sees this. 'Elinor and Marianne are in fact twin heroines, each embodying a mode of existence which is desirable, but each of which contradicts the other', p. 86.

[37] But to Litz 'in *Sense and Sensibility* the antitheses are resolved by a suppression of one position and an uneasy exaltation of the other', p. 102.

personae, her children. It is not Jane Austen who says, 'throw off your unworthy child from your affection for ever', but Mr Collins.

When Lord Brabourne remarks on Elizabeth Bennet, 'How cleverly is the line drawn which separates her and Jane from the rest of the Bennet family, to whom they were as much superior as if they had been the children of other parents!' he begins the solemn discussions of how remarkable it is, from a genetic point of view, that characters so unlike one another should appear together in Jane Austen's families.[38] Her families do indeed include such diversity, because life does. They are conceived as little paradigms of humankind itself. In them we see Jane Austen's characteristic embracing in her art of what is diverse, what is permanently contrary, without any irritable reaching out after an absolute 'truth'. If there must be such a truth, it is in the family as a whole. There all Jane Austen's ironic relativism, all her habitual retiring into a variety of points of view, is reconciled – to the extent that it ever is.

5

When Elinor has been infused with some sensibility by her softening toward Willoughby, Jane Austen considers her ready to marry Edward; and when Edward has passed through his affair with Lucy, he in turn is ready to marry Elinor. Predictably, he undergoes in the novel the same movement toward a middle ground as do the two sisters. There was a time when he had some of Marianne's sensibility. He thought Lucy was pretty,

---

[38] Brabourne, I 91. On this subject we encounter some of the oddest passages in Jane Austen criticism. In *Mansfield Park* Maria and Julia 'ought to belong to the London set who are . . . unprincipled . . . instead of being Mansfield products', Q. D. Leavis (cited below, p. 79 n. 3) X 135; in *Pride and Prejudice* 'it is difficult to conceive that Kitty and Lydia should have sprung from the same stem of which Jane and Elizabeth were the primary offshoots', Firkins, p. 30; at Longbourn 'the family circle comprises extremes of virtue and vice. . . . Upon what genetic hypothesis was this miscellany . . . founded?', R. W. Chapman, *Facts and Problems*, p. 184; and finally, for an answer that might make Mendel gasp, see Elizabeth Jenkins' musings on the workings of heredity in the Bennets, p. 242.

'at least I thought so *then*, and I had seen so little of other women, that I could make no comparisons, and see no defects' (p. 362). But by the time the novel begins he has already been disenchanted (p. 367). Thus he begins the novel in a melancholy state not unlike Marianne's after she has seen the truth concerning Willoughby: penitence without hope of amendment. He now lacks sensibility altogether (p. 18); he even knows nothing of the picturesque (p. 96). When Marianne asks him to admire the landscape all he can say is that 'It is a beautiful country . . . but these bottoms must be dirty in winter' (p. 88).

Edward's softening toward Elinor brings him, also, to a balance between sense and sensibility. By the end he is probably capable of saying, 'these bottoms must be dirty in winter, but it is a beautiful country'. She helps him to see Lucy in her true light, for it was his inability to make comparisons that hid her defects; and in the same respect he sees Elinor in her true light only because – o *felix culpa* – he had loved Lucy first. When Edward receives the letter containing the symbolic fact that Jane Austen has done him the favour of sending Lucy off with his brother, he is therefore immediately ready to ask Elinor to marry him. And he does, with a dispatch that does not seem to catch Elinor nearly so much off guard (p. 363) as it does most readers.[39] Here, as so often, Jane Austen's mind is intent on her plan rather than on verisimilitude.

Earlier, Colonel Brandon had learned of Edward's being cast off by his mother; and it happened that on that very day he also learned that the living of his Delaford had fallen vacant. Jane Austen has made it so, not so much to give Edward a living adequate to marry Elinor, for this could have been assured in any number of less awkward ways. The main reason for this remarkable turn in the plot seems to be that Edward's taking the Colonel's living brings him onto the same common ground

---

[39] This cataclysmic elopement and marriage seems to bother every critic who is determined to judge it by the standards of probability. '. . . there is something ludicrous in the rapidity with which, the very moment that his fool of a brother has conveniently taken [Lucy] off his hands, [Edward] hurries off to Elinor, to make her happy . . .', Brabourne, 1 86. See also Craik, *Jane Austen: the Six Novels*, pp. 50–1; Thomson, p. 235; Bailey, p. 33; Firkins, p. 5; Liddell, p. 29.

with the Colonel, figuratively – and so why not literally? Thus Jane Austen labours toward the end of the novel to fuse these two men into something of a single partner suitable for the now more closely related Elinor and Marianne. The Colonel now mentions, with no preparation whatever on Jane Austen's part, that he has met Edward from time to time in Harley Street and is 'much pleased with him' (p. 282); Edward now conveniently refers to his new acquaintance the Colonel as a 'sensible man'. The narrative now comes down heavily on 'Their resemblance in good principles and good sense' (p. 370).

The real resemblance between the two that makes them fit to be the collective partner for Elinor and Marianne is that both of them, outside the main action of the novel, have passed through that obligatory affair of sensibility and have arrived at the same state of mind as have the two sisters in the main action itself. In this early novel Jane Austen is thorough, if anything, in carrying out the idea that her four marriageable figures must pass through the same psychological course before she will unite them. But she does not seem technically able yet to keep Edward and the Colonel's reformation in suspension as an ingredient in the main action. In both cases it has settled to the bottom.

Edward's change of feelings concerning Lucy appears as a lump of narrative delivered when he and his author seem to have no choice, late in the third Volume (pp. 361–8); and the Colonel's similar adventure with the elder Eliza is delivered as much-criticised[40] retrospect in the second Volume (pp. 204–211). In every one of the novels the man destined to marry the heroine undergoes some significant change in character like the Colonel's and Edward's here. Even in *Northanger Abbey* there is a brief reference at the conclusion to something Henry Tilney has learned that may be intended by his author to have some lasting moral value (p. 247). But how to bring this change of character into suspension as part of the action proper remains a problem for Jane Austen throughout her career.

Colonel Brandon's new character is already established when the novel begins, and he is the steady moral beacon for the others.

---

[40] A 'rather lame device', Thomson, p. 96; 'barely necessary', Craik (above), p. 52; 'too late', Mudrick, p. 83; 'incredible', Ten Harmsel, p. 54.

He is already, as Elinor says, a sensible man (p. 50). He himself alludes to his forlorn and cheerless gravity, and no one would disagree. He even seems a little like a booby prize given Marianne to teach her a lesson for being too romantic – a man for whom one is destined to feel 'esteem'.[41] But he is intended nevertheless to be a tempered Willoughby. He too loved an Eliza, a girl with the 'same warmth of heart, the same eagerness of fancy and spirits' as Marianne (p. 205); and Marianne is indeed the second attachment of both of them. The Colonel had almost run off with his Eliza, and Willoughby actually did with her daughter. The Colonel makes a point of the 'unhappy resemblance' (p. 211) between the fate of the mother, whom he loved, and that of the daughter, whom Willoughby loved.

But Colonel Brandon is almost not a character at all. He is the steady, silent trustee of a moral value toward which the other three characters move; and which they have reached when at the conclusion they come to live at his Delaford, the one family enveloped in the property of the other. Marianne's marriage to him serves mainly to signify that at last she subscribes to the values he represents; and Mr Woodhouse's question, when he hears that Emma and Mr Knightley want to marry, could be asked here as well: 'Why could not they go on as they had done?'

Part of the answer seems to be that Jane Austen accepts without much question the convention that fiction ends with the heroine happily married. She complains of the novel *Olimpe et Theophile*, 'It really is too bad! – Not allowing them to be happy together, when they *are* married' (*Letters*, p. 450); and her great-nephew's typical attitude toward the convention is probably close to her own. He comments on the novels of Fanny Burney that Jane Austen knew so well: '. . . the heroine always satisfactorily escapes from her troubles . . . and marries the right person in the most . . . orthodox manner. This is only right and proper'.[42] This may be the sole explanation why at the conclusion the Colonel and Marianne occupy more than the same

---

[41] 'The embellishment of the Colonel . . . consists chiefly in his bestowal of a rectory upon Edward Ferrars . . . and his fetching of Mrs Dashwood to her daughter's sick-bed', Firkins, p. 6.

[42] I 69, speaking of Fanny Burney's novels. '. . . her characters are preoccupied with marriage', Bowen, 'Jane Austen', p. 103.

drawing-room. Jane Austen was after all rather cautious in all matters of convention. In the margin of Oliver Goldsmith's *An History of England* she wrote as a young girl, 'Every ancient custom ought to be Sacred, unless it is prejudicial to Happiness';[43] and an older Jane Austen, in long sleeves, wrote similarly to Cassandra, 'Mrs Tilson had long sleeves too, & she assured me that they are worn in the evening by many. I was glad to hear this' (*Letters*, p. 386).

So Marianne marries Colonel Brandon. And we are to suppose they will be happy. Willoughby gave a good first impression, but the Colonel's are inner attractions, to be esteemed. In a juvenile piece a young lady thinks that Mr Watts is 'quite an old Man, about two & thirty'; but her sister wisely puts it another way: 'He is not more than two & thirty ... rather plain to be sure, but then what is Beauty in a Man; if he has but a genteel figure & a sensible looking Face it is quite sufficient' ('The Three Sisters', *Minor Works*, pp. 58, 61). Colonel Brandon is the man for her, and apparently for Marianne too. Marianne's marriage to him is the final, ceremonial surrender of her self-centred romantic illusions to the world of the commonplace that she resisted at the beginning. Her first impressions have had to give way to the inner truth. Colonel Brandon wears a flannel waistcoat to ward off the rheumatism.

6

Sense and Sensibility began with old Mr Dashwood being cared for by the Henry Dashwoods and their daughters, 'not merely from interest, but from goodness of heart' (p. 3). But it is the will of the shadowy old man that his estate should go ultimately to his great-nephew John, who does not have the 'strong feelings of the rest of the family' (p. 5). Thus at the beginning the estate of this novel has been given over to him by the will of its creator; and one is not apt to remember at the end that he still

---

[43] See Mary Augusta Austen-Leigh, *Personal Aspects of Jane Austen* (London: John Murray, 1920) pp. 27–8. Jane Austen seems to have shared this sentiment with Fanny Price, who says, on the subject of morning and evening prayers, 'It is a pity ... that the custom should have been discontinued. It was a valuable part of former times', *Mansfield Park*, p. 86.

possesses it, and is managing it well. Furthermore, the Ferrars' estate goes to Robert, the genius of the toothpick case, and to Lucy Steele. Her final 'prosperity' is an 'encouraging instance of what ... an unceasing attention to self-interest ... will do in securing every advantage of fortune ...' (p. 376).

In Jane Austen's novels, calculating and prudent characters like these do inherit more than their share of the earth. We remember what Eleanor Tilney says of her father's abbey: 'I am but a nominal mistress of it, ... my real power is nothing.' The power is the General's, and at the end he has married her off profitably. Longbourn will go to Mr Collins, Kellynch to Mr Elliot.

This is the world into which the John Dashwoods push Elinor and Marianne at the beginning, and in which the two sisters must find a place. It is a world in which Lady Susan offers Reginald the shrewd advice: '... where possessions are so extensive as those of your Family, the wish of increasing them, if not strictly reasonable, is too common to excite surprise or resentment' ('Lady Susan', *Minor Works*, p. 300). It is a world in which Jane Austen's father offers advice to his son Francis on the value of 'prudence' when we are 'rising in life'.[44] A world in which Fanny Price's sailor brother speculates on his 'next step' upward when the first lieutenant on the *Thrush* is 'out of the way' (*Mansfield Park*, p. 375). A world in which the following heartwarming story is told of Jane Austen's own brother Charles: he was

> conning the roadstead with his glass, on the beach near Gosport. ... He saw the Captain's flag half-masted in the *Aurora*, took a boat out and learned that Captain Marshall had just died. Then he took a post chaise to the Admiralty. He was the first to report the vacancy, and asked for the appointment.[45]

Prudence, perhaps even Lucy Steele's 'sense', will always be

---

[44] J. H. Hubback, Edith C. Hubback, *Jane Austen's Sailor Brothers*, p. 18.
[45] Reported in John H. Hubback's 'Pen Portraits in Jane Austen's Novels', *Cornhill Magazine*, Third Series, LXV (July 1928) 24–33. Charles got the post.

very useful in such a world – so much so, that Sir Walter Scott is moved to make some critical comments in his review of *Emma*:

> ... before the authors of moral fiction couple Cupid indivisibly with calculating prudence, we would have them reflect, that they may sometimes lend their aid to substitute more mean ... motives of conduct, for the romantic feelings which their predecessors perhaps fanned into too powerful a flame.[46]

Romantic sensibility does indeed seem destined to have to make large concessions in Jane Austen's novels, if only to survive. What power does romance have when one finally enters the 'world'? Mrs Johnson sneers that Lady Susan's daughter indulges in 'that romantic tender-heartedness which will always ensure her misery enough' ('Lady Susan', *Minor Works*, p. 295); and Jane Austen seems ruefully to agree. Thus in *Sense and Sensibility* Marianne is allowed to escape such misery, by acquiring some more sense; and near the conclusion she is made to say, 'I wish to assure you ... that I see every thing – as you can desire me to do' (p. 349). She has gone a long way towards adjusting to the world.

Are we supposed to rejoice at this? Perhaps not quite. Near the beginning of the novel Colonel Brandon had commented, 'there is something so amiable in the prejudices of a young mind, that one is sorry to see them give way to the reception of more general opinions' (p. 56). The words apply so poignantly to Marianne; it is good to remember them at the end. She now sees everything as the Colonel could desire her to; and there is something necessary in that. But something sorrowful, for which Elinor is a consolation. For against Marianne's acquired sense Jane Austen has set Elinor's sudden new sensibility when faced with Willoughby – a circumstance 'which ought not in reason to have weight'. Near the end of *Northanger Abbey* were the words, '... there are some situations of the human mind in which good sense has very little power' (p. 239); and Elinor has discovered one – perhaps to her good fortune. Perhaps in the happy ending of this novel she is now just a little less well-equipped to deal with Jane Austen's commonplace world than

---

[46] Cited above, p. 23 n. 1.

she was at the beginning. And so the next to last paragraph turns a little wistfully to young Margaret Dashwood, who has 'reached an age highly suitable for dancing, and not very in-eligible for being supposed to have a lover'. Some day she too may sprain an ankle.

IV

PRIDE AND PREJUDICE
Irony in the Novels

1

Cassandra Austen's Memorandum records: 'First Impressions begun in Oct 1796/Finished in Augt 1797. Published afterwards, with alternations & contractions under the Title Pride & Prejudice.'[1] In its earliest form the novel even antedates *Sense and Sensibility*, which was not begun under that title until November 1797.[2] *Pride and Prejudice* is thus the third and last[3] of Jane

---

[1] *Novels*, VI (*Minor Works*), facing p. 242. A niece heard Jane Austen reading aloud from 'First Impressions' at Steventon in 1796 (Hill, p. 86); and there is some evidence that the novel may even have been begun a few months earlier than the date given in the Memorandum (*Life and Letters*, p. 73).

[2] Cassandra Austen's Memorandum; but the Memorandum notes in the case of *Sense and Sensibility* that 'something of this same story & characters had been written earlier & called Elinor & Marianne'. Jane Austen apparently finished 'First Impressions' and tried to publish it. On 1 November 1797 George Austen wrote to the publisher Cadell offering him a 'manuscript novel, comprising 3 vols . . .' (*Life and Letters*, p. 97); and this was probably 'First Impressions' (see *Memoir* (1871) p. 137). The manuscript shows up again in a letter of 8 January 1799 from Jane Austen to Cassandra: 'I do not wonder at your wanting to read "First Impressions" again, so seldom as you have gone through it, and that so long ago' (*Letters*, p. 52). In 1800 Mrs Holford published a novel, *First Impressions*; and thus Jane Austen may have been compelled to find another title. See R. W. Chapman, letter in *Times Literary Supplement* (28 Oct 1939), p. 625. The phrase 'pride and prejudice' appears prominently in Fanny Burney's *Cecilia* (1782).

Austen's 'gradual performances.' According to the *Memoir* she was apparently revising it as late as 1809–10;[4] and she tells in a letter how she 'lop't and crop't' it for publication (*Letters*, p. 298). It appeared early in 1813.

Pride and Prejudice is not Jane Austen's masterpiece, although it will survive such judgements. There are enough similarities between it and *Sense and Sensibility* to suggest that these two novels belong together as an early phase in Jane Austen's development. Both Elinor Dashwood and Elizabeth Bennet, for instance, are governed predominantly by 'sense', and both are critical of the world. Just as Mrs Dashwood says that Elinor would 'rather take evil upon credit than good' (*Sense and Sensibility*, p. 78), so Elizabeth says of herself, 'The more I see of the world, the more am I dissatisfied with it...' (*Pride and Prejudice*, p. 135). Another remarkable similarity between the novels is that Marianne Dashwood is the victim of 'first impressions', an expression that was actually the title of the original version of *Pride and Prejudice*; and, like Marianne, Jane Bennet is governed predominantly by an uncritical 'sensibility' (p. 208, although the context is ambiguous). She too has 'great strength of feeling' (p. 21), although there are of course significant differences between the two. Even Mr Bennet seems to owe something to Mr Palmer in *Sense and Sensibility*.

For the vexed question of *Cecilia's* influence on Jane Austen's novel, see Chapman in the Appendix to *Pride and Prejudice*, pp. 408–9; also Steeves, p. 342 n.

[3] But Q. D. Leavis, in a series of important articles ('A Critical Theory of Jane Austen's Writings', *Scrutiny*, X (June 1941) 61–87; X (Oct 1941) 114–42; X (Jan 1942) 272–94; XII (spring 1944) 104–19), argues that the later novel *Mansfield Park* was rewritten from 'Lady Susan', and that later still *Emma* was rewritten from 'The Watsons' (see p. 108 n. 1; p. 146 n. 1 below).

[4] *Memoir* (1871) p. 101. The *Life and Letters* says the novel was only 'far advanced' by 1811 (p. 243); and its chronology may even be based on the almanacs of 1811 and 1812. See R. W. Chapman, *Novels*, II (*Pride and Prejudice*) pp. 401 and xiii. She must still have been working on the novel close to the time she finally sold it, for Cassandra had not even read the whole of it in final form when it was published (*Letters*, pp. 302–3). On 29 November 1812 Jane Austen wrote that *Pride and Prejudice* was sold (*Letters*, p. 501). There was a second edition the same year as the first, and a third in 1817. Neither of these latter shows signs of revision by the author. See Chapman, pp. xi–xii.

Mr Palmer is taciturn, ironic, and aware that, 'through some . . . bias in favour of beauty, he was the husband of a very silly woman' (p. 112); in *Pride and Prejudice* Mr Bennet has much the same character, and, 'captivated by youth and beauty', he has married the 'silly' (pp. 236, 385) Mrs Bennet. Other more significant similarities between the two novels appear here and there in this chapter.

Like *Sense and Sensibility, Pride and Prejudice* has a double heroine and a double plot. The love affairs of Elizabeth and Jane Bennet are similar and inseparable. No one could deny that Elizabeth undergoes much more character development than does her sister, but as the plot progresses the two sisters again converge on an imaginary point that might be considered the ideal heroine of the novel.

Elizabeth, like Elinor, has more 'quickness of observation' than her sister (*Pride and Prejudice*, p. 15). She admits that she prides herself on her discernment (p. 208). But there is something new here; for the temptation to identify Elizabeth with Jane Austen herself[5] is very great. Elizabeth is the first of the young ladies in the novels – to be followed by Mary Crawford and Emma – whose cool sense consistently takes the form of an ironic detachment that is commonly imputed to Jane Austen herself. Indeed Darcy's comment to Elizabeth, that '. . . you find great enjoyment in occasionally professing opinions which . . . are not your own' (p. 174), could just as well apply to his author. Like Jane Austen, Elizabeth is often unwilling to commit herself directly to a truth, and she too is capable of withdrawing into the relativism of a variety of points of view. Likewise Elizabeth's lively mind comes into play best when she can put aesthetic distance enough between herself and her subject so as to regard it with ironic detachment. She loves 'absurdities'; she has a 'lively, playful disposition' which delights 'in any thing ridiculous'; she says 'Follies and nonsense . . . *do* divert me . . . and I laugh at them whenever I can' (pp. 152, 12, 57). Comments like these would not be out of place in her author's letters – and indeed we can find them there.

Elizabeth's irony is caricatured in her father. He too loves an

---

[5] 'As for Elizabeth Bennet, our chief reason for accepting her point of view as a reflection of her author's is the impression that she bears of sympathy between them . . .', Lascelles, p. 200.

'absurdity'; he too is diverted by 'folly'; he too sees the foibles of his family and is 'contented with laughing at them' (pp. 231, 236, 213). He holds himself entirely aloof from the world for most of the novel. His study door gives him distance from the family problems that would threaten his detachment by requiring moral decisions, some commitment to a truth. When he is finally forced to decide whether Lydia should be allowed to go to Brighton, he characteristically slides off from any serious concern in the matter by making the ironic comment that 'she cannot grow many degrees worse, without authorizing us to lock her up for the rest of her life' (p. 232).

Irony is therefore his métier; and in the first chapter he introduces his little Lizzy as his protégée. What happens to the two of them in the course of the novel is what seems to have happened to the ironic Jane Austen in the course of it as well. This is important in understanding *Pride and Prejudice*, and indispensable in understanding the novel that follows it. In the persons of Mr Bennet and Elizabeth, Jane Austen herself seems to be occupied with the question of just what part irony should play in her own fiction.

Irony requires a certain detachment. We find Elizabeth again and again assuming a position superior to her surroundings. She is proud as well as prejudiced. Caroline Bingley is not altogether wrong when she says that in Elizabeth there is a 'little something, bordering on conceit and impertinence . . .' (p. 52). Elizabeth acknowledges the impertinence herself (p. 380). She meets Bingley's sisters at Netherfield and immediately does not like them. When their temporary solicitude for her indisposed sister disappears, she returns to the 'enjoyment of all her original dislike' (p. 35). She does indeed enjoy disliking. It is a kind of artistic credo for her that 'The more I see of the world, the more am I dissatisfied with it.'

One manifestation of her sense of superiority is that she holds herself above her mother and her younger sisters. She feels 'mortification' when Mary sings at the Netherfield ball. She blushes again and again with 'shame and vexation' at her own mother (p. 100). Indeed whenever her family is in company her 'sense of shame' is severe (p. 209). She trembles 'lest her mother should be exposing herself again' (p. 45). And we find that telling phrase, 'exposing' oneself, more than once. At the ball it seems to her that, 'had her family made an agreement to expose themselves as much as they could during the evening, it would have been impossible for them to play their parts with . . . finer success' (pp. 101–2).

But Elizabeth is not so far above her family as she would like to think. When it comes to pride they are all of them, except perhaps Jane, members of the same family. Jane Austen is her systematic self in laying them all out as variations on the same theme of pride. When Mr Bennet makes his lady a mock compliment in the first chapter, she takes it seriously and says, 'My dear, you flatter me' (p. 4); and it is of course his pride not to have meant it that way. Mrs Bennet, having proudly gone to the Meryton ball in her carriage, thinks that Darcy did not talk to Mrs Long there because 'every body says . . . he is ate up with pride, and I dare say he had heard somehow that Mrs Long does not keep a carriage, and had come . . . in a hack chaise' (p. 19). Early in the novel her daughter Mary even gives a dissertation on 'pride' (p. 20) – of which she is of course very proud.

The Bennet family pride is vividly displayed in that fine scene, the Netherfield ball. Bennets are brought on stage here one by one, like five embodiments of one deadly sin, to exhibit their particular vanities. First Mrs Bennet runs on about her pride in Jane's prospects of getting a husband. Then Mary seizes the opportunity of 'exhibiting' her voice. Her cousin Mr Collins then follows with an aria of his own ('*The rector of a parish has much to do*'). It is easy to overlook the last two exhibitors. Mr Bennet sits in silence 'enjoying the scene' (p. 103). His pride is to be ironically detached from the spectacle of his own family's foolishness. By the end of the novel he will have paid a price for this. And the final exhibitor is his protégée Elizabeth, through whose eyes most of the ball is seen. Her pride, like her father's, is her seeming detachment, her illusion that she is not a Bennet herself, her shame as she watches them 'expose' themselves, her pride in being mortified by theirs. Eventually she will have to acknowledge that she too is a part of the family. Elizabeth will have to acknowledge that her last name is Bennet before it can become Darcy. Only then will she be ready for the world.

Elizabeth's general sense of superiority is of course partly justified. But it is partly an illusion that in the course of the novel will have to give way to facts. She makes the sensible pronouncement that first impressions are deceptive (pp. 22–3), and then is deceived by her own first impressions of Darcy (p. 11; see also p. 191). She gives Darcy the arch advice that 'It is particularly incumbent on those who never change their opinion, to be secure in judging properly at first' (p. 93), and makes the same mistake herself. When she hears Wickham's account of Darcy she says '. . . one knows exactly what to think' (p. 86), and turns out to be mistaken in what she thinks.

Her mistakes will bring her down into the world she is dissatisfied with. Her appearance at Netherfield early in the novel, with her petticoat six inches deep in mud, is a hint that she is not quite above the world. She says that her younger sisters are 'young in the ways of the world' (p. 150), and she should have included herself. She tells her mother she will never dance with Darcy, and then does. She enters into a dance from which she had held herself aloof. She tells Darcy, '. . . I had not known you a month before I felt that you were the last man in the world whom I could ever be prevailed on to marry' (p. 193); and then finally surrenders her ironic, superior detachment by marrying him.

Elizabeth's first step toward Pemberley is her rejection of Mr Collins. Her mother champions this wonderful specimen on the strength of the truth that a single man in possession of a good entail must be in want of a wife, and Mary champions him on the strength of his rhetoric (p. 64). But he is hardly a character at all. He is a caricature, climbing heavenward in the clergy while aggrandising his little kingdom here on earth, and his god is Lady Catherine. Elizabeth sums him up when she says that he 'is a conceited, pompous, narrow-minded, silly man . . . and . . . the woman who marries him, cannot have a proper way of thinking' (p. 135).

He is not in the novel because he is funny, but because Jane Austen's psychological scheme requires him. The significance of Elizabeth's rejecting his proposal is not that she sees through him, for it would be scarcely possible not to. In rejecting him she rejects marrying solely for worldly advantage. Her marrying him would effectively ensure that Mr Bennet's entailed estate would remain in the family. Thus rejecting him helps prepare her to accept a man as wealthy as Darcy for the right reason rather than the wrong one. After all, the prospects open to her in marrying Mr Collins, with all his preposterousness, are a suburban version of her worldly prospects when she marries Darcy. Mr Collins's humble abode borders on Rosings, the seat of Darcy's aunt; and when Elizabeth visits Hunsford, the place she could have occupied, Mr Collins points out to her the 'prospect of Rosings.' Indeed later 'she was tempted . . . to stop at the gates and look into the park' (pp. 156, 195). And it is at Rosings itself that Elizabeth meets some of the society she will take a place in when she marries Darcy. For that she has Mr Collins to thank.

When Elizabeth has passed from Hunsford to Rosings and finally to Pemberley itself, she feels 'at that moment . . . that to be mistress of Pemberley might be something!' (p. 245). And likewise when Jane at the conclusion asks her how long she has loved Darcy, she answers, '. . . I believe I must date it from my first seeing his beautiful grounds at Pemberley' (p. 373). But she had safely progressed beyond marrying for such a simple and material reason when she rejected Mr Collins. Her answer to Jane is thus ironic as it never could have been if she had not by then proved herself capable of a better reason. Jane sees the irony (p. 373), but it was lost on Sir Walter Scott,[6] and he is not alone.

As soon as Elizabeth rejects Mr Collins, her friend Charlotte Lucas accepts him. Jane Austen's plan required the Lucas sisters to be launched into the first chapter as the Bennet sisters' competition for a single man in possession of a good fortune; and Mr Collins, in possession of an entail and an abode bordering on Rosings, has immediately gone from Elizabeth to Charlotte. Jane Austen thus seems intent on forcing some comparison between the two victims of his affections.

Like Mr Collins, Charlotte exists for a reason; indeed in her case perhaps for nothing but the reason. She has plenty of cool, calculating 'sense'; and she therefore seems destined by Heaven for Mr Collins. He has gone about selecting a wife by 'design' (p. 105), and in turn Charlotte's motive for accepting him is more or less the same. She is just as immune to the ravages of sensibility as he is. She even has a 'design' (p. 22) for Jane to follow in capturing Bingley. She cannot help cautioning Eliza-

---

[6] In his review of *Emma* (cited above p. 23 n. 1): Elizabeth 'does not perceive that she has done a foolish thing [in refusing Darcy] until she accidentally visits a very handsome seat . . . belonging to her admirer'.

beth 'not to be a simpleton and allow her fancy for Wickham to make her appear unpleasant in the eyes of a man of ten times his consequence' (p. 90). Indeed she sacrifices 'every better feeling to worldly advantage' (p. 125). She has a 'prudent, steady character,' and says what no one could deny: 'I am not romantic you know' (pp. 135, 125).

She does not much resemble Elinor Dashwood's rival Lucy Steele, but the two do have in common that they marry solely from design, from unromantic and unalloyed 'sense'.[7] Both of them would subscribe to Mary Bennet's excellent pronouncement that every impulse of feeling ought to be guided by reason. Charlotte is therefore a fitting, if not quite perfect, mate for Mr Collins. Jane Austen has made her so. Mr Collins says that the two of them seem to have been designed for each other, and he may be right. Although Elizabeth is convinced they can never be happy together, Jane disagrees (pp. 135–6); and the novel comes a little closer to confirming Jane's disturbing opinion than her sister's (see p. 216).

When Charlotte has accepted Mr Collins, Elizabeth feels that 'all the comfort of intimacy was over' between her and her former friend (p. 146). The two part company. Elizabeth must go toward matrimony a different way; and Charlotte has served her purpose in helping define the way. The breach in the intimacy between these two has the effect of mapping out for Elizabeth some middle ground between Charlotte's designing sense and Jane's gushing and ingenuous 'strength of feeling'.

Elizabeth's second romantic possibility is Wickham. He drops into the novel in cavalier defiance of the logic of everyday life, and if Elizabeth had read the previous novel this would have been a clue. He has no ascertainable living relatives. He appears out of nowhere on a street in Meryton, a little like Satan materialised out of mist in the Garden of Eden. Unlike Darcy, he makes a good first impression. Soon he is 'universally liked' (p. 90). That includes Elizabeth, although some readers seem to wish otherwise.[8] Her second impression is that 'she had neither been

---

[7] At least Liddell comments on Lucy's 'lack of sensibility', p. 28.

[8] W. A. Craik says that 'Elizabeth sensibly refuses to be involved with Wickham', *Jane Austen: the Six Novels*, p. 81. The context of this remark curiously suggests that Elizabeth is not attracted to Wickham at all.

seeing him before, nor thinking of him since, with the smallest degree of unreasonable admiration'; and she goes away from their tête-à-tête 'with her head full of him' (pp. 76, 84).

There has been nothing like Wickham in Jane Austen's fiction before. The wicked characters in *Northanger Abbey* are hardly subtle. General Tilney discloses his inner nature by the uncomplicated act of throwing Catherine out of his house. John Thorpe exaggerates outrageously, and Isabella produces heavy-handed lies such as that James Morland is the 'only man I ever did or could love' and that Captain Tilney is the 'young man whom . . . I particularly abhor.' In the next novel Willoughby is somewhat more complex. He can hand Marianne a document, not written by himself, containing crafty expressions like, '. . . if I have been so unfortunate as to give rise to a belief of more than I felt, or meant to express.' He is even capable of enough wily ambiguity that at one point she has to exclaim, 'Willoughby, what is the meaning of this?'; and in order to render him clearly ineligible for Marianne, Jane Austen has to enlist against him the forthright syntax of Colonel Brandon, who pins on him the un-equivocal sin of fatherhood.

But Wickham is much more subtle still. His lie concerning the will is framed in words which, like his character itself, allow Elizabeth to draw out the implication she wants. He says of the living provided for him in the will, that Darcy 'chose . . . to treat it as a merely conditional recommendation' which Darcy had decided Wickham had forfeited out of 'extravagance' or 'in short any thing' (p. 79). When Elizabeth later tries to catch him up on this by telling him she has heard that the living 'was left you conditionally only, and at the will of the present patron', he has only to say, 'I told you so from the first, you may remember' (pp. 328–9). And he did indeed. It is easy to overlook the fact that her words can never quite expose the falseness of his, and that at the conclusion he is getting at least some part of the assistance from Darcy (p. 387) he had wanted all along.

But the fact of his perfidy, the fact that he has tried to warp Mr Darcy's will, is accessible to Elizabeth from the start if she were only receptive to facts. His 'wickedness' (p. 224) is overt in his very name, waiting for Elizabeth to draw it out. When she finally sees him as he is, he seems too obvious ever to have mistaken; and she alludes then to Lydia's having 'thrown herself into the power of – of Mr Wickham' (p. 277) – an expression that just faintly suggests the Devil.

Elizabeth's inability to see through him immediately thus shows something not only about his subtlety, but about herself. He is a splendid incarnation of Jane Austen's Protean false hero who will take almost any impression the heroine wants to give him. It is no wonder Elizabeth finds 'truth in his looks' (p. 86), for to some degree she is looking at herself. He answers her wishes, herself largely creating what she sees. He would be her Northanger Abbey if she were a student of the Gothic, the hero of her favourite story if she read romances, her picturesque ideal if she were an admirer of Gilpin. Willoughby answered Marianne's 'ideas of perfection'; and likewise Elizabeth is now 'convinced, that whether married or single', Wickham 'must always be her model of the amiable and pleasing' (p. 152). This arch, aloof young lady who has been so proud of her discernment is going to have to learn that, like all mortals and like all Jane Austen's heroines, she is capable of romantic illusions that lead to error.

2

Elizabeth's discovering the truth about Wickham is inseparable from her discovering the truth about Darcy. The two exist largely in terms of each other. To some extent Darcy is what he is in the novel because Wickham is what *he* is. Darcy's letter giving an account of Wickham's true character is therefore also a revelation of his own. It seems impossible to make a final separation between the two. This is remarkable and perhaps difficult to accept. Yet it is at the heart of *Pride and Prejudice*, and has received no attention at all. Darcy's father was Wickham's godfather; the young Darcy and Wickham were raised together; their pictures both hang over the mantelpiece at Pemberley; they both marry into the same family.

Wickham thus seems inextricably bound up in the romance of Elizabeth and Darcy. Only because he exists can they marry. That is clearly evident in the plot. It is Elizabeth's misconceptions concerning Wickham's character that are part of the reason Darcy writes the letter disclosing his own; then Lydia's elopement with Wickham causes Elizabeth to feel that she could indeed have loved Darcy (p. 278); then Wickham's willingness to marry Lydia for money allows Darcy to show the devotion and generosity that eventually bring Elizabeth and him together (see pp. 327, 365) in marriage.

The part Wickham plays in the happy ending of *Pride and Prejudice* is one manifestation of what comes as close as anything in Jane Austen's novels to being a metaphysical law: that dullness, foolishness, egotism and evil in all their discernible gradations are ultimately in the service of good. General Tilney therefore helps bring Catherine and Henry together: his 'unjust interference, so far from being really injurious to their felicity, was perhaps rather conducive to it' (*Northanger Abbey*, p. 252). Marianne needs Willoughby to bring her Colonel Brandon, Edward needs Lucy. Elizabeth and Darcy are 'indebted for their present good understanding to the efforts of his aunt', the proud Lady Catherine (p. 367). Emma needs Mr Weston to show her Mr Knightley as he truly is (*Emma*, p. 320). The reprehensible Mr Elliot helps to bring Captain Wentworth and Anne together (*Persuasion*, p, 241).

Evil thus has its place in Jane Austen's world – a state of affairs she can at least tolerate, although Mr Collins never would. Perhaps the most innocently boyish of all her characters is William Price, whose promotion in the navy he owes to Henry Crawford's lecherous uncle (*Mansfield Park*, pp. 363–4). Certainly the most impeccably upright of her characters is Edmund Bertram, who at the conclusion has taken his first step heavenward in the clergy on Dr Grant's apoplectic corpse (p. 473).

3

The romance of Elizabeth and Darcy separates naturally into two stages, the first extending up to the meeting at Pemberley. In this stage Elizabeth refuses Darcy's proposal chiefly because she herself is proud and prejudiced, although these two abstractions never of course come near covering the complexity of her character at any point in the novel. She is proud of her discernment, of her detachment, of her liking to dislike, of her superiority to her family; and these lead to her prejudice. Her prejudice is her habit of judging everything outside herself in whatever way best suits her own internal purposes.

'Pride' and 'prejudice' are thus more catchwords, like 'first impressions', unalloyed 'sense', 'sensibility', the 'Gothic', the 'picturesque' and 'wit', that point in Jane Austen's novels to that general self-conscious state of mind which for the most part generates its own appearances from the inside out rather than absorbing and adjusting to the real world outside. There is no denying that each of the heroines has a personality of her own. But behind all the heroines and propelling them is an idea: the heroines create a pleasing little aesthetic world to live in, and that world must be punctured by 'fact'. Elizabeth would rather live in her own world of smug ironies and critical dissatisfaction than in the real one. She showed this after the Meryton assembly when she said she could promise never to dance with Darcy in her life. Now she shows it again at Hunsford when she refuses his hand – no matter how ungraciously it was offered.

Her refusing Darcy causes her to receive from him a fact of such significance that Jane Austen has predictably founded it in a letter: his account of his relationship with Wickham. In the general scheme of the novels this account is a symbolic truth similar to Willoughby's letter to Marianne. Elizabeth is being forced to face facts, about Wickham, about Darcy, and about herself. She is '*now* struck' with the 'impropriety' of Wickham's confiding in her. As for Darcy, 'How differently did every thing now appear in which he was concerned' (p. 207). As for herself, the 'tumult' in her mind (p. 193) that had begun when Darcy proposed now comes to a climax in her discovery that, with all her discernment and enjoyment of dislike, she has made a mistake about the world outside. She exclaims what all Jane Austen's heroines could exclaim at this point when their illusions are forced to give way a little to the world: 'Till this moment, I never knew myself' (p. 208; cf. Emma's 'knowledge of herself', *Emma*, p. 412).

Elizabeth's acknowledging these errors does not itself make her ready to marry Darcy, although William Dean Howells and others have thought so.[9] She now returns to Longbourn. Thus at the end of Volume II the novel has come to a resting place, like

---

[9] He thinks that, after she receives the letter, 'it is a question merely of friendly chances' that lead eventually to the marriage, *Heroines of Fiction*, 2 vols (London: Harper, 1901) I 43.

Marianne's 'torture of penitence, without the hope of amendment'. For Elizabeth it is 'necessary to name some other period for the commencement of actual felicity' (p. 237). There is still something she has to learn, something that will require the offices of a mentor like the unironic Henry Tilney or Colonel Brandon. And so without much preparation Jane Austen brings in the Gardiners. She is carefully following her psychological scheme; that is why the Gardiners appear when they do. They will carry Elizabeth forward toward her final happiness at Pemberley, in Derbyshire. Mrs Gardiner has been in Derbyshire before. It is her country. Most important, it is her spiritual country. Speaking more like an allegorical guide to a Bower of Bliss than an aunt, she asks as Volume II closes: 'My love, should not you like to see a place of which you have heard so much?'

Jane Austen dwells on the 'suitableness' of the Gardiners to accompany Elizabeth on this journey (p. 239). From this point to the end of the novel they have an unusual part in bringing Elizabeth and Darcy together, not only at Pemberley but later at Longbourn after Mr Gardiner has turned over to Darcy the business of settling Lydia's marriage. Mrs Gardiner's letter to Elizabeth, for instance, reveals noble aspects of his character that he could never reveal himself. She also says in the letter that she personally likes Darcy. This is indeed the imprimatur he needs before Jane Austen will marry him to Elizabeth, and is similar to Colonel Brandon's giving Edward a living. Even the last sentence of the novel is devoted to Elizabeth's gratitude toward these two who had been the means of uniting her with Darcy.

The Gardiners are therefore Elizabeth's spiritual mentors; and they are an interesting solution to the structural problem Jane Austen always has to face: how to bring such figures of moral authority into the plot. In *Northanger Abbey* her solution is to try to make Henry Tilney first Catherine's romantic lover, then, after a certain amount of sleight-of-hand with his character, her serious guide. In *Sense and Sensibility* Willoughby is Marianne's actual lover, and Colonel Brandon is merely a mentor who seems to have been pushed into a final *mariage de convenance* of which Jane Austen is the real beneficiary. The same might be said of Mr Knightley in *Emma*, although many would disagree. When we try to envision his domestic life with Emma we are apt to be a little sobered by a serious statement he made to her in the shrubbery when he proposed: 'you hear nothing but truth from me'. But in *Pride and Prejudice* Jane Austen is content to involve the Gardiners only indirectly in the romantic plot, and has not contrived to marry Elizabeth to Mr Gardiner.

The Gardiners' main qualification to be Elizabeth's guides is that, in spite of the errors Elizabeth has now acknowledged, she still holds herself well above the rest of the world; and the Gardiners do not. To bring her down into their world is their main function in the novel. Elizabeth's family are still an 'evil' to her (p. 213)[10] in the respect that she does not yet see that her own newly-discovered errors are a part of theirs. She does not quite see yet that she is part of her family. She still unreservedly acknowledges the 'justice' of Darcy's 'objections' to them (p. 229); and thus, when she and her sister return to Longbourn, Jane Austen sends out to greet them the quintessential silliness of the family, just to keep Elizabeth's mortification alive. Kitty and Lydia appear, babbling about a bonnet they bought of which there were two or three much uglier in the shop, and about a lunch they are going to treat their sisters to if someone will only pay for it.

The Gardiners manage to belong to this family without mortification. Indeed they manage to belong to the world itself without mortification. That is not true of everyone. When Sir William Lucas gets a title he begins to feel a disgust for his business (p. 18). The Bingley sisters would like to forget that their family fortune came from trade (p. 15). But Mr Gardiner is not ashamed that he lives 'by trade, and within view of his own warehouses' (p. 139). He has intelligence, taste and good manners[11] without any self-conscious detachment from people who do not. The Gardiners are surrounded by a troop of happy little boys and girls. All is 'joy and kindness' in their house (p. 152). They seem to have the even, tolerant serenity and harmony of nature itself, which they are now going to share with Elizabeth. It is appropriate that their original plan is to take her to see rocks

---

[10] There is a danger however in attaching too Miltonic a significance to this word in the novels. See its uses listed in 'Miss Austen's English', *Novels*, I (*Sense and Sensibility*) Appendix.

[11] Mr Gardiner is the 'best-bred man in the book', Kennedy, p. 49.

and mountains (p. 154); what they finally do is to introduce her to this 'nature' in an even wider sense – the human nature that Elizabeth still archly holds herself above.

Mrs Gardiner had been suspicious of Wickham from the start, and had warned Elizabeth about him. Now at Pemberley she guides her niece to his picture, his true likeness, the equivalent for his physiognomy to what Darcy's letter was for Wickham's character. It is she who must do this. She asks smilingly how Elizabeth likes what she sees. Facts have begun to penetrate Elizabeth's illusions, she is learning to see, and now in front of the picture – she cannot smile (p. 247). Her self-satisfied illusions are vanishing. Confronting Wickham is inseparable from confronting Darcy, and inevitably in the next sentence Elizabeth is shown a picture of Darcy.

At the Meryton assembly Elizabeth had joined everybody else in the smug impression that Darcy's 'character was decided'. Since then she has been getting closer and closer to the true Darcy, building up under pressure a trapped reservoir of true knowledge that is fully released only when in this scene she now sees Darcy coming toward her at Pemberley. The main items of information came to her earlier of course in Darcy's letter. But she has also been learning to see him herself without knowing it. It is perhaps chiefly for this purpose that Darcy's cousin Fitzwilliam made his brief appearance. When Elizabeth met him at Rosings she was 'reminded . . . of her former favourite George Wickham; and though, in comparing them, she saw there was less captivating softness in Colonel Fitzwilliam's manners, she believed he might have the best informed mind' (p. 180). There she learned to 'see' Fitzwilliam by means of Wickham; and, although she was not aware of it, she was also learning to see Darcy – his honest lack of captivating softness – in his cousin.

Even Pemberley itself is something of an architectural manifestation of the true Darcy, and has thus subtly prepared her for the man she is about to meet. The same can be said of Woodston Parsonage, Henry Tilney's home. Catherine is taken there, finds herself in the 'most comfortable room in the world' (*Northanger Abbey*, p. 213), and marries into it. Elizabeth's similar installation at Pemberley was prepared for by the mention of Darcy's estate in the very paragraph that introduced him

(p. 10). Since then she has felt the curiosity to see Pemberley that came out when the Gardiners proposed their tour. Then at last she entered the park, then the house. Moving closer and closer to the true man, she confronted his miniature, then his large portrait. Finally, in the culmination of the process of discovery that began when she thought his character was decided, she confronts the true, three-dimensional Darcy himself.

This famous meeting is one of several almost purely symbolic scenes in the novels. Some improbable plot business is used here to convey what is essentially psychological action. The scene is little more than a correlative, made up of the physical acts of walking from place to place, of the process of arriving at the real Darcy that has been going on in Elizabeth's mind since the Meryton assembly. The scene is thus something of a gesture, a makeshift; and there is little use trying, as critics doggedly do, to explain away its improbabilities by finding in the geography or horticulture of Pemberley some plausible reason why Elizabeth and Darcy's love should suddenly prosper when they meet there.[12]

Elizabeth marvels at the 'perverseness' of the meeting (p. 252); and there is indeed a remarkable resemblance to the mock plot of Jane Austen's own 'Plan of a Novel'. The heroine there is pursued by a villain until 'at last in the very nick of time, turning a corner to avoid him, [she] runs into the arms of the Hero himself, who having just shaken off the scruples which fetter'd him before, was at the very moment setting off in pursuit of her' (*Minor Works*, p. 430). Thus the author of *Pride and Prejudice* seems to be doing with a straight face something not unlike what she laughs at elsewhere. In the other novels as well, there are coincidental turns of plot that recall absurdities in Jane Austen's juvenile burlesques. The rapid series of co-incidences that produces the marriages of the four principals

---

[12] A sample of the critical attempts to explain the scene in realistic terms: '. . . here Darcy and Elizabeth see one another for the first time in favourable . . . circumstances: he at his best on his own estate . . ., and she among congenial companions', Lascelles, p. 163; 'One of the first qualities to make him seem a possible husband is that he is a perfect landlord', W. A. Craik, *Jane Austen In Her Time*, p. 68.

in *Sense and Sensibility*,[13] for instance, is a little like the burlesque conclusion of 'The Visit', where three couples (one man
is named Willoughby) are engaged in six lines (*Minor Works*,
p. 54). Again and again characters in Jane Austen's fiction have
to account for these curious coincidences by quizzical references
to destiny and providence (see 'Lady Susan', *Minor Works*, p.
307; and pp. 198–201 below).

The coincidences and other improbabilities in Jane Austen's
plots are especially striking because she seems to work within
a tradition that utterly condemns them. In *Evelina* (1778), with
which Jane Austen was very familiar (*Letters*, pp. 64, 388),
Fanny Burney accounts for the superiority of the novel in just
these terms: she says that novels are preferable to romances because in the latter the 'sublimity of the Marvellous rejects all
aid from sober Probability'.[14] And Bishop Whately's famous
review of *Northanger Abbey* and *Persuasion* cites Aristotle on
the point that

> poetry (i.e. narrative, and dramatic poetry) is of a more
> philosophical character than history; inasmuch as the latter
> details what has actually happened, of which many parts
> may chance to be exceptions to the general rules of proba-
> bility . . .; whereas the former shews us what must naturally,
> or would probably, happen under given circumstances. . . .

Whately sees a moral dimension in this. He maintains that
'accidental events . . . are anomalies which, though true in-
dividually, are . . . false generally' and are therefore even morally
misleading.[15] The 'Pious and Learned' Doctor of Divinity in
Charlotte Lennox's *The Female Quixote* (1752; see *Letters*, p.
173) takes the same lofty position: 'It is the Fault of the best
Fictions, that they teach young Minds to expect . . . sudden
Vicissitudes, and therefore encourage them often to trust to
Chance'.[16] Jane Austen herself obviously took the matter of

---

[13] Firkins for one considers Robert Ferrars's marrying Lucy Steele
merely a 'makeshift expedient by which [Jane Austen] cleared
the path of Elinor and Edward', p. 5.

[14] *Evelina* (1778), Preface.

[15] Cited above, p. 23 n. 3.

[16] *The Female Quixote* (London: Oxford University Press, 1970)
IX xi (p. 379).

'probability' very seriously. She criticises Mary Brunton's novel *Self-Control* (1810) for not having 'anything of Nature or Probability in it' (*Letters*, p. 344); and she comments on her niece Anna Austen's novel: '. . . I have scratched out Sir Tho: from walking with the other Men to the Stables &c the very day after his breaking his arm – for though I find your Papa did walk out immediately after *his* arm was set, I think it can be so little usual as to *appear* unnatural in a book' (*Letters*, p. 394).

Why then are there so many conspicuously improbable events in Jane Austen's novels? In her early work some episodes, such as the last-chapter marriage of Eleanor Tilney to a 'man of fortune and consequence' and the remarkable circumstances that facilitate the marriage of Edward and Elinor, may be coloured just slightly by the juvenile burlesques themselves. In these cases the improbabilities may be striving for, or at least tolerating, a mildly comic effect. The young, rather snippety Jane Austen is here standing behind the plot saying, 'You and I know better than this, don't we?'

But as her art develops the improbabilities remain. She no longer uses them for humour; she seems in more and more cases simply to be ignoring them entirely, as if she were concerned with more important matters. She tends more and more to create events simply in order to cause a psychological change in a character when she wants it to occur; or, as in the Pemberley episode, even to serve somehow as a handy fictional representation of a psychological change that has mostly 'occurred' already and needs merely to be manifested somehow in the plot.

To some extent all novelists 'use' their plots like this, of course; but Jane Austen is unusually daring at it, and unusually careless about upholstering the improbabilities with some semblance of verisimilitude. Here we have one of the identifying characteristics of her art. We have to face squarely the fact that Jane Austen's conscience about making her plots totally believable is not very strong even at the beginning of her career, and that it relaxes more and more as she goes along. The novels begin to rise by fits and starts toward a plane where the plot is merely serving as a kind of thin, fragile, grudging allegory for a 'higher' psychological drama inside the heroine's mind. Jane Austen does not achieve this very often, and mostly near the end of her career; what is important is that she seems to have been striving toward it always.

The perverse meeting of Elizabeth and Darcy at Pemberley is moving in this direction; likewise a few other episodes such as the sudden arrival of Sir Thomas Bertram from Antigua, which Mary Crawford finds so marvellous (*Mansfield Park*, p. 360); the miraculous appearance in *Persuasion* of Mr Elliot out of nowhere on the seashore at Lyme; Anne Elliot's fantastic interview with a Mrs Smith who materialises 'to tell her what no one else could have done' (p. 212); and one of the most remarkable scenes in Jane Austen's fiction, the dreamlike final coming together of Anne Elliot and Captain Wentworth, who seem to have been guided toward each other by psychological forces that have left the plot far behind.

Thus the main reason Elizabeth and Darcy meet at Pemberley is that Jane Austen now considers her heroine ready to see the true Darcy. And what she is faced with on the lawn is intended to go far beyond anything that could ever be termed 'decided'. Here is a house with prospects beyond what the eye can reach. Through a window Elizabeth can make out the winding of a valley far into the distance. Flowing through his grounds is a stream which appears here and there at 'spots where the opening of the trees gave the eye power to wander' (p. 253). This is a feature of picturesque landscape which, according to Gilpin, 'gives the imagination a pleasing employment in making out the whole'.[17] Thus Darcy seems a little oddly to be taking on some of that wild and misty precipitousness Jane Austen smiled at earlier when Henry Tilney was touting the picturesque. We should remember that the Gardiners brought Elizabeth to Pemberley by way of a substitute for the Lakes, a district Gilpin considered rich in picturesque scenes;[18] and Darcy is a good substitute.[19] Here is something close to what Catherine and Marianne were looking for, the picturesque come true; and

[17] *Observations on the River Wye . . . relative chiefly to Picturesque Beauty . . .*, 3rd ed. (London: R. Blamire, 1792) p. 108.

[18] *Observations, on Several Parts of England, particularly the Mountains and Lakes of Cumberland . . . relative chiefly to Picturesque Beauty . . .*, 3rd ed., 2 vols (London: T. Cadell, W. Davies, 1808) 187 ff.

[19] Their tour has included Matlock in Derbyshire (pp. 239, 257). Gilpin's Cumberland book has a drawing of this mountain, reproduced in Chapman's edition, facing [243].

Elizabeth is to marry it. 'What are men', she had exclaimed,
'to rocks and mountains' (p. 154); and Darcy seems to be man,
rock and craggy mountain all at once.

When Elizabeth and Darcy finally meet face to face she finds
his behaviour 'strikingly altered' (p. 252). He has indeed undergone some subterranean changes in the course of the novel. But
the Darcy who appears on the lawn is more the result of changes
in Elizabeth than in himself. She has surrendered some pride
and prejudice to facts that have proved her wrong about
Wickham, about Darcy, and therefore about herself. She is now
humbled enough to see the world as it is; and so Jane Austen
has set Darcy before her.

What a change in Elizabeth's attitude! She had begun by
joining all the neighbourhood in disliking Darcy's forbidding,
disagreeable countenance (p. 10). Now at Pemberley she has
never seen him so 'pleasant' (p. 258). He in turn had begun by
thinking her not handsome enough to tempt him (p. 12). Now
she is 'one of the handsomest women of my acquaintance' (p.
271). When the eyes of these two meet at last, the novel has
come to its natural conclusion at Pemberley; and it is very significant that *Pride and Prejudice* has not ended here.

The novel has not ended here because Jane Austen is intent
on taking Elizabeth through a systematic course of psychological
reformation; and there is still one stage to go. Until this stage
is complete the novel cannot end, even though the coherent
plot may have. The heroine, now receptive to the world, has
yet to be brought down formally into it.

The plot business that lamely serves this purpose is Lydia's
sudden and unexpected elopement with Wickham. Many readers
are troubled by the gratuitousness of this episode,[20] but Jane

---

[20] Steeves thinks the elopement has no purpose in the novel at all.
It is 'extraneous', evidence of 'loose and lumpy plot construction'
(p. 347). W. A. Craik thinks the elopement 'has no direct effect' on
Elizabeth and Darcy's relationship 'except to let us see Darcy
actually behaving as the revised character Elizabeth's reproofs have
made him', *Jane Austen: the Six Novels*, p. 83. But Brabourne on the
other hand thinks the elopement may indeed have too much
effect: '. . . the sole doubt which remains upon my mind is the extent
to which gratitude for his generous behaviour to her sister Lydia and
her worthless husband really supplied the place of a warmer feeling
in Elizabeth's heart', 185.

Austen seems much more caught up in her psychological theme than the plausibility of her plot. Indeed she has strained both probability[21] and calligraphy by having the details of the elopement reach Elizabeth within three paragraphs of Darcy's ultimate compliment on her handsomeness; and in the form of two long letters from Jane that conveniently form a continuous narrative by arriving at the same time, the earlier letter having been ill-addressed and missent.

Jane Austen has not spent much delicacy on this elopement. Elizabeth thinks that Wickham simply wanted what she refers to nicely as a 'companion', an opinion confirmed by Mrs Gardiner (pp. 318, 323). And Lydia – she has apparently wanted one too. We are told that she has 'high animal spirits' (p. 45). The 'passions' of the two have been 'stronger than their virtue' (p. 312).[22] Lydia is thus something of a camp follower, which accounts for her presence at Brighton in the first place; and what is there to say about her mother, who laments that 'it was such a pity . . . Lydia should be taken from a regiment where she was acquainted with every body, and had so many favourites' (p. 313)? There has been nothing quite like this before in Jane Austen's fiction except for an eyebrow-raising passage in 'Lady Susan'. A friend writes that in her husband's absence she and Lady Susan can 'chuse our own society, & have true enjoyment'; in pursuit of which Lady Susan graciously lends the friend her young lover while she herself is occupied with somebody else (*Minor Works*, pp. 296, 302).

The elopement is the event that finally draws Elizabeth down into the world and brings about her marriage. That is its purpose in the novel. Elizabeth considers the elopement a 'proof of family weakness'; she feels 'humbled', and 'mortified' (pp. 278, 311). This mortification is very important in her psychological development. What is important is that the elopement is proof of 'family' weakness in a profound sense, for Elizabeth

---

[21] '. . . Lydia is too scantily presented in relation to her parents or to Wickham to prepare us adequately for her bad end', Brower, p. 167.

[22] But critics have trouble accepting this as a realistic motive. Liddell has an especially curious comment: '. . . a young man in distressed circumstances . . . is hardly likely to choose that moment to burden himself with a mistress', p. 54.

too has shown the weakness. She too has found Wickham a 'model of the amiable and pleasing'; and she owed the beginning of her disenchantment, not to her own discernment, but to Darcy. Elizabeth is thus a little like Lydia, from whom she has held herself aloof with such ironic detachment; Lydia is a little like Elizabeth, without having been given the benefit of truth in a letter.

All Elizabeth's dread at the Netherfield ball that her family would 'expose' themselves now takes a terrible form as she herself 'exposes' the news of her family weakness to Darcy (p. 277). Terrible because she is also in her own mind exposing herself. This is the necessary spiritual prelude to what will be the physical act in marriage. It makes Elizabeth a Bennet, a sister to Lydia, a woman, a woman of the world. Thus, no matter how awkwardly the elopement comes into the plot, it is crucial in Jane Austen's plan for her heroine's psychological reformation. The inevitable fruit of the elopement is that now Elizabeth is ready to marry. She is ready to accept Darcy. The effect of the elopement on him has been 'exactly calculated to make her understand her own wishes'. Never, she muses, 'had she so honestly felt that she could have loved him, as now, when all love must be vain' (p. 278).

Elizabeth now returns home, and this novel, like the two previous ones, seems to have come full circle. Jane Austen characteristically draws attention to the possibility that Elizabeth and Jane's loop out into the world has left them where they began. Again Bingley and his friend are coming to Netherfield, two single men in possession of good fortunes. Between Mr and Mrs Bennet the 'subject which had been so warmly canvassed . . . about a twelvemonth ago, was now brought forward again'; and 'Were the same fair prospect to arise at present, as had flattered them a year ago, every thing . . . would be hastening to the same vexatious conclusion'.

4

In order for Darcy to arrive back at Netherfield he has had to go through a course of psychological development remarkably similar to Elizabeth's. Jane Austen has overcome to some extent her previous difficulties in bringing the true hero's character change into the plot of the novel. But only to some extent. Darcy still seems to have saved up a formidable change to deliver as one lump in the scene at Pemberley. Consequently it is not easy to conceive how the Meryton Darcy could have developed into the charmer we see at Pemberley. He seems partly improved, partly inconsistent.[23] His difficulties may go back to Jane Austen's unfinished piece 'The Watsons'; for he may be a welding together of Emma Watson's two romantic attachments. At a ball the proud Lord Osborne notices her, although he refuses to dance with anyone (*Minor Works*, pp. 332–3); and in the continuation he was apparently going to propose and be refused before she married the good and gentlemanly Mr Howard.[24]

Like Elizabeth, Darcy of course holds himself aloof from the world at the beginning. Elizabeth notices a 'great similarity' in their minds (p. 91). He too is proud. She enjoys disliking; similarly he looks at her at the assembly 'only to criticise' (p. 23). He too has a 'satirical eye' (p. 24). He too is proud of his discernment. Indeed some of his early opinions are pronounced with such assurance that they might have come, not from Elizabeth, but from her sister Mary – or Doctor Johnson.[25] And when Bingley urges him to dance, he delivers himself of the lovely sentiment that 'Your sisters are engaged, and there is not

---

[23] To Mary Lascelles, the 'Darcy of Meryton assembly is quite inconsistent with the Darcy who is described and developed in the rest of the book', p. 22. Moler thinks the inconsistency is owing to his origin as a 'parody-figure', p. 93. Brabourne seems to show some admirable familial generosity here: he writes that when Darcy 'found himself vanquished by the charms of Elizabeth, he got rid of his pride' with 'commendable rapidity', 1 84.

[24] The similarities between the ball scene in 'The Watsons' and the Meryton assembly are very interesting. See *Novels*, VI (*Minor Works*) pp. 329–36.

[25] Let the reader decide for himself which of the following pronouncements is made by Darcy, which by Mary Bennet: (1) 'nothing is more deceitful than the appearance of humility. It is often only carelessness of opinion, and sometimes an indirect boast.' (2) 'Pride is a very common failing. There are very few of us who do not cherish a feeling of self-complacency on the score of some quality or other, real or imaginary.' (3) 'There is in every disposition a tendency to some particular evil, a natural defect, which not even the best education can overcome' (pp. 48, 20, 58, unfairly edited).

another woman in the room, whom it would not be a punishment to me to stand up with' (p. 11). Like the early Elizabeth, he is not yet ready to dance.

We have seen Jane Austen at work long enough to expect that Darcy's change will fall into the same two stages as Elizabeth's. It does. In the first he admits he was proudly mistaken about her, and proposes. But his very proposal, like her refusal, shows that he is not yet ready to marry her; for he still condemns the 'evils' of his friend Bingley's marrying into the Bennet family (p. 198), although he prides himself in having overcome this pride in himself. It is easy to overlook Jane Austen's subtlety here. Darcy has 'not yet learned to condemn' (p. 199) his disdain of the Bennets as in-laws for a single man in possession of a good fortune, unless that man is Darcy.

His second stage truly brings him down into the family. Here Jane Austen has worked out striking similarities between Elizabeth's case and his own. Again Lydia's elopement is crucial. The elopement humiliates Elizabeth by exposing the weakness of the Bennets; and in doing so it brings Darcy and her together in a mutual humiliation, for the same weakness is after all in Darcy's family too. Jane Austen has so contrived it that Wickham had eloped with Darcy's sister before Elizabeth's. The same Mrs Yonge was implicated in both affairs. Elizabeth had felt that no one's knowledge of her sister's frailty would have 'mortified' her so much as Darcy's knowing it (p. 311); and he in turn has had to submit himself to the same mortification in telling her of his own sister's frailty (p. 225). Elizabeth wants Lydia's elopement kept secret (p. 278), and Darcy wants Georgiana's kept secret also (p. 270). Thus Lydia's elopement has the effect of uniting these two in a common shame for a common 'family' frailty in their blood. Here is a crucial point in Jane Austen's psychological scheme. And the common shame of this couple had been exquisitely forecast in the final scene at Pemberley before Elizabeth received Jane's letters. Miss Bingley had meanly alluded to Wickham and had produced not only the distress in Elizabeth she had intended; Georgiana too had been distressed, and Darcy had blushed (p. 269).

Early in the novel Darcy had produced a resounding declaration worthy of Mary Bennet, that 'There is . . . in every disposition a tendency to some particular evil, a natural defect, which not even the best education can overcome' (p. 58). This has turned out to be true in a way he never meant. The natural defect in the Bennet family has turned out to be a defect that is in his own. He has therefore to some extent been falsely proud and falsely prejudiced in holding himself above the Bennets, with all their silliness. If he and Elizabeth are to marry, they will simply have to accept what their two families have appallingly in common.

Lydia's elopement now draws Darcy down into the world from which he had held himself aloof. Here Jane Austen's plot is a beautiful embodiment of her master plan. At the beginning Darcy had felt that the Bennet sisters' having an uncle near Cheapside 'must very materially lessen their chances of marrying men of any consideration in the world' (p. 37). Yet now he goes to this part of London himself. And at Lydia's wedding he appears 'among people, where he had apparently least to do, and least temptation to go' (p. 320). The same will be true at his own wedding.

The elopement thus unites Darcy and Elizabeth in one family. Their marriage is merely the ceremonial expression of this. Jane Austen now needs some little business to cause in the plot what has already taken place in the minds of her characters; and probably with tongue in cheek she has enlisted Lady Catherine for this purpose.[26] Here may be a last faint echo of the early burlesques. Many readers find Lady Catherine too absurd to pass as a character at all[27] – just the right neighbour for Mr Collins. At Longbourn she does indeed seem little more than the figure of Pride who has been sent at last by Jane Austen in a chaise-and-four to bring about in the plot what has already taken place where it matters. Lady Catherine suddenly appears to prevent the wedding; and in Jane Austen's beneficent and economic universe this of course causes the wedding to take place. Elizabeth and Darcy are 'indebted

---

[26] The *Life and Letters* has its own explanation of Lady Catherine's final appearance: '... while all fear of a commonplace ending is avoided by the insertion of the celebrated interview between Lady Catherine and Elizabeth', p. 264.

[27] Even Brabourne finds her 'a little exaggerated', I 106; see also Kaye-Smith, pp. 182–90.

for their present good understanding to the efforts of his aunt'.

These two proud people have come a long way from Hunsford, where Darcy proudly proposed and Elizabeth proudly refused. Their feelings, as Elizabeth remarks, are 'widely different' from what they were then (p. 368). Their pride and prejudice have been invaded by the real world, which they are now willing to accept in preference to their own. They have been brought down into the same family: Darcy will have Mrs Bennet to converse with during the long evenings at Christmas, and Elizabeth will have the similar consolation of Lady Catherine. Elizabeth's shame at her mother's silly behaviour in Darcy's presence already has had its counterpart in Darcy's shame at his aunt's 'ill breeding' (p. 173).

Their marriage gives them another relative in common – Wickham. We must never forget that. These two proud people must accept that Wickham is in their family, and in their blood. In another of Jane Austen's brilliant scenes where the plot business seems only a makeshift embodiment of what is essentially a higher, psychological drama that has already played itself out in the heroine's mind, Wickham comes to Longbourn when Elizabeth has returned there, and claims her' for a sister. She calls him brother, holding out her hand. That gesture is one of the most beautiful and profound in Jane Austen's fiction. Darcy too takes as brother-in-law the man whom Elizabeth thought 'every kind of pride' must revolt from (p. 326). Elizabeth and Darcy have accepted Wickham into their family – or perhaps they have accepted themselves into his. All three are now members of the same defective, Wickhamised family.

5

Early in the novel Jane and Elizabeth disagree concerning the Bingley sisters (I iv), just as Elinor and Marianne had begun with a disagreement concerning Edward Ferrars. In *Pride and Prejudice*, as in the earlier novel, such differences seem inevitable. The two sisters' characteristics are more or less antithetical. Elizabeth is cool and detached, and is clearly distinguished by 'sense' (p. 144); Jane on the other hand has 'great strength of feeling'. Elizabeth can be prickly and impertinent; Jane displays a 'steady mildness' (p. 129). Elizabeth enjoys disliking; and as for Jane, Elizabeth tells her, 'All the world are good and agreeable in your eyes' (p. 14).

In the course of the novel Jane undergoes a slight change in character which brings her that much closer to her sister. She discovers that she has been 'entirely deceived' by Caroline Bingley. She reluctantly acknowledges a 'strong appearance of duplicity' in the behaviour of Caroline and her brother in London (pp. 148–9). This is slightly reminiscent of Catherine's discovering 'fickleness' in the world when she reads the letter from her brother James (*Northanger Abbey*, p. 204); and of Elizabeth's own discovery of 'gross duplicity' when she reads Darcy's. Jane thus makes a discovery in the novel; one that is low-keyed but nevertheless not unlike those of Jane Austen's other heroines. Jane too has created an aesthetic illusion about the world that has had to give way slightly to facts. She is capable at the conclusion of making on the subject of Caroline Bingley the most 'unforgiving speech' her sister has ever heard her utter (p. 350). And when Caroline sends best wishes to her new sister-in-law, Jane – oh, the wonder if it! – 'was not deceived' (p. 383).

But Jane's bending toward her sister's critical dissatisfaction with the world is of course only very slight. She is too good ever to see the world quite as it is. She says she has 'no idea of there being so much design in the world as some persons imagine' (p. 136), and nothing in the world can ever change her much. Even at the conclusion she can consider Wickham's consenting to marry Lydia a charming 'proof . . . that he is come to a right way of thinking . . .' (p. 305). Jane Austen can be ironic in making her say it, but the irony is lost forever on Jane. Her sister tells her, '. . . you are too good. Your sweetness and disinterestedness are really angelic' (p. 134); and this is true to the end. Who would want it otherwise?

Bingley is the perfect husband for her. They seem to have been designed for each other – to borrow from Mr Collins. Bingley is perfectly uncritical, and incapable of learning anything about the world at all. The mud on Elizabeth's petticoat escapes his notice (p. 36). The people at the Meryton assembly are the most pleasant he ever met in his life (p. 16). He and Jane are thus at the start about as ready to enter the dance as they will ever be. Their marriage, as Elizabeth puts it, is the 'happiest, wisest, most reasonable end' (p. 347). Elizabeth loves them for all their blissful ingenuousness. She has enough sense for that. And Jane Austen obviously loves them too.

Elinor's softening toward Willoughby at Cleveland suggested that she was moving slightly toward the characteristics of her sister Marianne at the same time that Marianne was moving toward Elinor. Elizabeth too moves a little closer to Jane at the conclusion of *Pride and Prejudice*, but this is hardly very obvious or even very significant. It is just that Jane Austen seems reluctant completely to let go of any part of her master plan once she has worked it out. Her art changes as it evolves of course. But it is fascinating that, when the general scheme or skeleton of the early novels is superimposed on the later ones as a kind of anatomical guide, certain parts keep showing up where they always have been; even though the part may now be moribund or vestigial. And so at the conclusion of *Pride and Prejudice* Elizabeth takes on just a little of Jane's mild, uncritical and passive acceptance of the world. She seems to enjoy disliking less. When Lydia's new husband comes to Longbourn and parries her attempts to catch him in his lies, her pointed irony dies away into a kind of smile we have hardly identified with Elizabeth Bennet before now: a 'good-humoured smile' (p. 329).

There is no pursuing her dissatisfaction with the world now, no enjoyment of dislike. Later she even refrains from being witty at Darcy's expense, for he has not yet learned to be laughed at (p. 371). There is no laughing here at the world's foibles. She is mellowing a little. The more she sees of the world the more she seems fairly satisfied with it: an attitude her sister Jane will understand. If Elizabeth was wrong about Wickham, she was after all wrong too about Darcy. She has come to see that there is good in the world where she doubted it – which is what Jane has been too easily believing all along.

Thus Jane has become just a little more critical, and Elizabeth just a little less so. At the conclusion the gentle convergence of the two sisters seems again to point to some imaginary middle ground between their perhaps ultimately irreconcilable characteristics. That imaginary place of convergence would be the perfect heroine, in some other world where there were perfect heroines.

But what is perfect in *Pride and Prejudice*, what is at the very soul of this novel, is the two sisters together in the same family. They began with a disagreement and end living happily together on common ground, in Derbyshire. In the family all differences are reconciled. This cannot be emphasised enough. *Pride and Prejudice* is a generous and forgiving novel that for the most part must have been written with the same good-humoured smile that Elizabeth gives her new brother-in-law Wickham when she holds out her hand to him. She is 'unwilling for her sister's sake, to provoke him' (p. 329). She has let her critical temper relax to keep the family together, and so has her author. This must have cost Jane Austen very great effort. She is never quite able to achieve it again.

The family that is created in the course of *Pride and Prejudice* repels again and again the critical assaults made on it by the various characters. Darcy would have liked to marry Elizabeth but not her mother. Mr Bennet would have liked to exclude a daughter and son-in-law from Longbourn (p. 310). Lady Catherine would have liked Pemberley to remain unpolluted by Bennets (p. 357). Mr Collins would have liked his cousin Lydia driven out of the family forever.

But sentiments like these are futile. Jane Austen's irony is too strong. It has brought together the characters in a relationship that rises above absolute and final judgements on their relative merits. It has bound the characters together in a family relationship something like the symbiosis of the fungus and the orchid. Both are not equally beautiful, but each needs the other. Questions of good and evil are finally irrelevant. The Jane in the family will always need the Elizabeth to mediate between her and the world as it really is. Therefore it is up to Elizabeth to tell the truth about Wickham to Jane, who 'would willingly have gone through the world without believing that so much wickedness existed in the whole race of mankind, as was here collected in one individual' (pp. 224-5). But we must not overlook that Elizabeth will always need Jane as well. After Elizabeth has read Darcy's letter, she regrets that there is 'no Jane to comfort me and say that I had not been so very weak and vain . . . as I knew I had! Oh! how I wanted you!' (p. 226). So it is also with Bingley and Darcy. Bingley relies on his friend's judgement and cannot marry until Darcy gives his permission (pp. 199, 370). And Darcy himself cannot marry until he is ready to give

it. Only then has he finally overcome his disdain for the Bennets
not only in his Darcy self, but in the part of him that guides
his friend. Thus to some extent there will be a pooling of the
resources of sense and sensibility in the neighbourhood of Pemberley, as there was at Delaford.

Finally, the entire *ménage à quatre* in Derbyshire has needed
Wickham to bring it to its final bliss. Wickham's indispensable
presence in the novel is a profound expression of that 'general
though unequal mixture of good and bad' Jane Austen had hinted
in her first novel she was striving for. In *Pride and Prejudice*
the mixture has truly become a compound, and those moral
terms seem no longer to apply. Wickham has earned a grudging
place in the family. The conventional ending in this novel is
not just two weddings, but three.

It is true that Wickham is no longer the 'angel of light'
Meryton had thought him to be (p. 294). Indeed, now his
quarters are in the North, at Newcastle. But he cannot finally
be called bad. Jane Austen's irony has elevated her above such
a judgement. Let Mr Collins make it. Wickham is simply a
member of the family. He is carrying on his commerce with
it at the end, although excluded from Pemberley. But he is
even there, all the same. 'Are the shades of Pemberley to be thus
polluted?', Lady Catherine asked when Elizabeth seemed about
to marry into her family; and the answer is that Pemberley has
been polluted from the beginning. The large estate in Derbyshire
which was set up in the beginning (p. 10) to be Elizabeth's
final home has never been quite free of Wickham. His picture
may still hang there.

V

MANSFIELD PARK
The Scourging of Irony

1

Mansfield Park begins the series of three novels which were
written after Jane Austen moved to Chawton, and which were
published without any extensive later revision.[1] According to
Cassandra's Memorandum and Jane Austen's own note, the
novel was begun about February 1811 and was finished soon
after June 1813.[2] It was published in the middle of the next
year.[3]

The differences between *Pride and Prejudice* and the novel
that follows it are remarkable, very significant, and frustrating
for any critic who would like to see Jane Austen's powers rise
toward their zenith in a smooth elegant arc. One occasionally

---

[1] But Q. D. Leavis argues that 'Lady Susan' was rewritten to
become *Mansfield Park*. See x 63.

[2] *Novels*, VI (*Minor Works*) facing p. 242; Jane Austen's own note
appears in *Plan of a Novel . . .*, ed. R. W. Chapman (Oxford: Clarendon, 1926) [37]. She may not have been very far along as late as 29
January 1813; for it was then that she wrote to Cassandra: 'Now I
will try to write of something else, & it shall be a complete change
of subject – ordination' (*Letters*, p. 298). But a previous letter
(24 January, *Letters*, p. 294) does allude to a scene at the Grants'
about half way through the novel (II vii). By early in March
1814 Henry Austen was reading the completed work (*Letters*, p.
377).

[3] See Chapman in *Novels*, III (*Mansfield Park*) xi. A second edition
appeared in 1816, with some corrections by the author (*Letters*, p.
447).

encounters a reader who holds out for *Mansfield Park* as Jane Austen's best;[4] but the consensus is that something has gone wrong with her art here.

To begin with, there is a falling off in technique. In the early *Northanger Abbey* there are clumsy transitions like the following: 'Monday, Tuesday, Wednesday, Thursday, Friday and Saturday have now passed in review before the reader; the events of each day . . . have been separately stated . . .' (p. 97). Passages similar to this now reappear occasionally: 'And Fanny, what was *she* doing and thinking all this while? (p. 48). There is also an uncharacteristic diffuseness in the narration. Edmund and Fanny tediously discuss at length (pp. 25–8) the various small advantages of Fanny's living with Mrs Norris; and the discussion ends lamely with the words: 'So ended their discourse, which . . . might as well have been spared, for Mrs Norris had not the smallest intention of taking her'. And there is a stupefyingly painstaking inventory of Fanny's room (pp. 150–2). No one is likely to claim that either of these passages engages any large thematic issues in the novel; and whatever they do contribute could hardly justify their length. They sound like Edward Ferrars' voluble brother Robert on the subject of cottages.

Furthermore, the narrative for the most part seems leaden and witless. We find Jane Austen launching cumbersome sentences like, 'Fanny was tempted to apply . . . Dr Johnson's celebrated judgment . . .'; she is 'amazed at being anything in *propria persona*' (pp. 392, 398 and Chapman's note). It is true that there is at least one fine specimen of Jane Austen's wit in the novel. That is Sir Thomas Bertram's thought on Henry Crawford: 'He wished him to be a model of constancy; and fancied the best means of affecting it would be by not trying him too long' (p. 345). This compares favourably with the observation on Charlotte Lucas's quick marriage to Mr Collins: 'The stupidity with which he was favoured by nature, must guard his courtship from any charm that could make a woman wish for its continuance' (*Pride and Prejudice*, p. 122). But more characteristic of *Mansfield Park* is the following: '. . . there were shady

---

[4] See for instance Alistair Duckworth's chapter on *Mansfield Park* in *The Improvement of the Estate*.

lanes wherever they wanted to go. A young party is always provided with a shady lane' (p. 70).

And Jane Austen's lively, playful obliquity sags again and again, with the result that she often seems to be speaking to us in her own person like an essayist, rather than through the form of fiction. Occasionally in the earlier fiction there are such statements, delivered directly to the reader as if they were brief moral apothegms. The following is from *Northanger Abbey*: 'Dress is at all times a frivolous distinction, and excessive solicitude about it often destroys its own aim' (p. 73). Sometimes this solemnity is given to characters who can be suspected of merely sponsoring it on behalf of Jane Austen. Catherine Percival, for instance, 'considered that there were Misfortunes of a much greater magnitude than the loss of a Ball, experienced every day by some part of Mortality . . .' ('Catherine, or The Bower'), *Minor Works*, p. 208). Observations like these in the early work are recalcitrant particles which the fiction manages to hold in suspension. They could be strained from solution to form a moral residue that has never quite worked itself into the form of fiction. But these particles – of lead, perhaps – that are suspended more or less unobtrusively in the earlier works have become in many passages of *Mansfield Park* the very stuff of the novel.

The irony that makes a frame in fiction, keeping the characters' and even the narrator's sentiments removed some indeterminate distance from what could be conceived to be the author's own sentiments, has partly dissolved away in *Mansfield Park*; and its contents have flowed out toward the form of the essay – or the sermon. Jane Austen seems to lean toward us intently, making moral points. Sometimes she talks in what seems to be her own person ('that higher species of self-command, that just consideration of others, that . . .' p. 91). And often she seems to be talking through Fanny, Edmund and Sir Thomas Bertram. In these cases the characters come close to being *porte-paroles*, and there is no clearly discernible irony hedging off what they say from what their author is apparently saying.

Indeed the author has a great deal to 'tell' us in *Mansfield Park*. A lady who knew her says that Jane Austen held the 'belief that example, and not "direct preaching", was all that a novelist could afford properly to exhibit';[5] and in the 'Plan of a Novel' Jane Austen herself makes fun of characters who dispense propaganda for their authors (*Minor Works*, pp. 429–430). How she would reconcile this with *Mansfield Park* is hardly clear; for there is a dismaying amount of direct or diaphanous sermonising. Mary Crawford's last remark to Edmund tempts one to take an uneasy sidelong glance at Jane Austen herself: 'A pretty good lecture upon my word. Was it part of your last sermon?' (p. 458).[6] If the subject of the novel is indeed 'ordination' as Jane Austen says, in a sense it is her own.

It might even be fair to say that the heavy spectre of her most memorable clergyman hovers over *Mansfield Park*. Mr Collins says he never reads novels, and chooses Fordyce's Sermons when he comes to Longbourn; and now Jane Austen is making some concessions to him. His expatiation at Netherfield on the duties of the clergy pointed up his absurdity; Jane Austen was having fun at his expense. But where is the gaiety, the irony now? Edmund makes a speech astonishingly similar (pp. 110–112), and we are apparently to take it at face value, or with ironic qualifications that are only very slight.[7] Mr Collins was fond of referring to his 'abode', and Jane Austen was laughing at him for doing so. But now we encounter the same word used in dead earnest (p. 473) – and by the author herself. The thought is appalling, but is she now like Charlotte Lucas flirting with him?

2

There have been attempts to make *Mansfield Park* a predominantly ironic novel that is not quite accepting its own pieties at face value.[8] One should consider such interpretations

---

[5] *Personal Aspects* (cited above p. 74 n. 43), p. 86. See *Facts and Problems*, pp. 126–7.

[6] In a letter of 1816, Jane Austen wrote her nephew James Edward, 'Uncle Henry writes very superior sermons. – You and I must try to get hold of one or two, & put them into our Novels', *Letters*, p. 468.

[7] Avrom Fleishman does find some irony in Jane Austen's treatment of Edmund (although not in this speech), *A Reading of Mansfield Park* (Minneapolis: University of Minnesota Press, 1967) pp. 53–6.

[8] The most noteworthy is Lionel Trilling's fascinating and provocative interpretation in *The Opposing Self* (London: Secker & Warburg, 1955).

carefully, and then reject them reluctantly. For they are based on the assumption that attitudes which are not obvious in this novel must nevertheless be there because they are so obvious elsewhere. This may make the novel more interesting for some readers, but it will not do. We have to resist importing into this rather lugubrious work the grace, the coyness, the lightheartedness that seem to go a certain way toward characterising the earlier novels. On the other hand there have also been attempts to make all Jane Austen's other novels resemble *Mansfield Park*, by overemphasising or discovering their solemn moral earnestness.[9] Again there is some truth here, but not enough. *Mansfield Park* is remarkably different from the other novels. It is better to accept this with puzzlement than to try to minimise it.

Here then is a novel that must be faced squarely on its own stark terms. To understand the terms it is necessary to go back to the beginning of Jane Austen's career, and to trace the emergence in her fiction of a vague sense of guilt she comes to associate with irony and wit. This guilt culminates in, and perhaps was even purged by, *Mansfield Park* — a circumstance that may help to explain the novel, but certainly for unsympathetic readers will not do much to redeem it.

To begin with, Jane Austen's wit was never quite free to flourish unconstrained. In the climate that produced her there is a vague uneasiness concerning the propriety of such cleverness in a woman. Sir Edward Denham makes a remark in 'Sanditon' that is intended to be preposterous, but perhaps not quite preposterous at Chawton. He thinks that the 'Coruscations of Talent' may be 'incompatible with some of the prosaic decencies of Life' (*Minor Works*, p. 398). Surely the social decencies had their dampening effect on a lady's art. Jane West's *Letters to a Young Lady* . . . (1811) is probably a fair representation of the attitude of Jane Austen's rather prim society toward irony and wit in a woman. She writes that 'bitter irony is another solecism of the rules of politeness. To say what you are certain will give unnecessary pain, is not only a breach in manners but in morals'. Furthermore, 'Wit' should be 'restrained by the

---

[9] See for instance Alistair Duckworth's interesting *The Improvement of the Estate*.

fundamental laws of her own empire from lacerating by her keenness. . . .'[10]

Jane Austen's mordant art had to develop and survive in this close world of genteel decencies, beneath a lace cap,[11] in a sitting-room where she wrote on small sheets of paper that could be hidden under a blotter when a creaking door warned her of intruders.[12] The pressures on her can be sensed for instance in her mock 'Plan of a Novel'. A young lady there tries to make the acquaintance of the heroine. But because the lady has a 'considerable degree of Wit' the heroine, Jane Austen writes, 'shall shrink from the acquaintance' (*Minor Works*, p. 429).

Wit in a woman of her standing was something of a *bête noire*. Perhaps this is behind a comment she made in a letter after *Pride and Prejudice* had been published. A Miss Burdett apparently had learnt the name of the author, and Jane Austen writes, strangely, 'I should like to see Miss Burdett very well, but that I am rather frightened by hearing that she wishes to be introduced to *me*. – If I *am* a wild Beast, I cannot help it' (*Letters*, p. 311). In a famous description Mary Russell Mitford gives a similar impression of Jane Austen as something lethal loose in the parlour:

> . . . a friend of mine . . . says that she has stiffened into the most perpendicular, precise, taciturn piece of 'single blessedness' that ever existed, and that, till 'Pride and Prejudice' showed what a precious gem was hidden in that unbending case, she was no more regarded in society than a poker or a fire-screen. . . . The case is very different now; she is still a poker – but a poker of whom every one is afraid.[18]

---

[10] *Letters to a Young Lady*, 4th ed., 3 vols (London: Longman, 1811) III 43; cited in Frank W. Bradbrook, *Jane Austen and Her Predecessors* (Cambridge: Cambridge University Press, 1966) pp. 155–7.

[11] The author of the *Memoir* (1871) writes of Jane Austen's lace cap, 'I believe that she and her sister were generally thought to have taken to the garb of middle age earlier than their years or their looks required', p. 87.

[12] See *Memoir* (1871), p. 102, for this famous story.

[18] *The Life of Mary Russell Mitford* (cited above p. 16 n. 29) I 306 (1815). It is doubtful whether this description is founded on first-hand knowledge; see *Life and Letters*, pp. 84–5, 300–1.

The clearest indication of the social forces always pressing on Jane Austen's irony and wit is the effort her family made after her death to play down these most characteristic features of her art. The Austen-Leighs go as far as to report approvingly that one of Jane Austen's nieces had said, 'She was in fact one of the last people in society to be afraid of. I do not suppose she ever in her life said a sharp thing'[14] – which must be one of the least credible statements ever made about Jane Austen, unless it carries the sly implication that she reserved her sharpness for the surviving letters and the novels. In his edition of the letters Lord Brabourne, another family member, also takes pains to neutralise her. He writes rather defensively that 'a vein of good-natured satire might . . . be found' in the family letters, but that 'it always *was* good-natured, and no malice ever lurked beneath'.[15] And her brother Henry's 'Biographical Notice' seems to go out of its way to give us the assurance that she was '. . . fearful of giving offence to God, and incapable of feeling it towards any fellow creature' – a passage among those omitted from the revised notice that appears in Bentley's 1833 edition of the novels.[16] Henry Austen would have us believe that even on the 'vices' of humanity his sister did not 'trust herself to comment with unkindness'.[17] Finally, the commemorative plaque approved by the family[18] for Winchester Cathedral quotes a passage from Proverbs (31:26) that not everybody would consider the inevitable choice: '. . . in her tongue is the law of kindness'.

All these well-meaning sentiments must have their element of truth. But they must also reflect what Jane Austen's society uneasily wanted her to be, yet felt that she was not.[19] Thus she

---

[14] *Life and Letters*, p. 240.

[15] I 47.

[16] *Novels*, V (*Northanger Abbey, Persuasion*) p. 8. Henry Austen expanded and revised the notice for Bentley's edition of the novels, 5 vols (London, 1833).

[17] 'Biographical Notice', p. 6.

[18] Brabourne, I 57.

[19] Several of the best works of criticism make this point. D. W. Harding writes that Jane Austen 'has none of the underlying didactic intention ordinarily attributed to the satirist. Her object is not missionary; it is the more desperate one of merely finding some mode of existence for her critical attitudes. To her the first necessity was to

is hardly a 'natural' genius freely warbling her native wood-notes wild. Her art is always constrained and a bit defensive; and her irony and wit may never have been quite free from a vague sense of guilt.

The uneasiness, the guilt, are faintly evident even at the beginning of Jane Austen's career. At the outset the form of fiction itself presents her with a problem. For in narrative fiction the author's irony and wit are bound to 'characterise' himself unless he takes pains to make them characterise a persona he has created. Wittiness suggests a personality – a personality that must come to rest somewhere. In Jane Austen's very early 'The History of England', written when she was fifteen,[20] she is not quite certain yet whether she herself wants to take credit for her cleverness, or whether she wants it to characterise a fictive narrator. The question may have been in her mind at the conclusion, for she devotes much of the final paragraph to making the 'I' much more opinionated and scatterbrained than she (he?) has been before. The narrator now says, for instance, that she has been outrageously biased all along; and that '. . . the recital of any Events (except what I make myself) is uninteresting to me'.[21] The effect is that everything amusing in the piece now comes to rest on an 'I' who has suddenly been pushed a certain ironic distance away from Jane Austen herself.

This problem of settling on an immediate 'author' of her

---

keep on reasonably good terms with the associates of her everyday life', 'Regulated Hatred: An Aspect of the Work of Jane Austen', *Scrutiny*, VIII (Mar 1940) p. 351. Likewise Mark Schorer writes that Jane Austen's 'problem' is that of a 'satirist, who criticises the society within which he yet wishes to remain and . . . whose best values are his own', 'The Humiliation of Emma Woodhouse', *Literary Review*, II (summer 1959) p. 554. And Mudrick notes that Jane Austen 'was herself a person who . . . found it difficult to commit herself to anything, and who used her . . . wit . . . to guard herself against direct contact. Since irony implies a remoteness, since it requires, not an exposure and analysis of feeling, but suggestion and wit, it did not violate her sense of propriety . . .', p. 178.

[20] The manuscript is dated 26 Nov 1791. See *Volume the Second*, ed. Southam, p. 149.

[21] *Volume the Second*, ed. Southam, p. 148. See Southam's note, pp. 213–14, for the influence of Goldsmith on this cavalier attitude toward 'events'.

wit seems to have troubled Jane Austen throughout her career. Another of her early solutions is to cast her fiction in the form of letters.[22] The author of a letter is its writer. Thus the wit directly characterises the 'I' rather than Jane Austen herself. The convenience of this form is evident in 'Lady Susan'; and when Jane Austen abandons letters for narrative at the conclusion of the piece she quickly has to create a new author: a cynical, smart-alecky 'I' whose final comment on Sir James is, 'I leave him . . . to all the Pity that anybody can give him. For myself, I confess that I . . .' (*Minor Works*, p. 313). Here again the opinions of the narrator are just colourful enough to generate irony; thus the 'I' again splits away slightly from Jane Austen. It is the narrator who will have to take the credit or blame for all those naughty ideas; who will have to take whatever is due the author of this monstrous work itself. And how convenient for Jane Austen. The Austen-Leighs found it difficult to understand how their young aunt could ever have written it.[23]

When Jane Austen finally turned to full length fiction she had the problem once more of whom her irony and wit were to characterise. In her first novel, Henry Tilney escorts the young heroine to the top of Beechen Cliff. There, in a scene that just faintly suggests a Satanic temptation, he displays for her the riches of the world of wit that are hers for the taking; and this scene makes a suitable emblem for the entrance of Jane Austen herself into the novelist's profession.

In this early novel she again makes a sudden, nervous attempt at the conclusion to create a giddy narrator who will serve as the immediate 'author'. Thus the last two chapters are suddenly sprinkled with comments like the following: 'I leave it to my reader's sagacity to determine how . . .'; 'I have united for their ease what they must divide for mine'; 'my own joy . . . is very

---

[22] Jane Austen 'is quite incurious about the form of the novel: that is, she tries on . . . the two shapes that are in current use – the novel-in-letters, and the story directly and methodically related by an impersonal narrator – and then, having ascertained which is the better fit, adopts it and makes no further experiment', Lascelles, p. 124.

[23] See *Life and Letters*, p. 81; and Mary Augusta Austen-Leigh, *Personal Aspects*, p. 103.

sincere'; 'professing myself . . .'; 'I must confess that . . .'; '. . .
the credit of a wild imagination will at least be all my own'.

But for the first time she has also done something else. She
has made Henry Tilney himself a walking Pilgrim's Scrip of
witty observations that Jane Austen herself is obviously pleased
with. He and the 'I' actually divide the wit on the Cliff. His
opinions on history and the state of the nation, for instance,
flank a witticism in the narrative proper ('I will only add . . .',
p. 111). At this point in the novel both he and the 'I' thus
seem to be delivering their witticisms undisguisedly on behalf
of their author.[24] But occasionally Henry says something clever
that seems to set him slightly apart from her. When Catherine
receives her brother's letter, for instance, Henry's not quite
appropriate wisecrack moves him in this direction: 'You feel,
I suppose, that, in losing Isabella, you lose half yourself . . .' (p.
207). Here Henry is just a little unpleasant in his ruthless and
detached cleverness – just a little like Mr Bennet.

Jane Austen's treatment of Henry Tilney therefore reveals
a trace of ambivalence toward her own irony and wit. He seems
at times to speak cleverly for his author and then to be nudged
nervously away for having done so. What is important is that
the course of her later development continues in this direction.
She puts more and more distance between herself and these
qualities in her writing. She seems more and more reluctant to
take personal credit for them. That vague sense of uneasiness,
even guilt, begins to drift over them in her fiction. She tends
more and more to localise them in a character with whom she is
obviously not in complete sympathy.

Mr Bennet is the next notable example. He is the outlet for
much of Jane Austen's own irony and wit in the novel. Henry
Austen mentions his sister's 'keenest relish for wit',[25] and the
same certainly goes for Mr Bennet. He looks down upon the
defects of his family and is 'contented with laughing at them'
(p. 213); and this sentiment itself is echoed in one of Jane
Austen's own letters: '. . . if it were indispensable for me . . .

---

[24] So far as Henry is concerned, Mudrick may be identifying him
with his author in the following comment: 'Henry Tilney is the
willfully ironic and detached spectator as no one except the author
herself is in any other of Jane Austen's novels', p. 49.

[25] 'Biographical Notice,' *Novels*, v 6.

never [to] relax into laughing at myself or other people, I am
sure I should be hung . . .'(*Letters*, pp. 452–3). Mr Bennet seems
to have an uncommonly intimate relationship with his own
author. Indeed he is the character in *Pride and Prejudice* most
capable of having written it.

What happens to him in the course of the novel is therefore
of great importance. Jane Austen begins to pull herself away
from him and to look at him with some cold-eyed objectivity.
Elizabeth is made to see the 'impropriety' of his witty detachment. He is made to say, '. . . let me once in my life feel how
much I have been to blame' (pp. 236, 299). At the last he is
even made to attempt an uncharacteristically heavy-handed
spoof of a letter from Mr Collins; and for his efforts Elizabeth
can now give him only a reluctant smile. She wonders at his
'want of penetration'. 'Never had his wit been directed in a
manner so little agreeable to her' (pp. 364, 363). Thus at the
conclusion Elizabeth and Jane Austen seem to be turning away
from him; and in this scene he gives the impression of Milton's
Satan bragging of his conquests and being turned by his author
into a snake.

If Jane Austen has indeed always sensed the indecorousness
of her own sharp feminine wit, the social opprobrium of
Longbourn has now descended on Mr Bennet perhaps as a consequence. But in her rather rude treatment of him there is more
than merely this. For Jane Austen appears to see in Mr Bennet
more than the unseemliness of her own wit; she now for the
first time also sees a hint of her own moral irresponsibility.
To have been gay, flippant and witty has been an offence not
only against the social decencies, but also against the moral
ones.

This attitude, which looms up late in *Pride and Prejudice* and
suffuses *Mansfield Park*, deserves much more attention than it
has received. Jane Austen is becoming uneasy that her own art,
like Mr Bennet's, has been morally lax. It has run the risk of
merely using evil for the selfish and disinterested purposes of
art. It has often required of her and her characters an aesthetic
distance, a detachment, a suspension of moral judgement, a withholding of any commitment to declarable or doctrinal truth.
Thus Mrs Oliphant commented shrewdly on Jane Austen's
'silent disbelief of a spectator . . . who has learned to give up

any moral classification of social sins, and to place them instead on the level of absurdities'.[26]

Surely all this applies to Mr Bennet, that detached and bemused spectator of human folly. He is morally and physically passive if he is anything. With a book he is regardless of time (p. 12). In his library he has 'been always sure of leisure and tranquillity' (p. 71). He acts to any purpose only once, and that is to pay the social call on a single man of good fortune that ironically produces the rest of the novel. Other than that (and perhaps his trip to London) he refuses to exert himself in any attempt to correct the defects in his daughters, his wife, or himself. He is content to laugh at the whole family. When he is faced with the crucial moral question of whether to allow Lydia to go to Brighton, he retires into irony. He is the very spirit of irony and wit as a means of avoiding any engagement with the world's problems.

Toward the conclusion he is reprimanded for this attitude. Elizabeth bores in on his 'evils'; on the 'impropriety' of his 'behaviour as a husband' (pp. 237, 236). He is made to deliver his, or Jane Austen's, confession that it has not been enough for him to be light and bright and sparkling. He says now, '. . . let me once in my life feel how much I have been to blame'. He has been shown that he has an obligation to take moral attitudes and to act on them. He must open his library door and go out into the world; and there is some slight indication that he is doing so at the end (p. 385).

Elizabeth and even Darcy are taught much the same lesson. Darcy is made to upbraid himself for not telling earlier what he knows about Wickham. Mrs Gardiner reports that he feels 'It was owing . . . to his reserve . . . that Wickham's character had been so misunderstood . . .' (p. 324). And after Elizabeth receives his revelatory letter she too is confronted with the question 'whether I ought . . . to make our acquaintance in general understand Wickham's character' (p. 226). She decides not to, and is made to regret it. After her sister elopes she exclaims, 'that *I* might have prevented it!'; 'Wretched, wretched, mistake!' (pp. 277–8).

---

[26] An unsigned article, 'Miss Austen and Miss Mitford', *Blackwood's Edinburgh Magazine*, CVII (Mar 1870) pp. 294–305; reprinted in *Critical Heritage*.

These three characters have had to acknowledge their moral obligation to take an active part in combating the impropriety and wickedness around them. It is not enough to be silent, or to laugh. Therefore by the conclusion of *Pride and Prejudice* they have been primed with that grey virtue which Henry Austen in his 'Biographical Notice' felt he ought to ascribe to Jane Austen herself – 'usefulness'.[27] They are all helping in their modest ways to right some of the world's wrongs. The young lady who began the novel with a lively, playful disposition that delighted in anything ridiculous turns her sparkling, ironic intelligence, after Lydia's elopement, to the lugubrious problems of education. 'The mischief of neglect and mistaken indulgence towards such a girl. – Oh! how acutely did she now feel it' (p. 280). Elizabeth is sounding a little like Fanny Price, and Mr Bennet like Sir Thomas Bertram. Jane Austen's cool and often detached irony and wit are giving way to the aggressive moral activism that is so obvious in the next novel.

Thus at the conclusion of *Pride and Prejudice* we stand teetering on the edge of a significantly different attitude toward irony and wit. Jane Austen seems finally confirmed in what she has always suspected. Henry Tilney has been more nice than wise. Elinor Dashwood has loved too much to doubt where she can. Elizabeth Bennet has too much relished disliking and finding it 'such a spur to one's genius, such an opening for wit to have a dislike of that kind' (p. 226). Mr Bennet has not been right to recognise the unhappy defects of his family and then merely laugh.

Jane Austen's wit is giving way to 'wisdom', her 'satire' to 'morality'. And for her the difference between the one and the other seems remarkably rigid. She says of her last heroine that Charlotte's feelings about stinginess 'were divided between amusement & indignation'; and that Charlotte finds someone's sycophancy 'very amusing – or very melancholy, just as Satire or Morality might prevail' ('Sanditon', *Minor Works*, pp. 402, 396). This heroine seems to conceive amusement, wit, irony and satire on the one hand, and moral indignation on the other, as something like opposing forces that can never quite blend.

---

[27] *Novels*, v (*Northanger Abbey, Persuasion*) p. 3.

And so perhaps does Jane Austen herself throughout her career.

There is indeed some scattered, inconclusive evidence. In a letter she writes, 'Wisdom is better than Wit' (*Letters*, p. 410). No matter how playful the context, one senses here that for her as for Charlotte these two attitudes are to be chosen between, rather than ever to be completely reconciled. One of her nieces comments on Jane Austen's 'playfulness and fun', but goes on to add that 'When grave, she was *very* grave. . . .'[28] Can this help us understand how the author of *Pride and Prejudice* could go on to produce *Mansfield Park*? Toward the end of the former that playfulness flags, and in *Mansfield Park* the gravity and the wisdom come close to taking over. Mr Bennet had asked his daughter the frivolous question, 'For what do we live, but to make sport for our neighbours, and laugh at them in our turn?' (p. 364). But was the question so frivolous? It now seems to have been directed only superficially at Elizabeth, a little more pointedly at himself – and most pointedly of all at his author. *Mansfield Park* is a kind of answer: an answer suffused with that spirit of wisdom, moral indignation and activism that seems to have existed in Jane Austen's mind in a close to radical opposition to the spirit of amusement, satire and fun.

Thus in *Mansfield Park* the obliquities of 'play' are rooted out and all but destroyed. There is no place for aesthetic attitudes here. In an early letter she had tossed off the nice comment, 'I am proud to say that I have a very good eye at an Adultress' (*Letters*, p. 127) – surely an aesthetic rather than a moral pronouncement, and one that will do to typify her art before *Mansfield Park*. But now it is Mary Crawford who makes such comments. In a letter (and also to Edmund in person), for instance, she too speaks flippantly of adultery. And the result? Jane Austen hounds her with Fanny Price, who criticises the 'gaiety' and 'lightness' of her words (p. 456). Rather than being merely diverted by the world's troubles, this novel again and again takes arms against them. It declares guilt and innocence almost as forthrightly as Mr Collins does; it rewards them almost as he would like.

---

[28] William Austen-Leigh, Montagu George Knight, *Chawton Manor and Its Owners* (London: Smith, Elder, 1911) p. 164.

It searches out and chastises 'folly'. Jane Austen's characters who have retired into irony and detached aestheticism when confronted with moral matters have commonly used the word 'folly' where Mr Collins would use 'wickedness' or 'sin'. Elizabeth Bennet, for instance, says she is diverted by 'follies and nonsense'; her father is amused by 'folly'. This attitude is now summed up in the next to last chapter of *Mansfield Park* in a single italicised word from Mary Crawford's lips (p. 454). The word summarises how she feels about Maria and Henry's wickedness; and it seems for Jane Austen to summarise some important part of her own former attitude toward wickedness as well. Now Edmund is condemning the word and the attitude absolutely, and the word is '*folly*'.

In *Mansfield Park* laughing at follies and nonsense is condemned outright. It was wrong for its author ever to have turned the world's absurdities into an occasion for mere wit. This must be the profoundest meaning of Jane Austen's famous and at least partly serious comment in February 1813 that for her *Pride and Prejudice* is 'rather too light, and bright, and sparkling; it wants shade; it wants to be stretched out here and there with a long chapter of sense . . .' (*Letters*, p. 299). In *Mansfield Park* we now get the sense.

And the sparkle? Some of it is still there – but there to be got rid of. Jane Austen gives it to a character she can chastise for having it. The character is Mary Crawford. Mary is made the receptacle for virtually all her author's playful cleverness in the novel, and then is expelled from the Park. What happens to her seems not far from an outright condemnation of irony and wit as a controlling attitude toward the world's ills. Her attractions have proved too dangerous. Indeed, one of the 'Opinions' of the novel recorded by its author is that her nephew George was 'interested by nobody but Mary Crawford' (*Minor Works*, p. 431). She must finally be rejected, by Edmund, by Fanny, and by Jane Austen herself.

In banishing Mary Crawford, Jane Austen seems therefore to be banishing at least for the time being that aspect of her own rich intelligence which guiltily produced the lightness and brightness of the previous novels. To some extent she seems to see herself in Mary. It is Mary who has a 'mind of genius' (p. 129). Like her author, she has the keenest relish for wit. She enters the novel with a joke, and leaves with a smile (pp. 42, 459). She has a 'lively mind' that seizes 'whatever may contribute to its own amusement or that of others' (p. 64). Edmund gravely says that her mind 'can hardly be serious even on serious subjects' (p. 87). To Edmund's perplexity she speaks evil but 'she speaks it – speaks it in playfulness . . .' (p. 269). She speaks disrespectfully of the clergy, as she admits (p. 89). She might even have been able to create Mr Collins. She is capable of saying, '. . . as Dr. M. is a Clergyman their attachment, however immoral, has a decorous air' – which is actually a comment in one of Jane Austen's own letters (*Letters*, p. 258).

She is capable of saying, 'I am sorry for the Beaches' loss of their little girl, especially as it is the one so much like me'; or of saying, 'Mrs. Hall . . . was brought to bed yesterday of a dead child, some weeks before she expected, owing to a fright. I suppose she happened unawares to look at her husband' – both of which are comments from the early letters (*Letters*, pp. 4, 24). Indeed much of the wit in those which the Austen family has allowed to survive[29] could be transferred to Mary Crawford; furthermore, one serious comment in a letter, 'The loss of such a Parent must be felt, or we should be Brutes' (*Letters*, p. 145), seems actually to have found its way into Mary Crawford's letter written while Tom Bertram is ill: 'One should be a brute not to feel for the distress they are in'.[30]

Mansfield Park therefore seems the visible expression of subterranean sentiments that go back to the very beginning of Jane Austen's career. From the beginning she has been uneasy about the propriety of her irony and wit; and toward the end of *Pride and Prejudice* she begins to reveal uneasiness about their moral respectability as well. Her most obvious response to all this has been to invest her wit in characters toward whom she is not altogether sympathetic. This has now come to some kind of culmination in *Mansfield Park*. For she has sharply

---

[29] On this see *Life and Letters*, p. 82.

[30] P. 433. This last example is pointed out by Liddell, p. 70. Other critics who note similarities between Mary Crawford and her author are Q. D. Leavis, x 278; Mudrick, p. 169; and Lerner, p. 157. But Moler rightly observes (and I doubt whether anyone would deny this) that Jane Austen has nevertheless presented Mary's wit as evidence of an 'unattractive mind,' pp. 130–41.

localised practically all of her remaining wit in one character, Mary Crawford; and then has scourged Mary from the Park, and the novel. In doing so she seems also to have scourged part of herself. The light and bright and sparkling Jane Austen we have known has been expelled for a time. At the conclusion of this novel Edmund must 'learn to prefer soft light eyes', Fanny's, 'to sparkling dark ones' (p. 470). Jane Austen's, too, were dark.[31]

3

Fanny Price comes closer than any of Jane Austen's other heroines to having her author's unqualified approval. Henry Crawford says to her, 'You have some touches of the angel in you' (p. 344), and he may be right. It is indeed just possible to see her as faultless and unchanging[32] – a minor misconception that nevertheless takes away the very foundation of the novel.

Fanny Price is not quite that heroine of 'faultless Character' who appears in the 'Plan of a Novel'. She is therefore not fundamentally unlike the other heroines. This is an important point. Jane Austen is not deviating from her basic plot. Fanny begins in the usual state of mind over matter, although we tend to overlook this because it has now become such a formula that Jane Austen does not seem interested in dwelling on it any more. Fanny even has the same particular illusions as Catherine Morland and Marianne Dashwood.[33] She too loves the picturesque, the Gothic and the romantic; she too is determined to find them in real life, or to imagine them there. In her first

---

[31] Hazel. *Life and Letters*, p. 240.

[32] Many critics oddly do so. A sample: 'The necessity Jane Austen apparently feels to create such a paragon of virtue ... cancels any possibility of ... allowing [Fanny's] character to develop, since it is perfect from the beginning', Ten Harmsel, p. 105; Fanny is 'always right', Sherry, p. 73; she 'has really no faults to lose', Craik, *Jane Austen: the Six Novels*, p. 92; she 'behaves with a consistency, a steadiness, which ... show an unquestioned set of values', Andrew H. Wright, p. 125; 'her "right conduct" is consistent from the beginning', Duckworth, p. 72; she 'is set down in the Mansfield Park circle as Miss Austen's delegate and mouthpiece', Firkins, p. 77. But Moler rightly recognises that she 'grows painfully into self-knowledge', p. 146.

[33] Fleishman makes this point, p. 30. Moler even sees elements of parody in her, pp. 147, 149 n. 22.

sortie out into the world from the Park she visits Sotherton;
and in a scene strikingly similar to Catherine's first disappoint-
ing sight of Northanger Abbey Fanny predictably declares that
Sotherton does not quite measure up to her idea of the Gothic:

> This is not my idea of a chapel. There is nothing awful here,
> nothing melancholy, nothing grand. Here are no aisles, no
> arches, no inscriptions, no banners. No banners . . . to be
> 'blown by the night wind of Heaven'. No signs that a
> 'Scottish monarch sleeps below' (pp. 85–6).

Readers who like to see Fanny as essentially different from the
previous heroines tend to overlook this scene. We simply have to
accept that Fanny is 'romantic' – if feebly so. Like Marianne she
even has strong ideas on the picturesqueness of trees (p. 56).[34]

Fanny thus begins with the conventional romantic illusions,
although neither she nor Jane Austen asserts them nearly so
emphatically as in the previous novels. Indeed Fanny seems
incapable of anything emphatic. She has an 'obliging, yielding
temper' (p. 17); she seems tired and lacking in vitality; she is
the only heroine to get a headache cutting roses. But nevertheless her career in the novel will be the familiar one. She will
surrender her illusions before the onslaught of facts from the
real world. At the beginning she thinks of nothing but the Isle
of Wight (p. 18). Her trip to Sotherton takes her 'beyond her
knowledge'; everything there is 'almost as interesting as it was
new . . .' (pp. 80, 85). And as the novel progresses she will be
led out like the other heroines to an even wider experience of
the world.

The two most important episodes in her systematic introduction to the world are the theatricals at Mansfield Park and
her courtship by Henry Crawford. The first of these is perhaps
the single most perplexing episode in Jane Austen's fiction.
After the trip to Sotherton Mr Yates brings to the Park the idea
that the party there should put on a play for their own amusement. They finally settle on *Lovers' Vows*. From Volume I,
Chapter xiii, to Volume II, Chapter ii inclusive the novel is
devoted mainly to their elaborate preparation for the production

---

[34] See Chapman's note to p. 56 for Jane Austen's possible debt to
Gilpin here. But Fleishman maintains that Fanny is not being authen-
tically picturesque in this passage: see his pp. 31–2 and n. 15.

and Sir Thomas's final destruction of their scheme when he
returns from Antigua before he is expected.

Fanny has never before seen 'even half a play' (p. 131), and
she is faced during the preparations with the problem of what
attitude she ought to take toward them. Clearly Jane Austen
considers this a problem with profound moral implications, but
it is not quite clear what they are. There are certainly enough
possibilities.[35] Fanny, for instance, thinks that two of the parts

---

[35] The famous *Lovers' Vows* episode has generated a body of
literature all its own. What follows is a dizzying anthology that
gives some idea of the variety of explanations that have been
tendered. '. . . Edmund put his finger on the genuine objection to the
business when he drew the distinction between "good, hardened
acting" and the efforts of ladies and gentlemen. Anyone who has
seen an amateur company . . .', Jenkins, p. 190. 'The scheme of acting
the play is a bad one . . . not only because it threatens the integrity
of the self . . ., but also because it threatens the son's relationship to
his father and the father's relationship to his house', Wiesenfarth, p.
98. 'When Sir Thomas rejects the theatricals and the play itself, he
renders a judgment of the taste and pursuits prevalent among the
aristocracy of the time', Fleishman, p. 26. 'What the author may be
conceived, in agreement with Edmund Bertram, to disapprove, is not
"the amusement", but the occasion and the play chosen', Pollock,
p. 72. '. . . there were people who sincerely believed that *Lovers'
Vows* was a play of a dangerous sort . . .', William Reitzel, '*Mansfield Park* and *Lovers' Vows*', *Review of English Studies*, IX (Oct
1933) 451–6. '. . . it is hard to see why Miss Austen should have
selected this particular play for so severe a condemnation', Thomson, p. 151. 'The play . . . gave her an opportunity to justify her
personal disapproval of amateur theatricals', Q. D. Leavis, X
141. '. . . the theatricals constitute, in theological language, a "proxi-
mate occasion of sin" ', David Lodge, *Language of Fiction* (London:
Routledge, 1966) p. 109. The players 'attempt to replace a stable
world, in which the self relates to a pre-existing order, with a world
of process, in which the self extemporizes and directs', Duckworth,
p. 55. '. . . play-acting is . . . condemned on what cannot but seem
inadequate grounds', Craik, *Jane Austen: the Six Novels*, p. 123.
Finally, the comment for which I feel the deepest sympathy: 'A
careful American parent would find no fault with the securities for
propriety and innocence which accompany the rehearsals of the
play', Firkins, p. 68.
The controversy is enriched by the certain knowledge that there
were indeed amateur theatricals at Jane Austen's own Steventon
between 1784 and 1790. Prominent in them was the fascinating
Eliza, at that time wife of the Comte de Feuillide (guillotined in

are not fit for 'any woman of modesty'. Edmund in turn is uneasy because the theatricals would be taking liberties with the rooms in his father's house. And there is also a dark reference to 'all the dangerous intimacy' of the 'unjustifiable theatre' (pp. 137, 127, 462).

Most of the possibilities seem to have something vaguely in common. This could be put as the idea that it is perilous to be anything other than one's true self.[36] Such a formulation flattens the idea into a truism, which is perhaps why Edmund or Sir Thomas never delivers a formal statement on the subject. The idea exists in the novel only as the metaphor of acting, of 'play'.

Jane Austen has used the episode of the play to dramatise her attitude toward her art. The rehearsals are, among other things, a kind of metaphor for her own former 'irony'. Acting in a play is a means of being another self, of speaking with another voice; and irony and wit are 'dramatic' in the same respect. They have allowed Jane Austen and her characters to speak and act 'out of character'. Thus Darcy's comment on Elizabeth's wit: '. . . you find great enjoyment in occasionally professing opinions which in fact are not your own'. Likewise Jane Austen's own 'truth' has always been ducking behind the mask of a *persona* to become, as in the first sentence of *Pride and Prejudice*, someone else's 'truth'.

Now in *Mansfield Park* she is shedding her ironic voices to speak in what is predominantly her own. The destruction of the theatricals is the grand summary of this. Her pulling down the stage at the Park seems inseparable from her pulling down, or her letting collapse, most of the ironic framework that characterised the earlier novels.

The rehearsals have still another significance. For the ladies

---

1794). Jane Austen's brother Henry was Eliza's chief coadjutor in the theatricals – and became her second husband in 1797. For the Steventon theatricals see *Life and Letters*, pp. 63–6; *Facts and Problems*, pp. 32–3, 127; John H. Hubback's 'Pen Portraits . . .' (cited above p. 75 n. 45) pp. 26–8; and *Austen Papers 1704–1856*, ed. R. A. Austen-Leigh (privately printed, 1942) p. 126 (letter of 19 Eep 1787).

[36] Trilling makes this point. He says that behind the 'reasons' given in the novel is the 'fear that . . . the impersonation of any other self will diminish the integrity of the real self', *The Opposing Self*, p. 218.

and gentlemen at the Park, acting is not only an escape from their proper selves into 'irony'. It is also an escape from their own moral obligations. In *Lovers' Vows* Mary Crawford can do, from behind the mask of a dramatic character, what she knows she should not do *in propria persona* – to use Jane Austen's phrase. Mary can play Amelia, a 'forward young lady' (p. 144). Maria Bertram, who is understood to be engaged to Mr Rushworth, can play at flirtation with Henry Crawford in her dramatic role (p. 165).

Here again Jane Austen's own irony has served the same purpose for her and her characters as the rehearsals have for the young people at the Park. When Mr Bennet is confronted with the moral issue of whether Lydia should go to Brighton, he can merely take refuge in irony. And we must not forget that his author can also take refuge in him. Thus, by stepping behind a 'character', everybody has managed to avoid facing moral issues squarely. *Lovers' Vows* can be for the characters what they themselves have sometimes been for Jane Austen.

It is therefore a delicious luxury for the characters at the Park to be able to act within the ironic refuge of the play. Mary Crawford later says she had never known such 'exquisite happiness' as 'that acting week'. Henry never was happier (pp. 358, 225). These young people, and certainly Jane Austen too, are all caught between this delight and what they guiltily feel to be their moral obligations. Edmund feels the tension 'between his theatrical and his real part' (p. 163). And so, opposed to the play is a steady antiphony of references in the novel to that obligation to know one's true self. Sir Thomas's daughters lack 'self-knowledge'; Julia lacks a 'knowledge of her own heart'; Fanny alludes hopefully to Dr Grant's 'knowledge of himself'; Edmund reminds Mary of that 'most valuable knowledge we could any of us acquire – the knowledge of ourselves . . .' (pp. 19, 91, 112, 459).

The theatricals at the Park thus force Fanny to choose between acting and the obligation to know oneself, between the ironic freedom of art and the moral obligations of life, between wit and wisdom – although the episode is far from exhausted by such a formulation. Edmund, who has the same dilemma, weakens and decides to act. By a very subtle process of compromise Fanny too begins to drift into the play without ever formally deciding to. She teaches Mr Rushworth his part; she is Edmund's stand-in during rehearsal; she is the prompter. At the end of Volume I there is a crucial moment when she is asked actually to step onto the stage itself as Mrs Grant's substitute. It does not seem generally understood[37] that she does indeed agree to perform: 'she must yield' (p. 172). Like Edmund she too has now acquiesced to the exquisite irony of speaking in a voice not her own.

It is not her moral uprightness that now saves her from the part, but the remarkable, allegorical swooping down into the novel of Jane Austen's great figure of moral authority. Sir Thomas Bertram now arrives on beneficent winds from Antigua.

Henry Crawford remarks on the contrariness of fate in bringing Sir Thomas home just at this moment. His sister says to Fanny, 'To be sure, your uncle's returning that very evening! There never was anything quite like it' (pp. 225, 360). But she is not a student of the novels. Like the perverse meeting of Elizabeth and Darcy at Pemberley, the very flimsiness of the plot business in this case points toward a controlling thematic idea behind, or above, the plot. Here the idea seems to be that Fanny is simply not equal to the moral choice she has been called on to make. She is not quite able to resist the temptation of imposing between herself and the world an aesthetic mask, as she did at Sotherton, as she is now about to do at Mansfield Park. This passive, tired heroine, and perhaps Jane Austen herself, must be saved. And they are, by a figure whose moral authority is suddenly and apocalyptically thrust into the novel from outside; from some place outside so constituted spiritually and meteorologically that it can provide such a figure when one is needed.

Now he appears, like God (Julia says, 'I need not be afraid of appearing before him', p. 175) or Stephen Gosson. He sweeps away the wicked artifice of the play. He has the stage pulled down, and he burns every unbound copy of *Lovers' Vows* in the house. He then forgives his erring children, and rules his house, and his novel. He is not like Mr Bennet: there is never much laughing in his presence (p. 197).

---

[37] Wiesenfarth, for instance, comments mistakenly that 'no amount of pressure can overcome her resolution not to act', p. 99. Likewise Duckworth, p. 95.

Sir Thomas Bertram is Jane Austen's single figure of almost absolute moral authority – although the 'almost' here must bear some weight. None of the other fathers in her novels has any significant authority at all,[38] even though the conclusion of *Pride and Prejudice* has begun to push Mr Bennet in that direction. Sir Thomas is himself portrayed as capable of making errors, the chief being his attempt to coerce Fanny into marrying Henry Crawford; and like Mr Bennet he is made finally to acknowledge the 'errors in his own conduct as a parent' (p. 461). But the authority Jane Austen has invested in him is not much diminished by all this. By the conclusion Fanny has found in him 'a rule to apply to, which settled every thing. Her awe of her uncle, and her dread of taking a liberty with him, made it instantly plain to her, what she had to do' (p. 436). It would be cruel to look for irony here. His divined wish is her rule of right, his word is law.

Sir Thomas is therefore among Jane Austen's characters who seem almost to have no existence independent of the purpose they are serving in the spiritual development of the heroine. He stands for something. He is the power of conventional moral authority. He inveighs against 'that independence of spirit, which prevails so much in modern days . . .' (p. 318).[39] He descends on the novel to cut short the 'liberty which his absence had given' (p. 202) to his children, and his author.

Indeed *Mansfield Park* seems dedicated to compressing youthful energies, perhaps including the author's own, inside the conventional bounds laid down by him. In this novel youth is always attempting to trespass where it does not belong. At Sotherton, after the young people have viewed the chapel, they walk out into the grounds with 'one wish for air and liberty' (p. 90). Henry Crawford then induces Maria to pass around the edge of a gate in the wilderness while her fiancé has gone for the conventional key. And later the young people's play at

---

[38] The 'predicament of the Dashwoods, the Bennets, the Watsons, the Bertrams, and the Prices is largely due to the shortcomings or absence of the head of the family', Southam, *Literary Manuscripts*, pp. 84–5.

[39] What must be Jane Austen's single most evil character, Lady Susan, writes that a 'state of dependence' will not 'suit the freedom of my spirit', 'Lady Susan', *Novels*, VI (*Minor Works*) p. 299.

the Park threatens to spill over into life when for one horrible
moment on the stage Henry keeps Maria's hand after their revels
have been ended by her father's return (p. 175). But Sir
Thomas's return has the effect Mrs Grant said it would. He
'keeps every body in their place' (p. 162). There is no place in
his house for anything out of bounds. There is no place for
irony, for the play, or, finally, for his erring daughter.

Jane Austen's art has always respected the social conventions
of its time much more than does a novel, say, like *Wuthering
Heights*. The conventional social and moral boundaries mapped
out by the elder Lintons, for instance, are there to be broken,
like the famous windowpane, by Catherine and Heathcliff.
But Jane Austen's characters seldom transgress such boundaries
very far, or for very long.[40] Her young men reveal their cautious
waywardness by acts such as entering a ballroom without an
introduction (see 'Catherine', *Minor Works*, pp. 218–20). Anything like Heathcliffean window-opening is done only by
officially discredited characters. Thus Mary Crawford stands
before an open window at Mansfield Park (p. 108); and Mr
Woodhouse complains that Frank Churchill keeps opening the
doors at Randalls (*Emma*, p. 249). The attitude of both Jane
Austen and her characters toward the accepted forms seems
fairly represented in one of her letters: 'On receiving a message
from Lord & Lady Leven thro' the Mackays declaring
their intention of waiting on us, we thought it right to go to
them. I hope we have not done too much . . .' (*Letters*, p.
158).

Her art, therefore, always exists safely inside conventional
social and moral boundaries, or poaches cautiously on the
borders. The 'wilderness' at Sotherton, which takes on some
of the same significance as the heath in *Wuthering Heights* as
a place appropriate for behaviour outside the conventional,
would have made Emily Brontë smile.[41] It is a gardener's

---

[40] Mary Lascelles notes Jane Austen's 'strong natural bent towards
acceptance of life as she found it', p. 20.

[41] At any rate this miniature geography seems to have amused her
sister Charlotte. Charlotte describes *Pride and Prejudice* as 'a carefully fenced, highly cultivated garden, with neat borders', *The
Brontës* . . . (cited above p. 24 n. 5), letter of 12 January 1848 to
George Henry Lewes.

wilderness, a 'pleasant wood of about two acres', planted in larch and laurel.[42]

But *Mansfield Park* is even more conventional than Jane Austen's other works. The boundaries in it are very carefully kept. There must be more rooms, doors, walls, paths and gates in it than in any of the others. Its very title, of those certainly Jane Austen's own,[43] makes a narrow geographical, and ultimately moral, restriction. *Mansfield Park* curbs even more than the other novels that independence of spirit Sir Thomas objects to. And it curbs Jane Austen's own. It comes closest to exhibiting the qualities of mind Jane Austen's family seems to have wanted to find in her work.[44] In this novel the boundaries of conventional moral behaviour are not to be transgressed, even vicariously in the form of art. There will be no speaking from behind masks; no sparkling wit that turns wickedness merely into folly; no excursions across moral boundaries even on the wings of the irony and wit that have allowed Jane Austen to speak with another voice. When Sir Thomas returns from Antigua, there is no place for these in his house.

4

Sir Thomas undertakes in the first chapter to be Fanny's 'patron' (p. 8). Her settling physically and spiritually into his house is a sign that she is accommodating herself to the values he represents. First she moves from her little attic room to the East Room, then to an important place in the drawing room and in the Parsonage. By the next-to-last paragraph she is lodged permanently as a member of his family on the grounds of the 'paternal abode'; and she is assured of his 'perfect approbation' (p. 461).

Before she can take her permanent place on Sir Thomas's

---

[42] On the prim nature of an eighteenth-century gardener's wilderness see Chapman, 'Improvements', in the Appendix to the novel, p. 559.

[43] There is no evidence that the title *Northanger Abbey* is Jane Austen's own.

[44] Although the uncomfortable and guarded opinions of the family that are recorded in 'Opinions of *Mansfield Park*' would hardly seem to bear this out. See *Novels*, VI (*Minor Works*) pp. 431–5.

grounds she must pass through the second of her two important spiritual episodes. She must feel an attraction toward Henry Crawford and be rescued from it, just as she had almost yielded to Lovers' Vows before Sir Thomas returned to rescue her. A version of this romance with the false hero occurs in every one of the novels, and Jane Austen has no intention here of deviating from her general plan. Fanny can make Henry the embodiment of her own illusions. Like his counterparts he is 'every thing to every body', and so he can be for her what she wanted the chapel at Sotherton to be. He can be picturesque and romantic. Even his sister compares him to the heroes in old romances (p. 360). He has 'countenance' and good teeth (p. 44).[45]

Clearly Jane Austen has created Henry in the tradition of her earlier false heroes. But the similarity can take us too far. For even at the beginning Fanny has much profounder reservations about him than do any of the previous heroines. He never comes close to answering her idea of perfection. She sees quickly at Sotherton that his flirtation with Maria is 'wrong' (p. 99). She comes to recognise that 'he could do nothing without a mixture of evil' (p. 302). And when he proposes she does manage to turn him down in a speech that must employ more negatives than Jane Austen has ever put in one speech before (pp. 301–2).

But nevertheless Fanny's attitude toward him, even in this speech, is delicately ambivalent; and there is indeed throughout her courtship by Henry, as in the Lovers' Vows episode, the uncomfortable implication that her very attitude toward recognised evil is ambivalent. She is slowly and subtly drawn toward a man she knows is tainted by evil. She feels Henry's 'powers' (p. 232).[46] When he reads Shakespeare aloud her 'eyes

---

[45] I have not come across any notice in the criticism that Henry may owe something (but note the dates of the composition of *Mansfield Park*) to a Stephen Lushington, whom Jane Austen met in October 1813 and described as follows: '... very smiling, with an exceeding good address, & readiness of Language. – I am rather in love with him. – I dare say he is ambitious and Insincere. ... He has a wide smiling mouth & very good teeth', *Letters*, p. 353 (14 Oct 1813).

[46] And so have some of the distaff critics. Sheila Kaye-Smith comments on his attractiveness, pp. 79–80; and Margaret Kennedy makes the following excellent comment: '... it is one of the subtleties of the book that Henry Crawford, had he been a better man,

which had appeared so studiously to avoid him throughout
the day, were turned and fixed ... on him for minutes, fixed
on him ... till the attraction drew Crawford's upon her ...'
(p. 337). And when he prepares to leave the Park near
the beginning of Volume III she finds that her heart has
'softened' toward him, just as Elinor's had toward Willoughby;
and, like Elinor, at the moment of parting she takes his
hand.

The culmination of Fanny's romance with Henry takes place
at Portsmouth. Sir Thomas sends her to her parents' house
there in the hope that the humble surroundings will make her
reconsider Henry's offer, and she stays until summoned back
to the Park. Nevertheless why Jane Austen has gone to the
trouble of shifting the scene to Portsmouth is not at all clear.[47]
Sir Thomas's declared reason seems merely to follow from her
own, whatever that might be. In the previous novels the heroine
makes a loop out into the world and returns home near the
conclusion, and perhaps Jane Austen simply wants to follow
the pattern. But there seems also to be another good reason.
Again the plot has been used as a makeshift to further what is
essentially psychological action.

Fanny's trip to Portsmouth is a special humiliation for her,
and here as at Pemberley Jane Austen is much more interested
in her heroine's psychology than the scenery. The episode may
in this respect owe something to an earlier story, 'The Watsons'.
Emma Watson has been brought up by a wealthy aunt, and
returns to feel 'sensible of all that must be open to the ridicule
of Richer people in her present home' (*Minor Works*, p. 345).

---

would have been the right man [for Fanny]'. With him 'she would
have developed her latent capacities more fully and they might have
read Shakespeare together for a better reason than self-improvement',
pp. 74–5. Jane Austen herself calls him a 'clever, pleasant man',
Letters, p. 378.

[47] Following are a few of the critics' conjectures: '... variety is
introduced by the clever device of sending Fanny to visit her family
at Portsmouth, thus introducing fresh scenes and characters'. Thomson, p. 237; 'Fanny's going to Portsmouth ... was ... devised ... as
an opportunity for all the Bertram and Crawford complications to be
cleared up in letters', Q. D. Leavis, X 123: 'Jane Austen may have
wished for an opportunity to express her dislike of town life and her
longing for the country', Liddell, p. 65.

Fanny likewise is forced to endure the 'smallness' of her parents' house, the 'smallness of the rooms', the 'thinness of the walls', the 'narrowness of the passage and staircase'. Her feelings are 'sadly pained' by her father's 'language and his smell of spirits'. He is 'dirty and gross' (pp. 380–9).

Into these surroundings Henry comes in search of her; and so she feels a 'shame for the home in which he found her'. She is humiliated by the 'vulgarity of her nearest relations' (pp. 400, 402). Like Elizabeth at Lambton after the humiliating news of Lydia's elopement, Fanny feels certain that Henry will now give up the pursuit (p. 402). But what is important is that she feels more attracted to him than ever before. She is 'willing to allow he might have more good qualities than she had been wont to suppose'. She has 'never seen him so agreeable – so *near* being agreeable' (pp. 405, 406). It is as if the humiliation of having to appear in the squalour of her family has somehow propelled her toward Henry. He then insinuates himself into her family, and finally is walking along the Portsmouth ramparts arm-in-arm with Fanny and her sister on the family's Sunday outing.

Henry's powers over Fanny therefore reach their height when he comes into her sordid family. There seems to be a reason for this beyond the fact that Henry is now trying to be especially agreeable. Like all Jane Austen's heroines, Fanny needs to experience her own kinship with evil in the course of her spiritual entrance into the world. Elizabeth had her Lydia, Fanny has her family. Until she experiences this kinship, she is in the world but not truly of it. Jane Austen has therefore forced her back into the family, in a house filled with humiliating 'evils' (p. 385)[48] and unwashed cups.

And there is the implication, as in the previous novels, that whatever is unseemly in the house is also potentially present in Fanny. Elizabeth is a Bennet, Fanny is a Price. She may now live at the Park, but she is the daughter of a father capable of three 'By G—'s in one paragraph. She is not quite 'above' Henry. The culmination of her romance with him thus seems to belong here, in the midst of the family, with all its faults.

---

[48] But again, this word in Jane Austen's fiction does not necessarily bear much moral weight. See p. 91 n. 10.

What she sees now in the Price family she has always seen in him and now senses in herself. Therefore, here she feels closest to him. Here she meets him on common ground.

The Portsmouth episode thus seems to be Jane Austen's idea of a spiritual initiation into the world for Fanny. Fanny has been returned 'to the scenes of her infancy' (p. 369); she has been returned to her lowly origin. She has been forced down into the family whose blood she shares. She has been drawn onto the ramparts by what she knows is a mixture of good and evil. She now belongs to the world, with its evils, its Prices, and its Henrys.[49] Hence on the ramparts she is linked arm-in-arm with a sister and with Henry. Here may be the purposeful, hard core of 'meaning' in the scene so far as Jane Austen is concerned.

The scene on the ramparts is the final phase of Fanny's dangerous romance. It corresponds to that final rehearsal of *Lovers' Vows* when she was on the verge of being drawn into the play. Near the sea the air is mild; there is a brisk, soft wind; everything looks beautiful under the influence of the bright sky; the sea is now at high water, dancing in its glee (p. 409). Fanny is now on the edge of the sea. She seems now on the verge of yielding to Henry. She needs to be rescued again.

Therefore Jane Austen sends Henry away and then characteristically introduces a document that will dispel the half-illusion with which Fanny has invested him. This time the document is a newspaper, and it informs Fanny that Henry has suddenly eloped with Maria for reasons that, predictably, do not much interest his author.[50] The mere fact of this elope-

---

[49] Warre Cornish seems to agree on this matter, and has some harsh words for Jane Austen in consequence: '. . . I could wish Jane Austen had not lowered Fanny to the possibility of a marriage with Henry', *Jane Austen* (London: Macmillan, 1926) p. 150.

[50] Here again Jane Austen is guilty of a sudden elopement which seems to offend most critics' sense of what would be appropriate in a realistic plot. Thus Firkins comments on the 'seeming improbability of allowing a man to elope with a married woman whom he does not love to the certain ruin of his . . . prospects with the woman whom he does love sincerely', p. 70. 'Henry went off with her "because he could not help it" – which is absurd enough', Liddell, p. 54. The elopement 'does not appear to spring naturally from the previous action', Thomson, p. 159. 'In a quick and very unconvincing denoue-

ment is the crucial 'fact' in the novel. Now the 'truth' rushes on Fanny (p. 440). She begins to perceive the 'horrible evil', the 'gross . . . complication of evil' (pp. 440, 441) that Henry is capable of perpetrating.

It is now a fact that Henry is not what Fanny has always supposed: a mixture in which evil has merely its part. He has now been shown to be evil itself. He is not gray but black. In retrospect, there have indeed been times when he threatened to evaporate into some all-pervasive principle of wickedness swirling about the world in a Satanic mist. He once told the assembled company at the Park that 'From Bath, Norfolk, London, York – wherever I may be . . . I will attend you from any place in England . . .' (p. 193). Indeed his provenance has always seemed much grander than the house of a vicious Admiral (41). We recall – oh, the significance of it *now!* – that a chain necklace he once bought would not fit through an amber cross.

Fanny has felt his powers; and she has been rescued by – by whatever swept Sir Thomas home from Antigua. She is ready for a permanent place in his house. Jane Austen therefore casually introduces another little makeshift in the plot, Lady Bertram's indisposition, to hurry Fanny back to Mansfield Park. What is a little gratuitous illness to an author whose mind is on spiritual matters?

5

Sir Thomas now gives Fanny his perfect approbation, and throws in his son. Edmund has undergone a course of spiritual regimen that precisely parallels her own. Therefore in *Mansfield Park* again there is a double protagonist. Indeed Edmund and Fanny are so much alike at the beginning that they almost coalesce. Mary Crawford notices that they tend to look alike. Fanny can function as his stand-in at a rehearsal. The two seem always to be sitting where the other sat, and thinking what the other thought (see p. 207). Their relationship at the beginning is summed up in Edmund's comment to her, 'I am glad you saw it

---

ment, [Jane Austen] forces Henry back into the category of evil. He cannot resist an outrageous flirtation', Ten Harmsel, p. 119.

all as I did' (p. 64). More than any of the other heroines Fanny has flirted with perfection, and she in turn regards Edmund 'as an example of every thing good and great' (p. 37).[51]

Edmund passes through two important episodes in the novel, and we have seen Jane Austen at work long enough to guess that they will be essentially the same as Fanny's. First he yields, grudgingly, to the seduction of the play. He descends 'from that moral elevation which he had maintained before . . .' (p. 158); and he is of course extricated only by Sir Thomas's return. The second episode is his falling in love with Henry's sister Mary – perhaps more out of his author's passion for symmetry than his own for Mary herself. Here, as in the case of Henry's rehearsing with Maria, dramatic art threatens to break its bounds and ooze out dangerously into real life; for it was Mary Crawford that Edmund played opposite in *Lovers' Vows*.

The progress of this uninspired love affair is just as gradual and subtle as Fanny's with Henry. We can watch Fanny and her alter ego part company as he is slowly drawn toward Mary. The two cousins begin to disagree, and Edmund begins to make statements like, 'If you are against me, I ought to distrust myself – and yet . . .' (p. 155). Mary begins to grow more and more attractive. Fanny is 'a little surprised that he could spend so many hours with Miss Crawford, and not see more of the sort of fault which he had already observed, and of which *she* was almost always reminded. . . .' Mary's 'faults were what they had ever been, but he saw them no longer'. He is now what all the heroines have been at this point – 'blinded' (pp. 66, 264, 424). He is in that general state of illusion we have seen again and again: his mind is revising matter for its own aesthetic delight; he is creating art at Mansfield Park against his father's wishes.

The culmination of his romance with Mary comes when he goes to London to ask for her hand. This is his moment on the ramparts. He is ready to yield (p. 422). Again it is the elopement that provides the disenchanting fact. But here Jane Austen has encountered a difficulty. Henry can conveniently establish his

---

[51] Jane Austen apparently had a high regard for him too. The *Memoir* (1871) reports that Edmund was one of her 'great favourites', p. 157.

true character by the act of adultery; but Jane Austen has not been willing to let his sister do the same, even a sister who makes off-colour puns (p. 60). Apparently Jane Austen could not find, or did not bother to find, any suitable plot business to clinch Mary's evil – although the evil itself is presented as beyond question. Mary is simply made to respond to her brother's elopement with the inappropriate word 'folly'; and then Edmund is made to deliver a long lecture that slowly circles in on the 'faults of principle' (p. 456) suddenly revealed in the word.

Edmund gives the lecture directly to Mary, then second-hand to Fanny. But his real target is the reader. He and his author seem to apologise for the length of his address ('with the usual beginnings', p. 453); and perhaps by means of Mary's impish but apt comment on it ('Was it part of your last sermon?') Jane Austen is even apologising ruefully for its profundity. But it is very difficult to find any significant ironic qualification to what Edmund actually says. Jane Austen seems to be speaking directly through him. She has taken her cue from Fanny's father-to-be, and has temporarily allowed the fictive framework of the novel to collapse completely; although it is just possible that a part of her is secretly standing aside with Mary Crawford, smiling at the result – Wit smiling at Wisdom.

What Mary has mercifully revealed about herself, at least to Edmund, is that she is as evil as her brother. She has called 'folly' what she should have called wrong. The word 'evil' has been hovering over her for some time (see for instance pp. 376, 455, 456), waiting to settle. Now it does, and she begins to coalesce with Henry as that single force, evil itself, which has at last been given its proper name. Like her brother, she has always seemed not quite bound by time or space – as if she were a visitant from Dis, or London. She has been able to glide like a mist up Sir Thomas's stairs to find Fanny in the East Room; she has been able to tell her, 'I shall be at Mansfield Park for ever' (pp. 360–1).

Thus the two Crawfords are fast becoming one. Whatever differences there are between them lie very close to the surface of the novel. Most of the wit has been given to Mary, but the pair of them together often seem, like the Thorpes in *Northanger*

Abbey, to be a single value that Jane Austen has given two guises merely for the convenience of her romantic plot. It has even been suggested that the two are a split version of Jane Austen's earlier character Lady Susan.[52] The necklace hung around Fanny's neck, for instance, does not come from one of them or the other, but from both; Mary tells her that when she wears it the 'sister is not to be in your mind without bringing the brother too' (p. 259). Fanny's thinking later that she would never have accepted the necklace if she had known that Henry had anything to do with it (p. 362) is partly an indication of her own ambivalence toward the single value that the Crawfords seem to be embodying. Accepting the gift from Henry would have a special significance of course; but it is also true that Fanny seems to want to accept from the wicked left hand what she knows she ought to refuse from the wicked right. The Crawfords, then, are finally much more alike than different. At the end Edmund exclaims, 'Equally in brother and sister deceived!' (p. 459).

When Edmund has received his half of the truth concerning the Crawfords, he says, '. . . the charm is broken. My eyes are opened' (p. 456) – a formal declaration of disenchantment like Reginald's to Lady Susan: 'The spell is removed. I see you as you are' ('Lady Susan', *Minor Works*, p. 304). Edmund sees at last that Mary is a product of the bad world outside the Park. He generously comments on her character, 'This is what the world does' (p. 455).

And he is right. She and her brother do indeed know the world. Again they resemble their putative mother Lady Susan, who brings to the Vernons a 'knowledge of the world' ('Lady Susan', *Minor Works*, p. 251). Indeed the Crawfords seem to have been sent into the Park to share that knowledge with the inhabitants. Mary once told Fanny that Henry 'loves you with all his heart, and will love you as nearly for ever as possible' (p. 363) – a homely and oracular utterance that seems to have drawn on the hidden source of the world's laws. Fanny and Edmund's introduction to the wickedness of the Crawfords has thus completed their introduction to the world. They have had their little affair with the Crawfords, and with it. It has sought

---

[52] See Q. D. Leavis, X 128.

them out, in the East Room, at Portsmouth, and in the clergy. Their innocent illusions have been invaded by it.

They are ready to marry – and so why not marry each other? Their marriage seems little more than an impatient conventional gesture that Jane Austen has used to signify the rejoining of these two into a new, tempered spiritual product. Edmund and his cousin now collapse into each other's arms, and into each other, for reasons that have left the plot limping behind;[53] and Jane Austen has not wasted much energy even attempting to furbish up names, dates and places. If the reader still wants a plot, she says, let him make up his own (p. 470).

6

In Jane Austen's juvenile 'Catherine, or The Bower' the heroine is forced to endure life with a prissy maiden aunt who 'prided herself on the exact propriety and Neatness with which everything in her Family was conducted, and had no higher Satisfaction than that of knowing her house to be always in complete Order . . .' (*Minor Works*, p. 197). In *Mansfield Park* the hero and heroine end by snuggling into just such a household, and with relief.[54] Life at the Park proceeds 'in a regular course of cheerful orderliness'. There is a 'consideration of times and seasons, a regulation of subject'. There is 'propriety' in all things (pp. 392, 383).

These two have retired into a little fastness cut off from the wicked world that brought them together. Near the conclusion of 'Lady Susan' Mrs Vernon writes from the family home, 'Here we shall in time be at peace' (*Minor Works*, p. 297); and this seems to belong above the gate of Mansfield Park. Edmund and Fanny have been given a final home serenely free from con-

---

[53] Even Brabourne is a little uneasy here: Edmund 'went on comfortably considering his affection for his cousin to be of the most quiet and brotherly description, until the exigencies of the story compelled him to find out that it was something of a different nature', I 88.

[54] Miriam Allott's general comment on Jane Austen's art applies especially well here: 'Obedient to eighteenth-century notions of formal discipline, it is shaped by a rational, orderly temperament which . . . feels compelled to tidy up life's customary messiness', *Novelists on the Novel* (London: Routledge, 1965) p. 169.

flict. Even the threat of sexuality seems absent from it. Edmund began as Fanny's foster brother (see pp. 16, 374), and at the end he still seems closer to that than to a husband. Fanny finds herself 'pressed to his heart with only these words . . ., "My Fanny – my only sister. . . ." ' He manages 'to persuade her that her warm and sisterly regard for him would be foundation enough for wedded love' (pp. 444, 470). The chain he gives her fits through her brother William's cross, although Henry's would not. Even the trifling opposition of character that Elizabeth thinks will add sparkle to her marriage with Darcy has no place at the Park. To Edmund's relief, he need have 'no fears from opposition of taste, no need of drawing new hopes of happiness from dissimilarity of temper' (p. 471).[55] An evening in their home is going to be distinguished by a consideration of times and seasons, and a regulation of subject.

They are also free of economic cares. The first chapter sets up Mansfield Park as a kind of bank ('Sir Thomas Bertram had interest, which, from principle . . ., pp. 3–4);[56] a bank that rewards those with principle (for the word, see pp. 463, 468, and especially 'the sterling good of principle', p. 471). It seems inevitable then that the virtue of Edmund and Fanny is eventually rewarded handsomely and tangibly. The timely death of Dr Grant in the next-to-last paragraph gives them a generous income and a parsonage with an apricot tree. Thus their trials have brought them more than a knowledge of the world. And Fanny's brother William is destined for equally good fortune in the Navy. He is looking forward sweetly to the death of his First Lieutenant (p. 375). During the evenings at the Park we have seen him playing Speculation (p. 240). He and his sister have got their Thrushes at last, with Jane Austen's blessing. The key to one of the few charades she ever composed is 'Bank Note'.[57]

Most important, Edmund and Fanny are able to find shelter in the bosom of a family that Jane Austen is willing to purify

---

[55] 'Wherever we place the source of the failure, it is clear that the greater hope, the marriage of opposites who could spiritually complement each other, has been lost', Fleishman, p. 55.

[56] See Chapman's note on 'interest' as that word appears on p. 40 of the text.

[57] See *Novels*, VI (*Minor Works*) p. 450.

of all wickedness whatever. It is this most of all which sets off *Mansfield Park* from her other novels. True, something of the same purification takes place at the conclusion of *Pride and Prejudice;* but there it is not nearly so sweeping. Elizabeth looks forward to the time when she and Darcy 'should be removed from society so little pleasing to either, to all the comfort and elegance of their family party at Pemberley'. Likewise Jane and her husband feel that 'So near a vicinity to her mother and Meryton relations was not desirable. . . .' These two couples draw together into a tight little community, which from time to time takes in Kitty Bennet – presumably for her eventual purification. In 'society so superior to what she had generally known, her improvement was great' (pp. 384–5).

Pride and Prejudice is nevertheless remarkably tolerant in its willingness to give wickedness a place in the family circle. Wickham is subsidised by Darcy, Lydia visits Pemberley, Lady Catherine and Mrs Bennet perhaps meet at Christmas. But such tolerance, such ironic holding in suspension of moral contraries, has utterly collapsed in *Mansfield Park.* Nothing about the novel is more noteworthy. The final pages are riddled with the word 'punishment' (pp. 464, 465, 468). In a stupendous Last Judgement Jane Austen drives the wicked from the Park and shuts the gate.

Henry Crawford will of course never be admitted again. As for his sister, she is consigned to London. It seems the place for her. Lady Susan considers it 'the fairest field of action' ('Lady Susan', *Minor Works,* p. 294); whereas Fanny's impeccable opinion is that the 'influence of London' is 'very much at war with all respectable attachments' (p. 433). Mary will have to be content, at that distance, with Fanny's gracious thought that, wicked as Mary is, her friendship with Fanny herself 'had at least been blameless' (p. 433).

Maria also will never be admitted to the Park again. Fanny's generous opinion in this case is that 'the greatest blessing to every one of kindred with Mrs Rushworth would be instant annihilation' (p. 442) – a familial sentiment that might just strike a sympathetic chord in Mr Collins. Sir Thomas righteously refuses to admit his unworthy child into his home. She 'had destroyed her own character, and he would not by a vain attempt to restore what never could be restored, be affording his sanction to vice' (p. 465). Thus he takes seriously and without any clear demurring on the part of his author the lofty and vicious advice Mr Collins had offered Mr Bennet.

As for Mrs Norris, she is suddenly considered an 'hourly evil', and so must go the way of all the other evils in this book. Jane Austen sends her away to live with Maria 'in another country – remote and private'. 'Not even Fanny had tears for aunt Norris . . .' (pp. 465–6). And the Grants! They too are tainted. The 'continuance of the Bertrams and Grants in such close neighbourhood would have been most distressing' (p. 469). Who could deny it? And so Jane Austen sends them to London, and kills Dr Grant of apoplexy.

Mr Yates is grudgingly allowed to remain, even though he suggested the play. The moral atmosphere at the Park has of course its salubrious effect, and he begins to 'look up' to Sir Thomas, and be guided by him (p. 462). His wife Julia responds to the bracing atmosphere by becoming humble (p. 462); and Tom Bertram regains his health without his bad habits (p. 462). At the conclusion even Lady Bertram seems to have taken on a new moral dimension (p. 449), which will be her third.

By the final paragraph everything at the Park is 'thoroughly perfect'. The 'perfect happiness' that concludes Jane Austen's first novel is well undermined by playful irony; but in *Mansfield Park* even the faint self-mockery at the beginning of the last chapter cannot bring any valedictory irony into Sir Thomas's house. Here is a picture of perfection that apparently did not make Jane Austen sick and wicked. 'Let other pens dwell on guilt and misery' (p. 461). The Park has been absolutely purged of the impure world. It has been purged of that 'infection' brought by Mr Yates; an infection which had 'spread as those things always spread' (p. 184). It has been purged of Mary Crawford, whose mind was 'tainted' (p. 269). It has been purged of Henry, who suffered 'contagion' (p. 295) from his uncle's wicked habits. Fanny is safe forever from the 'stains and dirt' (p. 439) of her original home at Portsmouth.

The 'harmony' (see pp. 113, 191, 391)[58] that she loves, and that Jane Austen seems to have been yearning for at least since

---

[58] For the influence of the new romanticism on Fanny's 'harmony' effusions, see Bradbrook, p. 78.

Elizabeth Bennet began to smile only reluctantly at her father's irony – this harmony has been achieved by the expulsion from the Park, and from the novel, of everything not consonant with a uniform and self-congratulatory moral goodness. Irony, with its untidy obliquities and ambivalences, has for the most part been driven out. Wit has been localised in Mary Crawford and then driven out. Everything 'dramatic' has been driven out. The virtuous have withdrawn and have huddled together in a moral haven that is marked off by prim boundaries from the world outside. In Jane Austen's juvenile burlesque, 'Love and Friendship', she smiles impishly at a married couple who 'had on their first Entrance in the Neighbourhood, taken due care to inform the surrounding Families, that as their Happiness centred wholly in themselves, they wished for no other society'.[59] Now Edmund and Fanny seem to do the same in dead earnest, as they retire, with the other right-thinking Bertrams, into the grounds of the paternal abode.

---

[59] *Volume the Second*, ed. Southam, pp. 22–3.

VI

EMMA
Reality

1

Emma is the second of the novels written at Chawton and published without extensive later revision.[1] It was begun on 21 January 1814, finished on 29 March 1815,[2] and was published in December or early the next year.[3] By now Jane Austen was becoming famous, and the Prince Regent offered to allow her to dedicate the work to him – an offer she accepted.[4]

Emma is Jane Austen's masterpiece. It is the magnificent expression of the one large theme that has occupied her from the beginning. Again, a young lady enters the world. Thus at the end of Volume II Mr Knightley's brother tells her, 'Your neighbourhood is increasing, and you mix more with it'. But in this novel the entrance is largely metaphorical. It is true that Emma makes excursions further and further out into the actual countryside; but for the most part Jane Austen has simply abandoned such workaday plot business as a makeshift for psychological action. Emma's entrance into the world therefore does not have much to do with geography; she is the only

---

[1] But see Q. D. Leavis (X 63; 76–80) for the possibility that 'The Watsons' was rewritten to become *Emma*.

[2] According to Cassandra's Memorandum and Jane Austen's own note. See *Novels*, VI (*Minor Works*) facing p. 242; *Plan of a Novel*, ed. Chapman [p. 37].

[3] The title page is dated 1816. See *Novels*, IV (*Emma*) p. xi. There was no second edition during Jane Austen's lifetime.

[4] See *Life and Letters*, pp. 311–14.

heroine who does not take even one overnight trip into new surroundings.

In *Emma* very little of Jane Austen's customary plot business remains; a common observation is that nothing much happens in it.[5] 'Plot' is becoming less and less important to her. Indeed *Emma* does not have its full significance unless read as an abstraction of the previous novels, with many of their makeshift particularities of time, place and event refined away. *Emma* presupposes these novels. They are the visible flesh that prepares for the informing spirit. They are the particular forms, *Emma* the Idea – a conception that might send Jane Austen's Sir Edward Denham into a romantic ecstasy. He disdains novels made up of the 'vapid tissues of ordinary Occurrences' ('Sanditon', *Minor Works*, p. 403).

In *Emma* the heroine again comes into the world enveloped in an illusion that is eventually penetrated by facts. Jane Austen is no longer interested in giving specific causes of the illusion, although Mr Knightley does make a few formal remarks on Emma's early reading (see especially p. 37). But there are no bibliographies of romantic novels. Emma's illusion is conceived in the broadest terms – as if the illusion were simply the causeless state of the mind itself as a human being moves from his first parental house, close to the heart, out into the world. Thus Emma Woodhouse of Hartfield enters the world.

At the beginning Emma's mind is supreme over matter. That is her illusion; we have seen it before. She likes to be above 'sober facts'. Mr Knightley says she will never submit to 'a subjection of the fancy to the understanding'. Hers is a 'mind delighted with its own ideas'. Therefore she commits 'errors of imagination'. She always manages to take up an idea and make reality 'bend' to it (pp. 69, 37, 24, 343, 134). Indeed the words

---

[5] Jane Austen's own recorded 'Opinions of *Emma*' notes that one reader 'thought that if there had been more Incident, it would be equal to any of the others', *Novels*, VI (*Minor Works*) p. 438. An early reader of the novel, Susan Ferrier, put down the opinion that 'there is no story whatever', *Memoir and Correspondence of Susan Ferrier*, ed. John A. Doyle (London: J. Murray, 1898) p. 128 (letter of 1816); quoted by Hogan (cited p. 33 n. 22). And Firkins likens *Emma* to a 'picnic in which desultory groups of persons dispose themselves at random, or pursue nominal objects with devious strolls and pointless rearrangements', pp. 98–9.

Mr Knightley remembers from Cowper, 'Myself creating what I saw', seem to appear in the novel because they apply so well, not to him, but to her.[6]

Jane Austen has as usual installed her heroine in surroundings almost free from intruding facts that would threaten her illusions. Except for Mr Knightley Emma has no intellectual equals. She is therefore almost above contradiction. Her Hartfield holds itself apart from the village of Highbury to which it belongs; and the villagers all look up to the Woodhouses. Mr Woodhouse himself is a polite old gentleman who defers to his daughter on all important matters. Emma's sole confidante, Miss Taylor, is pliable, deferential, and has just been removed from Hartfield by marriage. Even Emma's sister Isabella is not distinguished for her intelligence (p. 92), and lives in London. *Emma* is thus the first of the full-length novels in which the heroine is not paired even with a sister, or an Edmund, of comparable stature; and the only novel to take its title from the lone heroine herself. At Hartfield Emma is the 'fair mistress of the mansion' (p. 22), and of the entire novel.

Indeed Emma comes close to creating the novel.[7] What appears in it is severely limited for the most part to what passes through her consciousness. There seem to be only two passages of any length (pp. 36–41, 343–9) where the point of view is clearly that of another character.[8] What appears to be objective narration is especially deceptive. Even the very first sentence ('Emma Woodhouse, handsome, clever, and rich . . .') cannot quite be taken as a neutral declaration of truth. It seems slightly coloured already by Emma's own vanity, although many would disagree.[9] When the novel goes on to declare that at Hartfield Harriet was 'artlessly impressed by the appearance of every thing in so superior a style to what she had been used to' (p. 23), again it is far from clear that this can safely be taken as completely objective narration that is free from Emma's own

---

[6] In *Jane Austen's 'Emma'* (Sydney: Sydney University Press, 1968) J. F. Burrows suggests these words as a motto for the novel, p. 106.

[7] Johnson makes a similar point, p. 164.

[8] For a discussion of the 'sustained inside view' in *Emma* see Wayne C. Booth, *The Rhetoric of Fiction*, chap. ix.

[9] Booth does, p. 257.

arch fancies. Again, Volume II Chapter ii begins with an account of Jane Fairfax's early life that might have been written by Dr Chapman; but by the tenth paragraph Emma's own nasty suspicions have begun to leach into even this apparently objective truth (for the very word 'truth' in the passage see p. 166).

A final example is the statement that Miss Bates and Jane Fairfax enter the ballroom at the Crown 'escorted by the two gentlemen' (p. 322). Certainly this seems to be conceived objectively. But even here there is something slightly peculiar. Which gentleman, Mr Weston or Frank Churchill, appears to be escorting which lady? It is likely that Frank is very subtly attending especially to Jane – a detail that is relevant indeed, although not yet to Emma, through whose consciousness ('any one who looked on like Emma', p. 322) this account is thus apparently passing on its way to us. The narrative of *Emma* seems constantly to be stealing into, and then part way out of, the central, controlling consciousness of the heroine.[10]

Emma is thus an encapsulated little world with Emma at its centre. It is a world made up largely of the private illusions of the heroine; and without much reference to any hypothetical 'objective' reality outside herself, although there are a few interesting exceptions (discussed below, pp. 167–9, 178). It is not easy to determine much more than the bare essentials of hard, external 'truth', for any seemingly objective vantage point is always threatening to erode into Emma's. Her imaginative consciousness is so subtly pervasive that it seems almost to have driven out the very possibility of objectivity. There are only a few facts that are firmly established in this big novel; only a few solid objects like pianos and pencil ends that stand firm in the sea of Emma's conjecture. At the conclusion, for instance, there is still little indication of what Harriet Smith is 'really' like. Again, many would disagree, but she does seem to remain more Emma's artistic creation than Jane Austen's.

---

[10] R. W. Chapman notes this in 'Jane Austen's Methods' (cited p. 25 n. 11). And Ian Watt comments on Jane Austen's successfully combining 'the internal and the external approaches to character', *The Rise of the Novel* (Berkeley: University of California Press, 1967) p. 297.

Emma therefore seems almost aloof from any world that could be conceived to exist outside its serene self. Like Emma herself it is arch, cool, detached. It seems largely self-sufficient and self-referential. There is not much impulse in it to make moral points that apply directly to the reader's world, except for several forthright declarations by Mr Knightley and the moralising in the final chapter. *Emma* has pushed itself a remarkable distance away from the aggressive wisdom of *Mansfield Park*. Jane Austen felt that readers who had liked the previous novel were going to find *Emma* 'very inferior in good sense' (*Letters*, p. 443), and it is indeed. This novel seems content for the most part to pursue its own disinterested aesthetic purposes inside its own close little world. Like Mr Woodhouse, it likes to keep the windows shut.

Thus when Frank Churchill comments on the sheet music that has come with the mysterious piano, 'I honour that part of the attention particularly; it shews it to have been so thoroughly from the heart' (p. 242), his words make a delicate arabesque of pretty and self-sufficient ironies. To the speaker himself they have a private meaning made piquant by his knowledge of how his hearers will mistake them; to Emma they have a nasty meaning she thinks she shares with him and which is mortifying to Jane Fairfax; to Jane they have a meaning she shares with Frank Churchill, although she must be puzzled as to what Frank intends them to mean to Emma. All this seems to exist merely for the richness of texture it gives to the novel. The ironies seem to stop at the edges of the novel, rather than to reach out with much moral significance that would directly apply in the world of our own experience; although if one is determined it is not of course impossible to find such significance in them.[11]

In *Pride and Prejudice* Miss Bingley's delivering such a *double entendre* (p. 269) as Frank Churchill's passes a direct moral judgement on her; but for Frank's ironies nothing seems quite so immediately appropriate as sheer admiration. Like much in the novel, they seem shut off from any world where moral judgements readily apply. The only clearly 'bad' character in the

---

[11] For someone's theory of how to find Jane Austen's 'own views' within the ironic framework of this novel, see Lascelles, pp. 201–2; see also Mudrick, p. 194.

novel is Mrs Churchill, who resembles Mrs John Dashwood; and it is interesting that Jane Austen has never allowed her to appear in person. She belongs where morality can make a judgement on her – in some other world, Sir Thomas Bertram's, or ours. One of the earliest reviews of *Emma* justifiably observes that it is 'amusing', but not necessarily 'instructive'.[12]

2

By the end of the novel Emma is no longer creating her own world. She has been forced to take merely a place in one outside herself. She takes her place in that 'real' world, that stylised 'reality' which until now in Jane Austen's fiction has always been signified by a relatively few carefully selected particular details that often bear great symbolic weight. To enter this world Emma must move from her father's side (p. 6), heart and house,[13] to Mr Knightley's; she must change her father's name for his. This is an expression in the plot of the psychic 'action' taking place within the heroine.

Mr Woodhouse seems to have been conceived as the extreme case of Emma's own state of mind[14] – a circumstance that does not at all interfere with his great charm. He and his daughter both lead imaginative lives more or less divorced from whatever is around them. The marriage of Mr Weston and Miss Taylor that Emma has 'made' in her own mind independent of however it actually did come about (p. 11), Mr Woodhouse has unmade in his. She is usually still 'Miss Taylor' to him. Likewise he 'unconsciously' attributes 'many of his own feelings and expressions' to his friend Mr Perry. He is 'never able to suppose that other people could feel differently from himself' (pp. 107, 8). Because wedding cake disagrees with him he is convinced that nobody should eat it. He is solipsism itself, sitting

---

[12] An anonymous review, *Gentleman's Magazine*, LXXXVI, pt II (Sep 1816), 248–9; reprinted in *Critical Heritage*.

[13] At least Jane Austen told her family that Mr Woodhouse 'survived his daughter's marriage, and kept her and Mr Knightley from settling at Donwell, about two years', *Memoir* (1871) p. 158.

[14] Mr. Woodhouse 'represents the danger of detachment from reality by way of egotism that she is liable to', Wiesenfarth, p. 114.

by a fire insulated from the weather, contemplating his own insides.[15]

Emma's pulling away from her father and entering the world falls into three main episodes, each terminating in a 'fact' she is forced to accept and adjust to. The first of the facts is Mr Elton's proposing to Emma herself rather than to Harriet Smith; then the news of Frank Churchill's engagement; and finally the revelation of Harriet's true parentage.

It is impossible to conceive Harriet as existing entirely independent of Emma. What Harriet is actually like when the two part company at the end only Robert Martin knows. The Harriet who appears in the novel is for the most part Emma's own creation. This is true, first, in the respect that we see Harriet mostly through Emma's eyes. Harriet's first words, for instance, appear as they have already been filtered through Emma's consciousness into indirect discourse (p. 27). And Harriet is Emma's creation in another respect. Emma has created for her impressionable friend a personality that is very much like Emma's own. When Frank Churchill commissions Emma to find him a wife, she archly suggests one who has been made 'like myself'; and we know just whom she has in mind (p. 373). Her protégée never amounts to much more than a projection of Emma's own personality onto a blank, reflecting surface. Harriet is blank to be sure; but one should be wary of readers who claim they know much more about her than that. To Emma her friend is 'exactly the something which her home required' (p. 26); and this seems to put Harriet in a category with Regency mirrors. The indefinite article belongs with her name – 'a Harriet Smith' (p. 26). Her telling Emma 'Whatever you say is always right' (p. 74) is not far from a summary of her character.

Jane Austen seems to be playing with the inseparability of the two from the very beginning. When Mr Elton tells Emma that Harriet 'was a beautiful creature when she came to you, but . . . the attractions you have added are infinitely superior to what she received from nature' (p. 42), the subject of this

---

[15] His origin may be Mr Watson in 'The Watsons'. That old gentleman is an invalid (*Minor Works*, p. 325) who sits by a fireside (p. 343) and loves his basin of gruel (p. 359). Q. D. Leavis has noted some of the similarities between the two characters, X 79–80.

studied compliment seems to be Harriet – at least Emma thinks so. But there is absolutely no way to keep Emma herself out of it. For Harriet's attractions are of course in imitation of Emma's; and Mr Elton's aiming a compliment at Emma through the transparent medium of her friend seems a fine illustration of this. But his magnificent illustration is his admiration of the water-colour. Emma thinks he must be admiring Harriet, but that would involve ontological problems beyond his modest capacities. One cannot praise art and not the artist – and in this case the subject being painted is itself something of a self-portrait!

The relationship of Emma and Harriet thus suggests that of an artist to her lifeless material. Emma thinks she made a Mrs Weston out of a governess; now as the novel begins she will try her hand at making something out of a Smith. Later when Mr Elton praises how Emma has indeed improved her friend, his words are 'Skilful has been the hand' (p. 43) – as if he were speaking, say, to a painter. The 'powers' of which she is so proud (p. 24) suggest an artist's powers. And the inevitable art form for her to try her hand at seems indeed to be the novel. After all, she is good at 'fancying interesting dialogues, and inventing elegant letters' (p. 264). She claims also that she has a talent for match-making – which is surely the novelist's province. And so, as *Emma* begins, Emma herself is about to create her own pretty little novel, with Harriet as the heroine.

In *Emma* therefore an artist is portrayed in the process of creating art, the art of fiction; and it is tempting to see the heroine as a kind of self-portrait of her author. There are enough similarities to support such an idea, and plenty of misleading conclusions to be drawn from it. It is interesting, for instance, that an author who claimed to have an eye for an adultress has created a heroine whose discoveries concerning Jane Fairfax and Mr Dixon are little short of that – and even the eye is the same colour (p. 39). It is interesting too that Emma dabbles in drawing and watercolour; and according to the 'Biographical Notice' Jane Austen had excellent taste in drawings.[16] And she too was a rather officious match-maker. She writes to her sister of a 'Match' which she likes 'because I had made it before'

---

[16] *Novels*, v (*Northanger Abbey, Persuasion*) p. 5.

(*Letters*, p. 231). Indeed she seems to have been intent on making one for her favourite niece[17] Fanny Knight; and writes to Cassandra that a young man named Wyndham 'is such a nice, gentleman-like, unaffected sort of young Man, that I think he may do for Fanny' (*Letters*, p. 379). If this is a Mr Elton, the letters reveal that he is soon succeeded by a Frank Churchill, concerning whom Jane Austen then writes: 'Oh! my dear Fanny, the more I write about him, the warmer my feelings become, the more strongly I feel . . . the desirableness of your growing in love with him again. I recommend this most thoroughly . . .' (*Letters*, p. 409).[18] Thus Emma has a Harriet Smith and Jane Austen 'a Fanny Knight' (*Letters*, p. 479) whose destinies seem to be awaiting arrangement by a mind delighted with its own ideas. Surely in Emma, then, we see something of her author. After Jane Austen had begun work on the novel she is supposed to have commented: 'I am going to take a heroine whom no one but myself will much like.'[19]

The Harriet that Emma succeeds in creating is a revelation of Emma's own imaginative inner life, as any work of art would be. Like all Jane Austen's heroines, Emma has a creative imagination that envelops her in an illusory world. Catherine creates a romantic abbey; Emma makes a Harriet who is going to thunder through a wild romance, complete with the obligatory rescue of the fainting heroine from gypsies by what appears, at least to Emma, to be the perfect hero (p. 334). Harriet herself of course is going to be the perfect heroine. She is an orphan, of parents unknown; and this in itself gives her everything an enterprising artist could wish for. Catherine Morland had to lament that in her entire neighbourhood there was 'not one young man whose origin was unknown' (*Northanger Abbey*, p. 16); how nice for Emma that she has been spared a similar fate! Somewhere in Harriet's obligingly misty past there

---

[17] The relationship of Jane Austen to Fanny Knight is remarkably like that of Emma to Harriet Smith. See *Letters*, pp. 216–17 (7 Oct 1808). Also Brabourne, II 119–20; II 221; II 246; II 248–9; II 330–1. Q. D. Leavis makes the interesting suggestion that in *Emma* Jane Austen has indeed 'divided' Fanny into Emma and a doppelgänger named Harriet Smith (x 82 and n. 6).

[18] The victim is a John Plumtre. See *Letters*, p. 409 n. (letter of 18 Nov 1814).

[19] *Memoir* (1871) p. 157.

must be an Italian count or a heartsick country gentleman – to a mind delighted with its own ideas. If one insists on descending to mere facts, however, all that is known is that Harriet has been placed at Mrs Goddard's school by a 'somebody'; an appellation repeated often enough (pp. 22–3) to be portentous, unless one has 'powers'. That 'somebody' will turn out to be somebody, of course. This would have been the case in Jane Austen's own juvenile burlesques or in Catherine's early reading; and Emma has 'no doubt' the same creative genius is going to descend on Highbury (p. 30).

As for Harriet's future, the water-colour portrait of her gives an indication of the aesthetic principles Emma is following. In painting the picture Emma means 'to throw in a little improvement to the figure, to give a little more height . . .' (p. 47). Likewise by letting her 'imagination range and work at Harriet's fortune' (p. 69) she devises a handsome denouement for her romance, and it is merely up to life to follow her plot. A gentleman's daughter always marries a gentleman. As a matter of fact Mr Elton is just the man. Emma thinks 'a young man might be very safely recommended to take Mr Elton as a model' (p. 34). Therefore, when Mr Elton presents an amorous riddle for the ladies' riddle book at Hartfield, Emma has the satisfaction of thinking, 'just so long have I been wanting the very circumstance to happen which has happened' (pp. 73–4). Mr Elton has just the right appreciation of good art, and so is obediently falling in love with Harriet. And when he takes the celebrated picture to be framed Emma knows the reason behind this too, without any troublesome reference to fact (p. 56). She also knows that he is going to propose to Harriet, in spite of what Mr Knightley thinks (p. 67). After all, that is the way she planned it.

But Emma's abbey now turns out to be like Catherine's. Mr Elton spoils her plot. He must be deficient in literary taste, in spite of his nice riddle. He proposes, but not to Harriet. He proposes to Emma herself! This is the first of the important symbolic facts in *Emma* which penetrate Emma's romantic illusion. She now makes the formal declaration of error that Jane Austen's plot requires of every heroine. Elizabeth Bennet had said, 'Till this moment, I never knew myself'; now Emma says, '. . . I have been in a most complete error with respect to your views, till this moment' (p. 131). She feels she has been 'disgraced by mis-judgement'. She resolves to repress her 'imagination'. She resolves to be humble. She resolves 'to do such things no more' (pp. 134, 142, 137).

3

The woman Mr Elton finally does marry is a truly memorable creature; and she was perhaps inspired by Eliza, the wife of Jane Austen's brother Henry. As a young girl Jane Austen was acquainted with her.[20] Mrs Elton's similarities to Eliza are remarkable, and it seems worth while to list some of them. Mrs Elton is vain, self-satisfied, and proud of the fine society that surrounded her at Bath and Maple Grove before her marriage; and as for Eliza, she was capable of the following modest sentiment in a letter written while she was still married to her first husband, the Comte de Feuïllide: 'My situation is everyways agreeable . . . mistress of an easy fortune with the prospect of a very ample one, add to these the advantages of rank & title, & a numerous & brilliant acquaintance. . . .'[21] When Mrs Elton comes to Highbury, she professes astonishment to find that Mrs Weston is actually 'lady-like' (p. 278); and Eliza, when she later went to England, wrote of life in Ipswich: 'The inhabitants of this place are much more fashionable people than I expected. . . .'[22] Mrs Elton feels that it is her right to be first in Highbury society (see pp. 298, 324); and Eliza writes from Ipswich: 'As everything is known in such small circles they are acquainted with my having been a *Comtesse*, & politely give me the precedence. . . .'[23]

Mrs Elton professes that, at Maple Grove, 'Blessed with so many resources within myself, the world was not necessary to

---

[20] See *Facts and Problems*, pp. 13–14, 32–34. The young Jane Austen dedicated 'Love and Friendship' (1790) 'To Madame La Comtesse De Feuillide.'

[21] *Austen Papers 1704–1856* (cited above p. 127 n. 35) p. 100 (27 Mar 1782). The editor makes clear that the 'originals' of Eliza's letters were in his possession; they were therefore in the family. In *Only a Novel* (New York: Coward, 1972) Jane Hodge finds similarities between Eliza's letters and Lady Susan's, p. 44.

[22] *Austen Papers*, p. 171 (16 Feb 1798).

[23] *Austen Papers*, p. 171 (16 Feb 1798).

me. I could do very well without it'. All she ever needs is her music (pp. 276–7). Surely here in particular Jane Austen is thinking of the stupendous affectation that could cause Eliza to write that she is '. . . a recluse the greatest part of the time, but Lady Burrell, Lady Talbot and one or two more neighbours having politely sought me . . . I have not found it possible to persevere in my plan of shunning all society to which I must honestly confess that I greatly prefer my books my harp, & my pianoforte'.[24] And one final example. Mrs Elton remarks coyly that it is dangerous to let husbands open letters addressed to their wives. Here and elsewhere she reveals, just beneath the surface of her sham gentility, a coarseness that is summarised in her exclamation, 'Oh! my dear, human flesh! You quite shock me' (p. 300; see her also on the subject of clean sheets, p. 306). Eliza's character must have been fascinatingly similar. A passage from her remarkable letters deserves to be quoted at length. She is now married to poor Henry Austen:

> I have not yet given you any account of my brother officers of whom I wish you could judge in person for there are some with whom I think you would not dislike a flirtation. I have *of course entirely* left off *trade* but I can however discover that Cap^{tn} Tilson is remarkably handsome and that Messrs Perrott & Edwards may be chatted with very satisfactorily, but as to my Colonel Lord Charles Spencer, if I was married to my third husband instead of my second I should still be in love with him. He is a most charming creature . . . but alas! he is married as well as myself and what is worse he is absent. . . .[25]

The inspiration for Mrs Elton, then, may have come from Jane Austen's own family. This has significance. If Jane Austen ever felt at all mortified by her sister-in-law, she has found a strikingly similar way of mortifying her own beloved Emma. For the unavoidable comparison in the novel is between Mrs Elton and Emma. The one was Mr Elton's first choice, the other his second. Indeed, toward the end of Volume II Mrs Elton comes rushing into the novel as if her destiny were to stand beside Emma for purposes of comparison. She comes to Hartfield and

---

[24] *Austen Papers*, p. 173 (29 Oct 1799).
[25] *Austen Papers*, pp. 170–1 (16 Feb 1798).

says, 'Very like Maple Grove indeed!' (p. 272) – as if she were the Gloucestershire Emma visiting her counterpart. In *Sense and Sensibility* Lucy Steele has the same relation to Elinor, and tells her: '. . . as soon as I saw you, I felt almost as if you was an old acquaintance'. Now Mrs Elton makes the same aggressive overtures of sisterly 'friendship' toward Emma. When the two of them are together, 'we' seems always on her lips (pp. 277, 283).

She is indeed Emma's Lucy Steele: a caricature who serves to show up the thin, delicate imperfections of the heroine herself. All of these seem comically exaggerated in this woman who is going to be her stand-in at the vicarage. Jane Austen has been uncommonly thorough in working out the similarities between the two.[26] Taken all together they are meant to tarnish slightly the Emma we thought we knew: that handsome, clever and rich young lady of the first paragraph.

To begin with, Mrs Elton is outrageously conceited. But what about Emma herself? When she meets the new bride, she is convinced that Harriet would have made Mr Elton a better wife: 'If not wise or refined herself, she would have connected him with those who were; but Miss Hawkins, it might be fairly supposed from her easy conceit, had been the best of her own set' (p. 272). There is something in this train of thought that would appeal to Mrs Bennet. By 'those who were' Emma of course has in mind herself; and thus her disdain for Mrs Elton's conceit has nicely brought out her own. Mrs Elton also seems proud to have been the 'best of her own set'; and Emma is just as proud to be the best of Highbury's, although she is not nearly so expansive on the subject in company. Mrs Elton thinks the Westons must be giving their ball chiefly in her honour; and what does Emma think? 'Emma must submit to stand second to Mrs Elton, though she had always considered the ball as peculiarly for her' (p. 325).

When Mrs Elton tells Emma that at Bath 'A line from me would bring you a little host of acquaintance' (p. 275), Emma appropriately recoils in indignation – although she herself supposes that Harriet must be deriving unspeakable social ad-

---

[26] Lerner mentions some of them, pp. 100–1. Mudrick refers to Mrs Elton as Emma's 'companion in motive', p. 194.

vantages from her own company. Mrs Elton is determined to 'bring forward' Jane Fairfax (p. 282), whether Jane wants to be brought forward or not; and Emma of course is doing the same for Harriet. Mrs Elton is 'constantly on the watch for an eligible situation' Jane can step into (p. 284); and likewise Emma tries to place her own protégée – first in Mr Elton's home, then in Frank Churchill's. Mrs Elton is not going to let Jane fall into 'any inferior, commonplace situation, in a family not moving in a certain circle' (p. 301); and Emma does the same favour for Harriet by keeping her away from the Martins.

Mrs Elton is gracious enough to show conspicuous surprise that Mrs Weston behaves like a lady; Emma shows similar surprise that Mr Martin's letter 'would not have disgraced a gentleman' (pp. 50–1). Emma is disgusted at the silliness of Mrs Elton's actually discovering that Mr Knightley is a gentleman (pp. 278–9); Emma herself is silly enough to tell him that his arriving at the Coles's in his own carriage 'is coming as you should do, . . . like a gentleman' (p. 213). At Maple Grove Mrs Elton had to endure the upstart pretensions of the Tupmans (310); Emma has the Coles (p. 207).[27] Mrs Elton declares that at Maple Grove, 'Blessed with so many resources within myself, the world was not necessary to *me*'; and now Emma's version: '. . . mine is an active, busy mind, with a great many independent resources' (p. 85). Finally, Mrs Elton has her nasty little joke about husbands and wives; Emma has Mr Dixon.

The significance therefore of Mrs Elton's appearance in the novel is not so much what she shows of her own busy vulgarity – although that is entertaining enough – but what she shows of Emma's. Jane Austen is using Mrs Elton to show some faintly unpleasant aspects of her heroine. And the reader is not the only beneficiary. For Emma too seems vaguely aware that Mrs Elton is showing her something about herself she would rather not know. Perhaps that is what she has in mind (or merely ought to?) when she says she feels Mrs Elton's overtures of friendship are an affront to her own 'dignity' (p. 276). Mrs Elton does disturb her very deeply. After their first meeting her 'mind

[27] Schorer makes this comparison in 'The Humiliation of Emma Woodhouse', p. 557.

returned to Mrs Elton's offences, and long, very long, did they occupy her' (p. 280).

Mrs Elton, then, is another of those heavily subsidised characters who are allowed to exist mostly for the sake of serving a purpose[28] in Jane Austen's plan. Mrs Elton's 'character' is intrinsically interesting of course – probably to no one more than Jane Austen herself. But, more important, her presence in the novel serves as a nagging, persistent embarrassment to Emma: an embarrassment that seems to be saying over and over in a shrill self-important voice, 'I am Mr Elton's Emma. We *do* have so *much* in common!' Emma's introduction to Mrs Elton thus seems to follow her episode with Mr Elton as a humiliation she must endure before Jane Austen considers her ready for Mr Knightley.

When Mr Knightley has finally proposed, Mrs Elton's usefulness to Jane Austen has disappeared; and Jane Austen is not much interested in fictive drones. She therefore sets up a scene that seems to turn her creation at last into nothing more than a caricature, a joke. She makes Mrs Elton sound more stupendously foolish at Miss Bates's than even Mrs Elton seems really capable of (see especially p. 456). Her author has used her up, and is discarding her.

4

At the same time that Emma is enduring the new Mrs Elton, she is passing through the second important episode in the novel: her romance with Frank Churchill. He has no more claim to an existence in the novel quite free of Emma's conception of him than Harriet Smith does. The match Emma eventually thinks of creating between the two would have been perfect – one mirror blankly reflecting the other. What is he 'really' like? Again we should be wary of those many readers who think they know. When he arrives at Highbury he tries to hide whatever could be conceived to be his true self (see p. 437). And when his subterfuge at last comes to light, we do not even then get the true Frank Churchill – only some rough notes for one,

---

[28] Firkins on the other hand is among those who think Mrs Elton is merely 'deputed to amuse the reader in the . . . suspension of the other interests', p. 98.

in the form of a sincere valedictory letter from him (pp. 436–43; he does however appear again briefly in III xviii). Between this entrance and exit we get mostly a character who has shrewdly permitted Emma's own imagination to create him to suit herself.

He makes his first appearance early in Volume II, not long after Mr Elton's presumptuous proposal to Emma. She manages to wring a good deal of suspense out of the interval. She asks Mr Knightley, 'Cannot you imagine . . . what a *sensation* his coming will produce?'; and when she hears that he is going to arrive the next day, the 'worn-out past was sunk in the fresh-ness of what was coming' (pp. 149, 188).

The reason his arrival is going to be so sensational for Emma is that she has already to some extent created in her mind the sensational Frank Churchill who will now arrive. He seems to wait patiently at Enscombe in the form of rumours of letters (p. 18) until his author, Emma, has leisure to decide what to make of him. When she knows what she wants, he will appear obligingly in that form. Thus before he ever arrives we see her engaged in creating him. To begin with, there is that 'distin-guished honour which her imagination had given him', the honour of being almost in love with her. She, in turn, has the 'decided intention of finding him pleasant'. He is going to 'belong to her', for he will be exactly the man to marry her, if she were ever to marry (pp. 206, 119). At the height of her creative frenzy she seems to know almost everything there is to know about him. She declares to Mr Knightley, 'My idea of him is . . .'; and she follows with a thoroughgoing itemisation of particulars, including his general knowledge of farming (p. 150).

It is not easy to make any objective judgement about him, but the Frank Churchill who finally arrives will probably do as well as any man for Emma's aesthetic purposes. He is typical of Jane Austen's false heroes in that he presents a blank, glossy exterior that will reflect almost anything that is put in front of it. Emma's idea of him is that he will be able to 'adapt his conversation to the taste of every body, and has the power . . . of being universally agreeable'; and in this respect he is indeed everything she could hope for. There was 'truth' in Wickham's looks; and likewise Frank Churchill declares, '. . . I will speak the truth, and nothing suits me so well' (p. 200). He is like nothing quite so much as a mirror, one that says, 'I smile because you smile . . .' (p. 216). Soon Emma thinks she must be a little in love with him (p. 262). That is not surprising. To some extent he is a reflection of herself. He is the perfect partner for a mind delighted with its own ideas.

Thus Emma's relationship with Frank, like her relationship with Harriet, is not so much that of one character to another as one character to her own creation. Frank Churchill seems at least partly that: a projection of Emma's own personal desires into another, willing body. Again and again the amenities that pass between the two faintly suggest that he is somehow not quite 'separate' from her – not quite his own man. He tells her, 'You are always with me'; he writes at the conclusion that he and Emma always 'seemed to understand each other'. She in turn points out the 'likeness' in their destinies (pp. 369, 438, 478). And in one of Jane Austen's strange scenes that seem a little closer to fantasy than real life, the Box Hill picnic, Emma is seen sitting apart with him, whispering with him as if she were actually communing with her own innermost soul. He tells her there, 'You order me, whether you speak or not'. He seems to know her most secret thoughts without her having to give them voice. Indeed he seems to be the embodiment of those thoughts; and so he turns to the others and speaks to them as if from her own mouth: 'Ladies and gentlemen – I am ordered by Miss Woodhouse to say . . .' (pp. 369, 370).

Frank Churchill is therefore partly a figment of Emma's own briskly imaginative inner life. We have seen this again and again in the novels. What she thinks he is saying and doing tells almost as much about her as about him. Thus his arrival makes it obvious that the post-Elton Emma is still more inclined to create a personal romantic world than accept the real one. He is Mr Elton's replacement, or revision, in the second volume of her determined little romance. Now it is Frank who is just the one to carry off the heroine. As for the heroine, Emma has in mind that this time it ought to be herself – except of course that like all young ladies on the lookout for a husband, she has little intention of ever marrying (p. 84). Does she sense that an artist has to maintain a certain detachment from her material? Does she sense that for her there is another knight in shining

armour waiting, somewhere? Who knows? Certainly not Emma.
All she knows is that the perfect heroine to complete the plot is
going to have to be Harriet (p. 266) – again.

As a fabricator of romances Emma is nothing if not systematic. Jane Austen has concentrated sharply on the doggedness
of Emma's devising a new 'scheme' (p. 266) so hopefully like
the old one that failed. When her first romance had given way
to facts, Emma had resolved 'to do such things no more'. But
perhaps just *once* more. Even if the world did not bend to her
aesthetic purposes that time, certainly it will now. And so, when
Harriet throws her precious treasures behind the fire and declares '. . . there is an end . . . of Mr Elton', Emma insists on
thinking 'And when . . . will there be a beginning of Mr
Churchill?' (p. 340). Here is a truly Olympian disregard for
the inductive method. And later, when Harriet and Frank are
thrown together in the Udolphan splendour of an attack by
gypsies, Emma once more tries hard to let nature simply take
its course. 'No, she had had enough of interference'. But what
self-respecting artist could be satisfied with that? 'There could
be no harm in a scheme, a mere passive scheme' (p. 335).

What Emma wants to make of Frank Churchill is, after her
adventure with Mr Elton, another indication of a persistent
headstrong romanticism that still seems almost impervious to
mere facts. But there is something special about Emma's
romanticism in this second case – something we have only
glimpsed in the earlier heroines, something Jane Austen may
not have dared to reveal fully before now. For she has used Frank
to expose in her heroine a touch of coy, nasty sexuality. Emma
seizes on a slight hint from him and creates an unpleasant
affair between Jane Fairfax and a Mr Dixon. She tells Frank,
perhaps with something closer to a leer than any of the other
heroines are capable of, that if she had been in Ireland with
Jane and the Dixons, 'I think I should have made some discoveries' (p. 218). Frank then becomes merely a receptacle for
the sour, smug discoveries of Emma's own creative imagination.
He smiles when she smiles. He simply listens, and says, 'Conjecture – aye, sometimes one conjectures right, and sometimes
one conjectures wrong' (p. 242).

Emma's conjectures on the subject of Jane and Mr Dixon
reveal a quality of mind that it is not easy to find in the previous

novels. There is something unusual, and disturbing, about Emma's 'powers' here. She has created a racy little joke. She likes to goad Frank into reminding her of the punch line, 'Dixon', so that she can snigger, even though 'it was something which she judged it proper to appear to censure'. When that mild young man obligingly titillates her imagination, she 'wished he would be less pointed, yet could not help being amused . . .' (pp. 348, 243). In these scenes she is more than a little like a lady eagerly listening to an off-colour story while protesting with a giggle that it isn't fit for ladies' ears – more than a little like a lady who would say, 'Oh! my dear, human flesh! You quite shock me'.

This is the heroine Jane Austen thought no one but herself would much like. After the novel was published she did indeed record among the 'Opinions' that a Miss Isabella Herries 'did not like it – objected to my exposing the sex in the character of the Heroine'.[29] Emma is a creature to raise eyebrows, at Highbury and Chawton too. It seems impossible that her author could have brought her to light without at least a little self-consciousness and apprehension. Jane Austen is after all a lady novelist, one whose family went out of its way to explain that she could never have created Lady Susan out of her female self 'without having constantly before her the thoughts and proto-type of this exceptional character';[30] a lady novelist whose family was defensively anxious to point out that the 'innate purity of her soul shines . . . upon every page. . . .'[31]

5

Frank Churchill seems to bring out the worst in Emma, but he also brings out the best. From the moment he enters her mind she is moving toward the man she will marry. He first causes her to think of the very possibility of marrying (p. 119), thus preparing her to marry Mr Knightley; he causes her to conceive of what a man should be (p. 397), thus helping her finally to see that Mr Knightley is such a man. As Emma draws closer and closer to Frank, she is therefore drawing closer to

[29] *Novels*, VI (*Minor Works*) p. 438.
[30] See *Life and Letters*: cf. p. 116 n. 23 above.
[31] Brabourne, I 58.

Mr Knightley without knowing it. The two rivals seem to coalesce in Emma's mind at a specific point in the novel, the ball at the Crown (III ii). It is here that Emma's love seems to begin to flow from one to the other. She says later that she 'was very much disposed to be attached' to Frank at one time, 'nay, was attached – and how it came to cease, is perhaps the wonder' (p. 396). But the novel is clearer on this matter than Emma is: here, at the Crown, the wonder begins.

At the Crown Emma begins to see clearly what has been before her since she was a child (see p. 37); she begins to see clearly that fate and Jane Austen's plan have long intended Mr Knightley to be the true hero. Emma is growing ready for him now, and so the whole world seems to conspire to make him appear before her. She has seen Mr Weston many times before, but now at the ball for the first time he too helps her to appreciate Mr Knightley. She looks at Mr Weston and thinks, 'a little less of open-heartedness would have made him a higher character. – General benevolence, but not general friendship, made a man what he ought to be. – She could fancy such a man' (p. 320). She has also seen Mr Elton before, but now he too leads her to Mr Knightley. He boorishly refuses to dance with Harriet. 'This was Mr Elton!', she thinks; and then she sees the silent and gentlemanly Mr Knightley leading Harriet to the dance.

Emma now sees what has always been there to see: Mr Knightley's 'tall, firm, upright figure'. She thinks that, 'excepting her own partner, there was no one among the whole row of young men who could be compared with him' (p. 326); and with that 'excepting' she seems to have begun the subtle transference of her romantic affections from her false partner to the true. In the restrained and precise movements of Jane Austen's dance, Emma has now changed partners. Frank Churchill has led her to the dance; Mr Knightley will lead her away. This is a crucial moment. In one of the most beautiful passages in any of the novels, these two come face to face at last in a ballroom scene that is only a sketchy, perfunctory bodying forth of silent, intangible psychological action. Jane Austen's mature art is retiring inward. Here is a dance that is taking place only nominally at the Crown, and truly in the characters' souls:

'I am ready', said Emma, 'whenever I am wanted'.
'Whom are you going to dance with?' asked Mr Knightley.
She hesitated a moment, and then replied, 'With you, if
you will ask me'.
'Will you?' said he, offering his hand (p. 331).

She has said she is ready. Her author is beginning to agree,
and takes her now to Donwell Abbey. Emma has been there
before, but not since Frank Churchill helped prepare her to
see it as it truly is. Jane Austen is relentlessly pushing her
heroine's psychological development, and is here merely con-
triving her plot for that purpose. Like Elizabeth Bennet, Emma
is ready to be introduced to the true hero; and as before Jane
Austen finds architecture and landscape a handy means of
bringing this about. Emma is now shown a variety of family
collections in the abbey by her father; just as Elizabeth had been
introduced to portraits of her lover's ancestors by the house-
keeper. Emma now feels an 'increasing respect' for Donwell,
'as the residence of a family of such true gentility, untainted in
blood and understanding' (p. 358); just as Elizabeth found
Pemberley elegant without ostentation. At Donwell as at
Pemberley there is a river that winds out of sight: there is more
to Mr Knightley too than meets the eye.

From the beginning Emma has been proud of her 'quick
eye', her 'quick observation' (pp. 31, 316). Over and over the
words 'she saw it all', 'she had heard and seen it all' have
appeared like an ironic refrain in the novel (some examples: pp.
298, 327, 363). But now they are coming true. She is learning
to see the world. She is ready for one of the most remarkable
scenes in fiction, the Box Hill picnic. This is the symbolic and
magnificent expression of the confrontation between Emma
and the real world – a world that began to dawn at the Crown
and Donwell Abbey. In the chapter following her visit to
Donwell she and the other major characters all ascend Box
Hill; and what happens there must be the thematic summit
of Jane Austen's fiction.

The picnic seems to be a dream-like idealisation of the novel
itself, existing somewhere between Surrey and fantasy. On Box
Hill Emma sits aloof, elevated above the hard, factual world.
When she wants something from it to serve the purposes of

her private imaginative life, she snaps her fingers and demands it. Her spokesman Frank Churchill declares to the rest of the company, as if from her own mouth, 'that she desires to know what you all are thinking of'; that she 'requires something very entertaining from each of you. . . .' These requests seem to be the epitome of Emma's fastidiously aesthetic attitude toward everything outside her handsome, clever and rich self. Her requests are particular instances of what must be the single ultimate wish of any mind delighted with its own strong imaginative powers: the wish to make the world serve one's own inner purposes; the wish to use the world, rather than accept it as it is.

There is in the novel a minor character who seems just the opposite: a character who seems to accept the world absolutely as it is. She too appears at the picnic. Jane Austen has invited her there, and now brings her face to face with Emma in an encounter that has a profound significance in that young lady's psychological development. The character is Miss Bates, and she is one of the most unusual and fascinating in Jane Austen's fiction.

Comparisons between Miss Bates and Emma seem inevitable. Harriet actually suggests one, and Emma replies huffily, '. . . between *us*, I am convinced there never can be any likeness, except in being unmarried' (p. 85). Indeed Jane Austen does seem to have designed Miss Bates as her heroine's opposite in some important respects. Emma is introduced as 'handsome, clever and rich'; Miss Bates as 'neither young, handsome, rich, nor married' (p. 21).[32] Emma thinks too much of herself; Miss Bates and her mother think 'so little of themselves' (p. 418). Emma has a sharp, critical intelligence; Miss Bates 'loved every body' (p. 21). Let Emma congratulate herself on her ability to make 'discoveries'; Miss Bates, having been favoured with one of them, can only reply humbly, 'I do not think I am particularly quick at those sort of discoveries. I do not pretend to it. What is before me, I see' (p. 176).

The heart of Miss Bates's character, and of her chief significance in the novel, seems to be expressed in an exclamation she makes when she enters the ballroom at the Crown – 'Everything so good!' (p. 323). She is open and affirmative, and she seems

[32] Mark Schorer notes this in 'The Humiliation of Emma Woodhouse', pp. 556–7.

willing to embrace all the world.[33] She makes no demands on it; she has no particular aesthetic vision to which she must bend the facts. What is before her she sees. She is the ideal receptor of unmediated reality in this novel, and indeed in the entire scope of Jane Austen's fiction. Miss Bates is capable of registering everything truly as it passes by: 'Two steps . . . take care of the two steps. Oh! no, there is but one. Well, I was persuaded there were two. How very odd! I was convinced there were two, and there is but one' (p. 329). She is constitutionally incapable of bending facts to her own purposes. When Emma comes to call she overhears Miss Bates promising to tell her a fib on Jane's account; but the simple, kind lady is finally able to say only, ' "My dear," said I, "I shall say you are laid down upon the bed:" but, however, she is not . . .' (p. 379).

Buried in her massive rambling monologues is the raw material of Jane Austen's novel, and of Emma's, unorganised yet by syntax or by the particular reforming bias of any artist. Buried in these undiscriminating hotchpotches of soup, chimneys, baked apples and ribbons are the simple truths of the real world, waiting for Emma to learn to accept them, rather than invent them or revise them to suit herself. The crucial 'fact' in the novel, Frank's secret engagement, is there,[34] in Miss Bates's natterings on his odd interest in her mother's spectacles (p. 237); again in her first monologue at the Crown ('but Mr Frank Churchill was so extremely –', p. 323); then again shortly afterwards ('. . . Jane on one arm, and me on the other!', p. 329); then again buried in her musings on Mr Perry's carriage (see p. 346); and again in her chaotic account of Frank's sudden trip to Richmond after the picnic (see p. 383).

Jane Austen's style is characteristically spare, exquisite, and efficient. Yet she has larded *Emma* with huge blocks of Miss Bates's desultory prose. Miss Bates seems to have been permitted to break her bounds as a character,[35] and to become a little more

---

[33] Yasmine Gooneratne makes a similar comment about Miss Bates, in *Jane Austen*, p. 158.

[34] Apparently this point was first made by Mary Lascelles, *Jane Austen and Her Art*, pp. 93–4.

[35] One of the 'Opinions of *Emma*' recorded by Jane Austen reads 'Miss Bates excellent, but rather too much of her', *Novels*, VI (*Minor Works*) p. 438.

than one. She takes on a special significance in Jane Austen's scheme for Emma's reformation. She suggests reality itself, before it has been passed through the discriminating intelligence of someone determined to make something of it. Thus she succeeds almost completely where even her author has so often fallen short. All Jane Austen's stylisation, her rigid and purposeful selectivity, have here in Miss Bates given way before a flood, a hubbub, of undiscriminated, unsymbolised particular details. Here is a hole in the fabric of Jane Austen's fastidious art, exposing, in this late, mature work, the busy world, the humming reality that has seemed always to be waiting just beyond her prim fiction. Reality, the world – in its bustling, garrulous, inartistic disorganisation. Miss Bates seems to select nothing. What is before her she sees. And everything is so good. She is the simple unintelligent world that Emma has been disdaining in favour of her own heightened romantic one. She has brought into this close, over-heated world of Emma's gusts of the reality waiting outside. It seems perfectly appropriate that Jane Austen should have brought these two face to face on Box Hill, so that Emma can insult her – and for being dull.

Since the dance at the Crown Emma has been Mr Knightley's partner. He must lead her aright. He must lead her down the hill and into the world. He tells her now, 'I will tell you truths while I can'; and the truth he tells her is that it was wrong to insult Miss Bates. One does not insult the world, one accepts it. That is the single, fundamental truth he has to tell. Emma blushes. 'Never had she felt so agitated, mortified, grieved, at any circumstance in her life' (pp. 374–6). Her blush marks an epoch. The two are now closer to having danced down the set. In a scene at Hartfield resembling their scene at the Crown, Mr Knightley now takes her hand:

> . . . whether she had not herself made the first motion, she could not say – she might, perhaps, have rather offered it – but he took her hand, pressed it, and certainly was on the point of carrying it to his lips – when, from some fancy or other, he suddenly let it go (p. 386).

They are still not quite ready for the happy end. Mr Knightley has his reason for thinking so (p. 432), and Jane Austen seems to have hers. She knows exactly what must still 'happen' to the heroine. That simple fact which Miss Bates has been airing for so long has yet to ventilate Emma's smug little romance; until it does, Emma is not spiritually ready for Mr Knightley.

6

The fact is now sprung cleanly by Mrs Weston in one compact clause: '. . . that Frank Churchill and Miss Fairfax are engaged' (p. 395). There had been previous hints that Frank was disposed to go his own way regardless of what Emma chose to think about him; but she has been blind to hints. At the moment when he first appeared, for instance, Emma was thinking, '. . . by this time to-morrow . . . I may be thinking of the possibility of their all calling here' (p. 190). She then opened the parlour door and he was there already. Mrs Weston's news simply confirms again what anything but a mind delighted with its own ideas should already have known: that the mind cannot bend matter to its own aesthetic purposes; that the hard furniture of fact – a piano for instance – cannot be made into what it is not.

The revelation of Frank's secret engagement is the crucial symbolic fact in the novel; the fact that has a profound effect at last on Emma's knowledge of the world, and of herself. She is now entering the world beyond ruined abbeys, fascinating adulteries, fatal love-struck meetings amid gypsies; the world that demands those 'common feelings of common life' Jane Austen alluded to in *Northanger Abbey*; the world that demands what Emma now refers to as 'common sense'. She admits now that 'with common sense . . . I am afraid I have had little to do' (p. 402).

Jane Austen has conceived the revelation of Frank Churchill's secret engagement to Jane Fairfax as something roughly equivalent to the revelation of the secret sexual lives of the other false heroes. Whatever there is of badness in him has finally been discovered; and Emma wastes no time before giving her version of the official pronouncement that occurs in each of the novels: 'I have escaped. . . . But this does not acquit *him* . . .; and I must say, that I think him greatly to blame' (p. 396).

But Frank Churchill is no Wickham. Many of the strong elements of plot in the previous novels have been refined away

in *Emma*; and Jane Austen has chosen not to have Frank perform any of the conventional acts of wickedness that occur in
the earlier novels. There is no elopement, for instance; it is more
likely that the reasons Frank gives for a secret engagement (p.
437) exist in the novel to prevent such an elopement, than the
other way around. The result is that it is not quite clear just
what he has done wrong.[36] Emma alludes to his coming 'among
us with affection and faith engaged, and with manners so *very
disengaged*' (p. 396). This is true to some extent, but it is hardly
clear that his manners were so disengaged as she seems to have
wanted to think they were; and his final letter is very gentlemanly indeed in taking all the blame for the 'intimacy' (p. 438)
of the two, when a good part of the blame belongs to Emma.

What then is he guilty of? Mr Knightley declares that Frank
'wants delicacy of principle' (p. 448). This ought to be the
final word; but Mr Knightley has also criticised his handwriting
(p. 297), and has shown certain other signs of justice tempered
with a little jealousy. Indeed every one of the attempts on the
part of the characters in the novel to make a moral judgement
on him seems open to such qualifications, or to be vacillating and
indecisive in itself (see especially pp. 400–1). Perhaps Mr
Woodhouse's opinion is as good as any: 'Do not tell his father,
but that young man is not quite the thing. He has been opening
the doors very often this evening . . .' (p. 249).

Here again, as in the case of the theatricals at Mansfield Park,
there is an issue that Jane Austen does not seem quite able to
translate adequately into fictive terms – an issue both moral
and aesthetic at the same time. Thus Frank's 'sin', which is
also to some extent Jane Fairfax's, cannot adequately be condemned by the characters within the novel in purely moral
pronouncements. There is an aesthetic dimension. This dimension of whatever one chooses to call his wrongdoing is that he
has not simply temporised and lied; he has delighted in making

[36] Some examples of the critical puzzlement on this point: '. . . the
mystery, when it is brought to light, is, though interesting, on a
smaller and more homely scale than the real badness of Wickham',
Jenkins, p. 198; 'A secret engagement was, in 1815, a very bad
business', Kennedy p. 83; and, finally, an American critic on the subject of secret engagements: though 'Miss Austen does her best to
uphold its solemnity by speaking of it in the tone appropriate to
a . . . burglary, the reader declines to excite himself', Firkins, p. 96.

his lies into art.[37] With more than a little help from Emma he has made up a beautiful story featuring mysterious pianos, cryptic gallopings to and fro, coincidental meetings and veiled flirtations. He has skilfully done what she herself did with her watercolours: he has taken what was real and thrown in a little improvement, added a little more height.

His charming subterfuge brings him to that point where morals and aesthetics meet in Jane Austen's fiction. To lie is a moral transgression, but to lie beautifully is an aesthetic one. Frank has dared to make a delightful little world of his own, rather than humbly surrender to the one that already exists. He has forsaken the commonplace real world that his author has dedicated herself to. He has blasphemed the world as it is, and has set up a false, golden one. And he has enjoyed doing so. He has felt the exhilaration of manipulating characters. He has created delicate ironies out of their ignorance. He has revelled in his artist's powers, as Emma recognises (p. 478).

If such pride in artistic creation is a sin, it is Emma's sin as well. Frank is Frank; but he is also a projection of her imagination, and of the sin of her imagination. The two have understood each other instinctively. He has sat beside her on Box Hill and spoken her silent thoughts. The final revelation of the falseness of his art is thus also a final revelation of the falseness of hers. In understanding him, she now understands herself. That is Jane Austen's plan. And so these two end the novel, as they began, profoundly the same. In a beautiful scene they stand communing together one last time, apart from the rest of the company at Randalls; and they seem both to be bidding farewell to the art that has delighted them so much. Their little play is over. Emma says to him:

> I am sure it was a source of high entertainment to you, to feel that you were taking us all in. – Perhaps I am the readier to suspect, because, to tell you the truth, I think it might have been some amusement to myself in the same situation. I think there is a little likeness between us (p. 478).

[37] Lerner comments on Frank's delight in his subterfuge: '... our strong moral disapproval is played off against the delight we take – and he takes – and despite herself Jane Austen takes – in his skilful managing', p. 102.

Learning of Frank's deception is the most dreadful humiliation endured by any of Jane Austen's heroines. Emma is forced to admit that she has been 'completely duped' (p. 399). Frank has reduced her to a child who has played for his amusement. He has made her play a game with a children's box of alphabet letters; a game Mr Knightley perceived was 'a child's play, chosen to conceal a deeper game on Frank Churchill's part' p. 348).[38] He has let Emma tell him her girlish fantasies, such as the charming one on the subject of the mysterious piano; to which he solemnly replied, 'I smile because you smile, and shall probably suspect whatever I find you suspect. . . .' A pert, self-assured little girl has officiously declared that it was the big bad wolf who brought the piano; and her uncle, throwing up his hands in mock wonder, has answered, 'You don't say'. This may be the first time in Jane Austen's fiction that the heroine has been the victim of irony that is beyond her own comprehension. For the first time the heroine has been manipulated inside the novel itself by an artistic talent greater than her own. Frank, not Emma, is the master of the alphabet.

Frank's disclosure of his secret engagement seems to be the final good deed exacted from him by Jane Austen's beneficent universe. He has helped to bring the hero and heroine together. Emma hears the news, and within paragraphs she exclaims (a little unfairly?), 'So unlike what a man should be! – None of that upright integrity, that strict adherence to truth and principle . . . which a man should display. . . .' It is not really Frank she is describing, but Mr Knightley. Elizabeth Bennet had to come to Darcy by the same devious route. The false hero always has his uses.

When Emma was planning Harriet's first match, she cited the line, 'The course of true love never did run smooth –', and hinted that Hartfield would prove it wrong: 'There does seem to be a something in the air of Hartfield which gives love exactly the right direction, and sends it into the very channel where it ought to flow' (p. 75). Events have proved her wrong, and then right. She seems to have had to fail in her match-making in order to gain the knowledge that will make her own marriage.

---

[38] According to the *Memoir* (1871), Jane Austen told the family 'that the letters placed by Frank Churchill before Jane Fairfax . . . contained the word "pardon"', p. 158.

Mr Elton proved not to be the perfect hero for her romance, nor did Frank Churchill; but they have led her to her true knight, who is now appearing.

Harriet now confesses her love for him, which is just what Emma needs finally to realise her own (pp. 406–7). Jane Austen then characteristically bends the plot into a circle. The heroine returns home and makes a gesture at beginning life again as if nothing had happened – except that in *Emma* most of the geography has been dispensed with. Emma goes to sit by her father's side again, as she had done in the first chapter. The scene reminds her 'of their first forlorn tête-à-tête, on the evening of Mrs Weston's wedding-day' (p. 422). The deceptive circularity serves as usual to emphasise just how much has changed, in the heroine's mind, if not in the plot. She began by saying she had never been in love: 'it is not my way, or my nature . . .' (p. 84). Now it is. She began with little intention of ever marrying at all: 'I must see somebody very superior to any one I have seen yet, to be tempted . . .' (p. 84). Now at last she sees him.

7

Mr Knightley undergoes a process of spiritual discovery that is faintly like Emma's own. Many readers mistakenly think that he is perfectly fit for Emma even at the start, and that he never changes.[39] He is indeed almost a recalcitrant particle of perfection – but not quite. When he considers Emma's future and exclaims at the beginning, 'I wonder what will become of her!' (p. 40), he still honestly does not know. He has yet to learn something about himself. The same is true when he claims testily that he is not 'prejudiced' against Frank Churchill (p. 150). Eventually he learns of course that he is. He learns that he 'had been in love with Emma, and jealous of Frank Churchill, from about the same period, one sentiment having probably enlightened him as to the other' (p. 432). Thus Frank has obligingly worked a little alteration even in the lofty character of Mr Knightley.

---

[39] Booth for one considers him 'completely reliable', p. 254 (although see his p. 263). J. F. Burrows on the other hand treats him with great scepticism (*Jane Austen's 'Emma'*). See especially the Introduction.

The two lovers now drift together in the shrubbery at Hartfield, moved gently by forces that have risen out of the brittle, outworn plot to live a life of their own. The particularities of plot are fast coming to the end of their usefulness for Jane Austen. There have been sounds of her shutting up shop since Mrs Churchill suddenly gave her life (p. 387) that Frank might make his engagement public. Just why are these two standing together now? Because their carefully worked-out psychological reformation is complete. It hardly matters any more what 'happens' in the plot.[40] Mr Knightley says he has come to Hartfield in his 'anxiety' to see how Emma is bearing the news about Frank; and as for the rest, Jane Austen simply tosses off that the 'rest had been the work of the moment. . . .' He proposes, and she accepts. 'What did she say? – Just what she ought, of course' (pp. 432, 431). Readers anxious to know much more will have to consult Miss Bates. She said earlier that it 'is such a happiness when good people get together – and they always do' (p. 175, but note the context).[41]

At the beginning Mr Knightley had looked upon Emma as a sister (p. 40). If these two were destined to live at Mansfield Park they would probably end on much the same footing. But when he leads her into the dance at the Crown, he exclaims, 'Brother and sister! no, indeed' (p. 331). Jane Austen has thus made a gesture at preparing the two for a sexual life together. But is it any more than a gesture? No one would deny that Mr Knightley is one of Jane Austen's finest, most upright characters.

---

[40] W. A. Craik takes what seems the conventional view that Mr Knightley's proposal at this point is to be explained as a stroke of good luck for the heroine: 'It is ironically fitting that Emma, who has ruled the action and so made all her own problems, should have those problems solved for her by matters in which she takes no active part at all, Mr Knightley's proposal . . ., Frank's engagement . . ., and . . . Harriet's engagement to Robert Martin . . .', *Jane Austen: the Six Novels*, p. 154.

[41] She bears listening to. She is allowed to utter some profound truths Jane Austen would never have dared burden her principal characters with. In this respect Miss Bates resembles that other oracle of homely wisdom, Mrs Jennings in *Sense and Sensibility*. It is Mrs Jennings who observes fairly early in the novel that Colonel Brandon will marry Marianne sooner or later (p. 196). And truer words were never spoken than her pronouncement in the same paragraph, 'One shoulder of mutton . . . drives another down'.

Only Mrs Elton could find anything to criticise. But was he really destined to be anybody's husband? There is something discomforting in the fact that not many readers, when asked, know his Christian name.[42] It seems impossible to imagine his honeymoon without recalling that playful but ominous statement he made to Emma when he proposed: 'You hear nothing but truth from me'.

Like Colonel Brandon, he is the safe, cool repository of the spiritual values the heroine is prepared at last to wed. He has 'watched over her from a girl, with an endeavour to improve her, and an anxiety for her doing right . . .' (p. 415). He comes into the novel ready-armed with the virtue of strong moral activism that has been developing in Jane Austen's fiction since Mr Bennet was urged to do more than smile at the world's follies. When Mr Knightley sees Emma doing wrong, he is determined to 'speak. He owed it to her, to risk any thing that might be involved in an unwelcome interference . . .; to encounter any thing, rather than the remembrance of neglect in such a cause' (p. 350). He brings the heavy moral vocabulary of *Mansfield Park* into the novel also. He is far from afraid of the words 'truth' (p. 430; for further examples and variations see pp. 446, 375), 'duty' (p. 146), and 'principle' (pp. 147, 448, 462, 474). He knows how to find 'faults' (pp. 10, 11, 446, 448). He declares that Jane Fairfax did a 'wrong thing', and that this ought to make it easier for Emma to bear that Jane 'should have been in such a state of punishment' (p. 447). Indeed one of his last services in the novel is a running moral gloss of Frank Churchill's letter – a gloss that takes up more than half a chapter (pp. 444–8).

But at Mr Knightley's very core is a value that even his grave moral vocabulary cannot quite project. He lives in the real, workaday world, and accepts it as it is. Farming interests him; Emma catches him discussing agriculture even with a lady (p. 361). He is familiar with the solid earth, and takes it at its word. In the drawing-room at Randalls the company engage in elaborate conjectures concerning how deep the snow is outside; and Mr Knightley does what it is so uncongenial to the minds of Jane Austen's characters ever to do. He goes outside

---

[42] It is George. On this matter see *Facts and Problems*, p. 201.

and looks at the snow. He has the annoying habit of putting conjectures to 'proof' (p. 145). In short, he respects the commonplace world Jane Austen dedicated her art to, long ago. One would expect him to have a high regard for Miss Bates and her mother, and he does (pp. 224–5). He sends them apples (p. 238) – a little offering at the world's altar.

The earth under foot, and its physical laws, have been at the centre of Jane Austen's art since the beginning, when Catherine Morland rolled down the hill, and Elizabeth Bennet's petticoat was six inches deep in mud. To be 'above' the earth, to imagine it romantically heightened, more picturesque than it really is, to imagine its inhabitants obeying one's own aesthetic laws rather than the world's laws – this could be conceived as the 'sin' of all Jane Austen's heroines. But the earth itself, with its rocks and trees, has not figured in her art much until lately. But beginning with *Mansfield Park* she does indeed celebrate more and more that solid object on which her delicate drawing-room artifice has been founded. Her art begins to move outdoors. (There are a remarkable number of scenes laid there in *Persuasion* and the unfinished 'Sanditon'.) She goes with Mr Knightley to stand on something that repels conjecture. She even begins to celebrate 'nature' occasionally.

We can see this in *Mansfield Park*, for all its fences, gates and doors. Fanny Price actually delivers several effusions on the beauty, serenity and harmony of nature (see pp. 106, 113, 209) – effusions that Jane Austen is receiving with a straight face, and may even be sponsoring. Near the conclusion Fanny is even made to appreciate trees without any thought of their usefulness in picturesque landscapes (pp. 446–7). She and Edmund are described in the next-to-last paragraph as 'Equally formed for domestic life, and attached to country pleasures'. As for the wicked characters, there are no country pleasures for them. Henry is in favour of 'improving' streams. And his sister insults farmers. She sees 'nature, inanimate nature, with little observation' (p. 81).

Thus in *Mansfield Park* Jane Austen seems to be calling attention to the substantial, silent earth that has endured unperturbed through all the fantastic headstrong reveries of her characters. And we see this again in *Emma*. The heroine begins inside a house – a house she seldom leaves (p. 41). She is the fair mistress of a mansion; and the mansion itself is set off from Highbury, which surrounds it. The countryside is a threat to her. She has a 'horror of being in danger of falling in with the second rate . . . of Highbury . . .' (p. 155). She lives in a private, romantic world she herself has helped to make, and she prefers it to the one outside.

Yet the countryside is quietly there, even at the beginning; and is already exerting its calm, steady pressure. Hartfield, 'in spite of its separate lawn and shrubberies', does 'really belong' to the village of Highbury (p. 7). In the course of the novel this natural world has its quiet way. It invades Emma's mind; it absorbs her into itself. It makes her belong to it. We see her standing in the door of Ford's shop and observing outside in the street a kind of sprawling natural scene that has seldom been admitted into Jane Austen's novels before:

> . . . the butcher with his tray, a tidy old woman travelling homewards from shop with her full basket, two curs quarrelling over a dirty bone, and a string of dawdling children round the baker's little bow-window eyeing the gingerbread . . . (p. 233).

Finally, we see her at the last moment before Mr Knightley arrives to propose to her. She has left her father's side, and is walking outside in the shrubbery. 'Never had the exquisite sight, smell, sensation of nature, tranquil, warm, and brilliant after a storm, been more attractive to her' (p. 424). She is leaving her house to enter the world – a world with considerably more dogs, children and greenery than Jane Austen has ever before permitted as part of the neat, elegant, functional furniture in her novels. Emma is surrendering her private little world, and her private little epithet, 'Miss Woodhouse, of Hartfield' (p. 276), for another world, another house,[43] another heart, and another name.

8

Even after Emma consents to live in Mr Knightley's world rather than her own, there is still in the plot one 'fact' she has yet to accept. In an unusual strategy, Jane Austen has saved

[43] See note 13 above.

this final disclosure until the very end; and thus it makes a kind of coda to Emma's romantic career in the novel. It is the fact that Harriet is the illegitimate daughter of a tradesman; and Jane Austen quickly huddles it into the last chapter.

Is she simply tying up a last loose thread? That is just not Jane Austen's way. She has probably been planning this from the start. It seems likely that she has saved this racy bit of news until now so that Harriet's illegitimacy can make a last, rather snide comment on – not Harriet, but Emma herself. Harriet is now a tradesman's daughter, true, and an illegitimate one; but that would hardly be very important if Emma had not destined her to be something else. In Emma's pretty romance Harriet was destined for something grander, something wonderful; and therefore the truth is making a final comment on Emma's romantic mind. Here is the commonplace truth (and then some?) about whatever is 'conceived' romantically.

And this final episode is saying even more about Emma than that. For Jane Austen's condemnation of Emma's protégée at the end is so energetic, so meanly self-righteous, so reminiscent of *Mansfield Park*, as to suggest that the real recipient is someone more important than poor Harriet. At the beginning Emma had told her that 'there will be plenty of people who would take pleasure in degrading you' (p. 30); and surely there must be some reason why Harriet's author now becomes one of them. For plainly Jane Austen is bullying her. Emma is now made to suggest a comparison between Harriet – and an ox (p. 473)! And another passage applies to illegitimacy that word so characteristic of *Mansfield Park* – 'stain'. Harriet, it seems, will have to live with the Martins at a kind of moral finishing farm. Perhaps she will show 'improvement' there. At least she will be, shall we say? – stanchioned, out of harm's way. She will be 'retired enough for safety'; she will never be 'led into temptation, nor left for it to find her out'. The 'intimacy' between Emma and her must of course 'sink' – a circumstance that, the narrative concludes with a sniff, 'was not to be regretted' (p. 482).

Does Harriet truly deserve all this? Perhaps not. But if there is a character who does, it is certainly Emma herself. Indeed the 'temptation' Harriet is going to be so safe from at Abbey-Mill Farm may not be her own so much as Emma's. After all, it was Emma herself who encouraged her to think of Mr Elton and Frank Churchill in the first place; perhaps the same could be said of Mr Knightley. The only man who ever tempted Harriet in her natural state of glazed innocence was Robert Martin. As for the 'stain of illegitimacy', it was not Harriet who claimed she would ever turn out to be a gentleman's daughter. And as for that 'worst of all' Emma's 'womanly follies – her wilful intimacy with Harriet Smith . . .' (p. 463), does the folly really lie in the fact that Emma was intimate with this rather silly young lady, or in the fact that Emma went a long way toward making her so silly?

Thus the moral fervour in the final chapter may be directed only nominally at Harriet, who is certainly a safe target for it. Perhaps Jane Austen has actually intended her treatment of Harriet to reflect primarily on Emma. If so, Emma ends in an ambivalent state – to say the least. She has to accept a good deal of what Harriet has coming, as well as the 'perfect happiness' the last sentence of the novel has in store for the heroine herself. Jane Austen may therefore have found a way to heap blame on Emma while rewarding her – a suitable treatment for a heroine whom the author thought no one but herself would much like.

Indeed Jane Austen seems to have conceived Harriet as a kind of embodiment of a 'part' of Emma herself: a young lady whose career goes along with the heroine's own to make up the totality of Emma in the novel.[44] The fortunes of the two have run parallel from the beginning. Each of the matches Emma proposes for her friend comes finally to focus on herself: the matches with Mr Elton, Frank Churchill and Mr Knightley. When the second of these matches falls through for both of them, and Emma is forced to break the news, it occurs to her that 'she should have the very same . . . office to perform by Harriet, which Mrs Weston had just gone through by herself' (pp. 403–4). Here and in other places Jane Austen seems to suggest similarities that go beyond what can be accounted for by the fact that Emma is Harriet's teacher. When Harriet displays her precious treasures, for instance, Emma thinks to herself, 'Lord bless me! when

---

[44] For Q. D. Leavis's suggestion that Jane Austen 'divided' the character of Fanny Knight into the Emma and Harriet of the novel see note 17 above.

should I ever have thought of putting by in cotton a piece of court plaister that Frank Churchill had been pulling about! – I never was equal to this' (p. 339). But of course she is, in her own way. She has managed to interpret Frank's running off after only a quarter of an hour in her presence as a mighty 'dread of her returning power' (p. 316)[45] when there was no such significance to it at all.

There is a distinction in the novel between Emma's 'head' and her 'heart' (see for instance p. 412); and Emma seems at times even to have invested her protégée with the qualities of her own heart until that cool and self-sufficient heroine is ready to embody them herself – although there is a danger of making more of this than Jane Austen has. On the subject of 'tenderness of heart' Emma thinks 'Harriet is my superior in all the charm . . . it gives. Dear Harriet! – I would not change you for the clearest-headed . . . female breathing' (p. 269). And when Harriet finally accepts Robert Martin, Emma thinks to herself, 'Such a heart – such a Harriet!' (p. 475), as if the one object had come to have some immediate relation to the other in her mind.

Emma seems, without knowing it, to have sent her Harriet out as an advance scout in search of the proper husband for a young lady who is handsome, clever, and rich. Early in the novel she recommends her young friend to Mr Knightley with the words, 'Were you, yourself, ever to marry, she is the very woman for you' (p. 64); and perhaps it is not Harriet she is really recommending, but herself, in the only form as yet acceptable to her own arch mind. Harriet's subsequent romance with Mr Knightley is inseparable from her own. Mr Knightley's dancing with Harriet at the Crown seems to lead inevitably to his dancing with Emma. When Harriet later hints darkly at being in love, Emma thinks, 'It's [sic] tendency would be to raise and refine her mind – and it must be saving her from the danger of degradation' (pp. 341–2). Here Emma is thinking that Harriet is referring to Frank Churchill. But Harriet has

---

[45] Likewise the giddy heroine of one of the juvenile pieces manages to explain to herself why Edward Stanley has gone off to London without saying goodbye: 'He could not trust himself to see me – Charming Young Man! How much must you have suffered!', 'Catherine, or The Bower', *Novels* VI (*Minor Works*) p. 239.

begun to think of Mr Knightley – as indeed Emma has also. Emma's thought thus has an ironic application to herself: her own growing love of Mr Knightley, rather than of Frank Churchill, is now going to refine her own mind.

Finally, when Emma herself begins to feel worthy of Mr Knightley, she thinks, 'could he even have seen into her heart, he would not, on this occasion, have found any thing to reprove' (p. 391); and this appears to be her version of Harriet's own statement on the same subject: '. . . now I seem to feel that I may deserve him; and that if he does choose me, it will not be any thing so very wonderful' (p. 411). When Harriet at last makes a declaration to Emma of her love for Mr Knightley, Emma has therefore had something else declared to her at the same time: 'A few minutes were sufficient for making her acquainted with her own heart' (p. 407). At last she, and not her Harriet, seems to be in possession of her heart; this indeed may account for the strangely turgid expression 'development of self' that appears at this point in the narrative (p. 409).[46] Mr Knightley now finally (pp. 429–30) proposes to the whole Emma – and for a moment she thinks he must be discussing Harriet!

Thus by the end of the novel Jane Austen has established an intimacy between these two young ladies that makes it difficult indeed to imagine either one of them quite separate from the other. And so, when we get the last-minute news of Harriet's true parentage, what are we to think? What Emma herself thinks is clear enough: 'Such was the blood of gentility which Emma had formerly been so ready to vouch for!' But is this the final word? Haven't we also been given a final, oblique comment on the gentility of the heroine herself? After all, she too is no longer what she thought she was. The fair mistress of the mansion has had her own comedown, into the commonplace world.

By the final chapter these two have both come to rest there. Emma marries Mr Knightley; and Harriet – perhaps she marries him too. Robert Martin seems like a yeoman's version of him. One should not overlook this. Mr Knightley has been sponsoring

---

[46] For this expression see K. C. Phillipps, *Jane Austen's English*, p. 41.

him from the start. He lives on Mr Knightley's land, and they share more than that. They both stand firmly on the earth, and believe firmly in it. Harriet assured us at the beginning that Robert Martin's reading was weak on Gothic novels but strong on the Agricultural Reports; and he and Mr Knightley will be able to discuss farming together as they walk the fields. It is right that, after Emma and her Harriet have accepted this pair, Emma should find it in her heart to think at last, 'It would be a great pleasure to know Robert Martin' (p. 475). For she could no more marry without accepting him than she could without accepting Mr Knightley himself.

The two couples are destined to settle eventually at Donwell Abbey and its adjoining farm. Mr Knightley had laid out the prospect before Emma and Harriet on the day they came to pick strawberries. There is nothing deliberately picturesque on his land ('all the old neglect of prospect', p. 358), only rich pastures, spreading flocks, an orchard in blossom. Apples, strawberries, and the more spiritual fruits the novel has been cultivating all ripen there naturally. The outing to Donwell that day was arranged according to his view of the 'simple and natural' (p. 355). If he has an aesthetic, that is it. It has replaced Emma's in the novel.

Mr Knightley's world is that general though unequal mixture of good and bad that Jane Austen long ago promised it would be. 'What is good and what is ridiculous are most unfortunately blended' there – as Emma had earlier remarked snidely of Miss Bates (p. 375). It is a world that accepts Harriet within its boundaries, if not in the abbey itself. She has her place on Mr Knightley's estate. This is important indeed in our understanding of the novel. Harriet can use a little 'improvement', it is true, but not the way Emma had in mind at Hartfield. She requires a little husbandry, but no forced hybridisation, or match-making.

She was destined to be what she has turned out to be; and that is good. Everything produces its fruit after its kind. The world intended her for Robert Martin, and it has had its way. The two tended always to be growing together whenever Emma's interference lapsed (see p. 187). On the farm they will take whatever is their natural bent.

And the world intended Emma for Mr Knightley. The loss

of Miss Taylor that she lamented in the first chapter occurred so that Frank Churchill could come to visit his new step-mother, and could thus lead Emma to Mr Knightley. Emma claimed at the beginning that it was she herself who promoted Miss Taylor's match. Now she knows it was the world, working in its quiet, commonplace, unromantic way. It always produces the 'perfect happiness' of the last sentence. It is not the perfection of a romantic novel or a watercolour, but perfect for the world.

As the novel closes, how can Emma ever explain to herself the fact that Harriet and Robert Martin have done what she tried so hard to keep them from doing? 'The fact was, as Emma could now acknowledge, that Harriet had always liked Robert Martin; and that his continuing to love her had been irresistible'. That seems indeed to be one version of a last, fundamental 'fact' at the core of this great novel – a fact that must appear somewhere in the Agricultural Reports, and that Emma is at last acknowledging. Left to itself, the world produces – whatever the world produces. Beyond this, it is not possible to make discoveries. 'Beyond this', the marriage of those two 'must ever be unintelligible to Emma'.

Unintelligible? That is perhaps the most poignant admission a mind delighted with its own ideas can make. It is an admission that is a magnificent summary of the lives of Jane Austen's heroines. Emma began as an 'imaginist' (p. 335), proud of her powers. But the world urged upon her some angular, symbolic facts that her powers could never bend to her own aesthetic purposes. Not even an artist can master the world. She began the novel containing the world; now it contains her.[47] She has taken merely a modest place in one she never made. She will have to learn to prefer the world's art to her own.

---

[47] Mark Schorer makes the interesting comment that in each of the four 'blocks') of the novel Emma 'bulks less large' than in the one before, 'The Humiliation of Emma Woodhouse', p. 551.

VII

PERSUASION
Romanticism

1

At the time of her death Jane Austen had written more than eleven chapters of a work now entitled[1] 'Sanditon'. But her last completed novel is the two-volume *Persuasion*. Cassandra's Memorandum and Jane Austen's own note show that it was begun on 8 August 1815.[2] She had completed a first draft and then some significant revision by 6 August 1816.[3] In July of the next year she died. The novel was published posthumously in the same volume as *Northanger Abbey*.

In Heaven all things have their appointed places; and when Kipling's mess-waiter, Brother Humberstall, comes before the celestial Janeites to stand for his initiation, the question he will be asked is, not which of Jane Austen's novels is best or second-best, but which is third. For surely *Emma* is her pro-

---

[1] In *Novels*, VI (*Minor Works*) p. 363 n. 2, Chapman notes that Jane Austen may have intended to entitle this work 'The Brothers'. The title 'Sanditon' originated in the Austen family.

[2] *Novels*, VI, facing p. 242; *Plan of a Novel*, [p. 37]. According to *Life and Letters* (p. 334) she had completed the first draft by 8 July 1816. Later she cancelled the chapter that brought about the re-engagement of the hero and heroine, and replaced it with two new ones (see *Memoir* (1871), pp. 166–7). The cancelled chapter has survived, and appears in *Novels*, V.

[3] Again according to the Memorandum and the note. Thus it is probably *Persuasion* that Jane Austen refers to in a letter dated 13 March 1817, as 'something ready for Publication, which may perhaps appear about a twelvemonth hence' (*Letters*, p. 484; also p. 487).

foundest novel, *Pride and Prejudice* her most brilliant. And *Persuasion* is her most beautiful. It is serene, dreamlike, and even less concerned with the busy particularities of plot than *Emma*.

Indeed *Persuasion* seems to belong last: it seems to have grown out of the previous novels, and to be looking back on them with an achieved serenity that could only have come after great trials – the trials perhaps of a Marianne. For this reason, and for many others, *Persuasion* has always been the darling of the Janeites. Here is a novel that gives the impression of having been written by a quiet, bemused, resigned and intelligent lady who has profited by her private suffering, and has now come, at middle age, to stand at last amid Mr Knightley's rich pastures, spreading flocks, and orchards. *Persuasion* has an earned beauty, and is mature, confident, and autumnal. The bloom is off the world now – and the heroine too. The novel begins in autumn, and Anne walks the fields, taking pleasure

> from the view of the last smiles of the year upon the tawny leaves and withered hedges, and from repeating to herself some few of the thousand poetical descriptions extant of autumn, that season of peculiar and inexhaustible influence on the mind of taste and tenderness . . . (p. 84).

None of the other novels is quite like this. Tartness must be the characteristic taste of Jane Austen's fruit; *Persuasion* alone is mellow, and ripe.

2

When this novel begins, the heroine is already twenty-seven – an age Marianne Dashwood seems to have considered as somewhere on the long, slow descent into the vale of senility.[4] Anne Elliot is 'faded and thin'; her 'bloom had vanished early'. Seven or eight years ago she and Frederick Wentworth had fallen deeply in love; but Anne had been persuaded by Lady Russell to believe the engagement a wrong thing, and the two have separated.

---

[4] At any rate she thinks a woman of that age could 'never hope to feel or inspire affection again' (*Sense and Sensibility*, p. 38); Liddell makes this comparison, p. 134.

The heroine of *Persuasion* thus begins the novel having already passed through the precarious romantic experience that makes up the main action in all the previous novels. This is highly significant. Anne and the true hero have already found each other, and have been put unnaturally asunder. This gives to the ensuing action a sense that 'nature', through the firm supervisory agency of Jane Austen, is simply reasserting itself in its mild, slow, inexorable way. Less is left to the dangerous vagaries of human volition here than in any of the other novels. The destined couple, having finally come together in the penultimate chapter, discuss how it is that they have done so – gazing meanwhile at a display of greenhouse plants (p. 246). Ripeness is all.

As a consequence, the cardinal virtue Anne Elliot is called upon to exercise in the novel is the one Mr Knightley has to draw upon while waiting for his apples – patience. She is nothing short of admirable in this respect. At Uppercross Cottage, for instance, she is described as displaying a 'little farther perseverance in patience' while submitting to her sister's querelousness. As the Musgroves one by one impose their troubles on her, she mildly resolves to 'listen patiently, soften every grievance, and excuse each to the other . . .' (pp. 39, 46). Many readers think therefore that all she has to do in the novel is suffer without changing, and wait for the happy end;[5] that indeed *Persuasion* has no 'middle' at all: no plot development to lead necessarily from the beginning to the end.[6] This is not

---

[5] The belief that Anne does not undergo any real character change is commonplace in criticism of the novel. The following are samples. Anne is a 'heroine who never changes fundamentally', Babb, p. 204. She 'is morally irreproachable; her character, therefore, undergoes no significant development', Ten Harmsel, p. 166. 'Jane Austen agrees with her heroine much more than she has ever done before, because Anne has really no faults', Craik, *Jane Austen: the Six Novels*, p. 167. Having 'made the initial blunder of allowing herself to be over-powered by Lady Russell's judgment . . ., she never afterwards makes a single error in morality, judgment or taste', Jenkins, p. 235. In a letter to Fanny Knight, Jane Austen herself refers to Anne as 'almost too good for me' (*Letters*, p. 487).

[6] Thus William Dean Howells writes of the conclusion, 'Nothing can be quite said to determine it among the things that happen . . .,' *Heroines of Fiction*, I 51. Likewise, Firkins thinks the reason Anne and Wentworth do not marry immediately upon his

true, of course – although surely such criticisms are more easily directed at this novel than at any of the others. Jane Austen is never without her careful plan for the psychological reformation of her heroine. Anne does indeed change, and she will be a better mate for Wentworth in the last chapter than she is in the first.

The novel begins at Kellynch Hall, the ancestral home of the Elliots. Anne's elder sister Elizabeth is now mistress of it, and is her father's favourite. As for Anne, 'her word had no weight'; 'she was only Anne' (p. 5). She is like a prisoner in the house. She 'had been too little from home, too little seen. Her spirits were not high. A larger society would improve them' (p. 15). She is now going to enter the world.

Her entrance differs profoundly from that of the previous heroines. The home she leaves is disintegrating. Sir Walter's estate can no longer support him: he has decided to let it, and move to Bath. The fundamental order of his little world is changing fast. The neighbouring village of Uppercross used to be all in the 'old English style', with a squire's mansion: 'high walls, great gates, and old trees, substantial and unmodernised'. But now there is also a modern cottage with a 'viranda, French windows, and other prettinesses' (p. 36). The elder Musgroves, who live in the old mansion and are themselves in the 'old English style', are being subjected to an 'overthrow of all order and neatness' by their children, with 'more modern minds and manners' (p. 40). The social order that gives Sir Walter's life its meaning is thus changing before his eyes. It is 1814. The sailors are returning home from the war. The navy, as he complains, is 'bringing persons of obscure birth into undue distinction' (p. 19). Indeed, he is being supplanted in his own halls by an admiral. He has tried too long to sit huddled in his Kellynch consoling himself with his book of the Baronetage while 'domestic affairs' (p. 3) outside have passed him by.

---

return is that Miss Austen is bound to . . . postpone . . . the arrival of a consummation . . .', p. 116. According to Andrew H. Wright, 'Anne's reconciliation with Captain Wentworth stems . . . from a series of fortuitous circumstances', p. 161. And Cornish thinks that 'if Frederick Wentworth had known the state of Anne's heart at the moment of meeting her again after so long an absence, he must have flown to her side and forgiven all', p. 200.

Thus the heroine of this last novel is taking leave of a grand home that will never be hers to call home again (but see pp. 125–6). This is important.[7] There can be no return home in the novel, as there is in each of the others (assuming that in *Sense and Sensibility* the Dashwood sisters' home is Barton Cottage). Anne must find a new one. She must complete the movement that the heroine of *Emma* was still not quite able to endure at the conclusion: the removal forever from the paternal abode. It takes place now. And is it taking place for Jane Austen as well? Kellynch may be bankrupt for her, too. From the old, dignified inland houses of the valetudinarian Mr Woodhouse and the superannuated Sir Walter Elliot her art is moving now, toward the sea. In that final fragment 'Sanditon' she is beginning to build a new home there, in a resort on the Sussex coast.

Jane Austen has not spent much subtlety on Sir Walter's house. It comes very quickly to represent little more than the Elliot family's general state of mind. It is a state of mind that seems to subsume so many of the attitudes we have encountered in the heroines before. At the outset of every one of the novels the heroine is under a spell that prevents her from seeing the world as it really is. As Jane Austen's art has progressed she has conceived the illusion in more and more general terms. The Gothic novels and the novels of sensibility that serve to produce illusions in Catherine Morland and Marianne Dashwood are left behind. The very words 'Gothic', 'romantic' and 'picturesque' that we see even as late as *Mansfield Park* – these slowly fade away, and we are left, in Emma Woodhouse, with a heroine who exhibits what seems close to a pure, idealised, and ultimately causeless illusion: the propensity of a strong mind, when unobstructed by fact, to assert its supremacy over matter by whatever imaginative means are most congenial to it; the propensity of a mind to be delighted with its own ideas rather than with the world's.

Conceived in such general terms, the states of mind of all the previous heroines tend to collapse into one for which 'egotism' is as good a word as any; and in *Persuasion* Jane

---

[7] Alistair Duckworth is excellent on this: 'In *Persuasion* the estate is defeated where in *Mansfield Park* it triumphed', p. 185.

Austen has indeed concentrated on just this. Kellynch Hall is the home, the palace of egotism in the novel. Sir Walter Elliot is the presiding spirit of the place; and the first chapter sets him up as nothing short of a caricature of vanity. For amusement he reads nothing but his Baronetage, which falls open obligingly to the page recording the history of his family. The centre of his world is a dressing-room in which he is surrounded by mirrors. Other rooms are furnished with a Mrs Clay, whose reflexive function is to tell him, 'We are not all born to be handsome';[8] and by a Mr Shepherd, who simpers, 'I venture to hint, that Sir Walter Elliot cannot be half so jealous for his own, as John Shepherd will be for him' (pp. 19–20). Other than himself the apple of his eye is Elizabeth; and she is – who would have believed it? – 'very like himself' (p. 5).

In short, 'Vanity was the beginning and the end of Sir Walter Elliot's character' (p. 4); which is as much as to say that Jane Austen is not much interested in giving him any character at all. She has no intention of turning him loose to live a full life in the novel. He exists to perform a function in her careful plan. He is little more than a representation of the essential nature of the house which Anne was born into, and is now about to leave.

He is also the inheritor of the generations of Elliot blood chronicled in his book; and Anne – she is the inheritor of his, no matter where she lives. She may be able to leave his house, but will that free her of the family vanity Kellynch merely represents? This is the issue that begins the novel. Can Anne truly leave the Elliot 'house'? Surely she can: she is mild and self-effacing, the one Elliot who could tolerate the word 'only' next to her name; the only Elliot willing to concede, as Anne now does on her arrival at her sister's Uppercross Grange, 'that another lesson, in the art of knowing our own nothingness beyond our own circle, was become necessary for her' (p. 42). The entrance into the world that is taking Anne away from Kellynch thus seems to be taking her safely away from a family to which, perhaps, she never really belonged.

---

[8] Constance Hill quotes a family source on Jane Austen's own father: 'As a young man I have always understood that he was considered extremely handsome, and it was a beauty which stood by him all his life', *Jane Austen: Her Homes and Her Friends*, p. 31.

She seems already to have left behind at Kellynch that ego-
tistical little world that enclosed the previous heroine for so long.
Emma finally came out of her shell, left her house, when she
consented to take a man from the real, apple-producing world
as a husband; and to change her name for his. If Anne too is
free of her father's house she will do the same. And so now at
Uppercross Jane Austen brings into her presence Captain
Wentworth, the man whose name she was once offered.

What brings him to Uppercross at this opportune time?
'Coincidence', most readers seem to think. Indeed we can find
this everywhere; *Persuasion* more than any of the other novels
seems to jolt along to its happy end on quirks, chances and
coincidences. But surely that is not the impression Jane Austen
is aiming at, any more than when she brought Elizabeth and
Darcy together so fortuitously at Pemberley. She is simply
saying more boldly in *Persuasion* than she has ever said before,
'I am the author and I have a plan for altering my heroine's
psychology. I make events happen where I need them. Is it
all that important that they seem relentlessly plausible? Every
wind has its Prospero'. The cause of Wentworth's return just
now after so many years thus cannot be laid to the Admiralty
so much as to an experienced, confident author who is less and
less interested in concealing her fictive legerdemain. Her subject
is, as it has always been, her heroine's psychology; the plot,
with its names, dates, and perfunctory clamberings in and out
of carriages – in *Persuasion* that will have to follow gamely
behind. 'Plot' in this sense is becoming a husk.

At Uppercross the two lovers are now moved slowly and
purposefully toward each other. Wentworth comes into the
neighbourhood on a visit. He moves closer and closer to Anne
as he first pays his respects to the elder Musgroves in the Great
House, then visits the Cottage itself. Their eyes finally meet
(p. 59). Soon the two are sitting on the same sofa, buffered only
by Mrs Musgrove. Soon he is touching a child who is touching
her. Soon the two are sitting together at the same table on a
visit to the seaside, at Lyme.

It seems inevitable that Anne should now be in sight of the
sea. Nature is drawing her away from her father's traditional,
inland house, and is preparing her for something new in Jane
Austen's repertoire: a morally reclaimable male who is destined

for the heroine in the last chapter and who is also – a sailor. This will require some acclimatisation on Anne's part, and perhaps her author's; and so at Lyme Jane Austen presents her heroine with Wentworth's friend Captain Harville. He is a sailor too: a kind of pale imitation of Wentworth himself; and he seems to exist in the novel primarily as Anne's safe introduction to the nautical type. He brings into her widening experience a sense of the strange and faraway places that Wentworth himself has seen since he went away. In Captain Harville's house she sees collected something 'curious and valuable from all the distant countries' he has visited; a collection 'more than amusing to Anne: connected as it all was with his profession . . .' (p. 98). He brings to her a sense of the beauty that comes from living in an atmosphere of danger. His sailor's life has left him a little lame, and he lives now on the edge of the sea, where he has to 'defend the windows and doors against the winter storms to be expected' (p. 98). He brings into Anne's experience, and into this last novel, a new sense of turbulent, fascinating and dangerous energies over the horizon, a sense of impending weather, a sense of the sea.

He has living with him a Captain Benwick. This man too is going to do his part in introducing Anne to a sailor's life. Like Harville, Benwick has been maimed, for he was engaged to Harville's sister, and is mourning her death. The 'friendship between him and the Harvilles seemed . . . augmented by the event which closed all their views of alliance, and Captain Benwick was now living with them entirely' (p. 97). How gently, how subtly nature works. There is someone else whose fiancée died to him, and who has been spending a great deal of time with her relatives. When Anne thinks there is still hope that romance can bloom for Captain Benwick again (p. 97), she thus seems to be conceding, without really knowing it, that romance can bloom again for Wentworth too.

Anne's mind is reaching out toward Wentworth now. Standing near the sea in the presence of the Harvilles and Captain Benwick, she thinks regretfully, 'These would have been all my friends' (p. 98). She comes to think 'how much more interesting to her was the home and the friendship of the Harvilles and Captain Benwick, than her own father's house', now in Bath (p. 124). She is being drawn slowly toward Captains

Harville, Benwick, Wentworth, and the sea; and she is leaving her father behind.

Jane Austen now puts Anne's new allegiances to the supreme test by transporting her at last to that mecca of egotism, Bath, where she rejoins her father. It is important to recognise that her stepping into his rooms there has the effect of a return to all the vanity of the Hall, with its mirrors. Elizabeth and Mrs Clay are installed there. All the familiar delights of self-consequence are there, merely scaled down to a house in Camden Place. If Anne had been able to resist them at Kellynch, what threat are they here? She has come a long way.

3

But there is a new mirror in Sir Walter's new house – a mirror Anne has never yet stood before. 'Various as were the tempers in her father's house', it pleases them all (p. 161). Perhaps it will please her, too. It has indeed already given her a flattering glimpse of herself on the seashore at Lyme. It is glossy and blank just as it ought to be. It is Jane Austen's last false hero, and his name is Mr Elliot.

Like Wentworth he has appeared in the novel in blithe disregard of the laws of time and place. He simply materialised on the edge of the sea while Anne was visiting Lyme, and he has proceeded to Bath according to his author's instructions, there to await the heroine's arrival (but see pp. 206–7). Captain Wentworth jokingly referred at Lyme to the part Providence has played in these 'extraordinary circumstances' (p. 106), and someone else has plainly had a hand as well.

Jane Austen could doubtless have brought Mr Elliot in with a formal introduction and good reasons for being at Lyme; but in this late novel she is not much interested in making such events plausible. She does not try very hard to conceal that his life is in her hands, not his own. She is using him to subject Anne Elliot to her great spiritual trial in the novel, and consequently he appears only when Jane Austen is ready to put him to work. He is thus one of her most cog-like characters. He has been designed to perform a function. When she is through with him she has so little inclination to subsidise his further existence that she quickly packs him off to London with another bit of worn-out machinery, Mrs Clay; and leaves them there, dazed, to work out their own plot (see p. 250).

Jane Austen has neglected almost all the rich irrelevancy of detail that could have made him a believable character. She is not much concerned with his hair, teeth and eyes. It is true that Anne was immediately struck with him at Lyme, but the reader has to accept her reasons more or less on faith (see pp. 104, 143). As is usual with this figure in the novels, his real power lies not so much in what he is as what he 'reflects' back to the heroine from her own consciousness. And Anne, like the previous heroines, does indeed have such a consciousness to be reflected. It has been gathering force in her since she left her father's house, although we are apt not to notice the change.

As she has moved out into the world from the tight Kellynch enclave, as she has thought less and less of her family and more of Wentworth and the sea, she has actually been going 'home' – as is nicely indicated by her arrival in her father's rooms in Bath. She has been slowly and subtly increasing in Elliot self-awareness to the point where all the family vanity she seemed to have left behind is beginning to have its appeal for her too. This is the crucial development that 'makes' Mr Elliot appear in the novel at just the point he does.

At home Anne was indeed 'only Anne'. When she leaves she becomes somebody at last, and thus begins the journey 'home' toward the satisfactions of self-consequence. At Uppercross she is immediately 'treated with too much confidence by all parties', and is 'too much in the secret of the complaints of each house' (p. 44). She then begins to receive little attentions from her former lover. She begins to hear comments on her personal appearance (p. 60, but note her reaction). At Lyme she is described as 'having the bloom and freshness of youth restored by the fine wind . . ., and by the animation of eye which it had also produced';[9] and she is aware that the mysterious stranger on the shore has noticed her (p. 104). Then again at Lady Russell's Kellynch Lodge, 'either Anne was improved in plumpness and looks, or Lady Russell fancied her so;

---

[9] As usual Firkins is sceptical, here of the physiology involved. See his p. 122. But Jane Austen's implication seems clearly to be that Anne's radiance is not so much a result of the sea breeze as of a dawning awareness that Wentworth may still love her.

and Anne, in receiving her compliments on the occasion, had the amusement of connecting them with the silent admiration she had received at Lyme (p. 124). When she arrives in Bath even her father compliments her 'on her improved looks' (p. 145).

These little touches serve to indicate that Anne too is eligible for the Elliot vanity. To tempt her, Jane Austen has invested the seductive powers of the family in the person of Mr Elliot. When Anne is ready to appreciate them, he appears. His significance in the scheme of the novel thus seems clear and relatively uncomplicated. He is for Anne at Bath what the dressing-room mirrors have been for her father: a means of admiring her own Elliot self in a form outside herself. He too is an Elliot, and the heir to her father's Kellynch. And so it is right that Mr Elliot should confront her now and talk to her of 'our family'. He calls her cousin. He points out a disturbing similarity between the two of them: 'You talk of being proud, I am called proud I know, and I shall not wish to believe myself otherwise, for our pride, if investigated, would have the same object . . .' (pp. 150–1). We remember that the two do indeed share the common purpose of trying in their own ways to protect the family from the adulteration of Mrs Clay. Their cousinship goes deeper than is revealed in Sir Walter's book – deep enough for Mr Elliot to hint darkly of marriage (p. 188).

If marriage for Jane Austen's heroines has always been a formal celebration of a final willingness to accept a world outside themselves, here is a marriage which, if anything, would celebrate the opposite. Sir Walter has always hoped that his estate could be 'transmitted whole and entire, as he had received it' (p. 10), and his hopes for this have rested on Mr Elliot. By marrying one of Sir Walter's daughters Mr Elliot can preserve the family from the adulteration of the impure world outside. Elliots can be Elliots still, gazing, as in that mirrored room, at their own inviolate Elliot family selves.

Elizabeth had earlier loved him 'for being her father's heir' (p. 8), but he had spurned her. Now he seems to be beckoning to Anne. Lady Russell points out that the match would indeed make Anne 'the future Lady Elliot'. And Anne's own 'imagination and . . . heart' are bewitched for a moment at the 'idea of becoming what her mother had been. . . .' Here then is the prospect 'of being restored to Kellynch, calling it her home again' (pp. 159–60) – and living forever with the mirrors. It is as if Anne's long journey outward from her father's house has merely carried her back into it; it is as if taking leave of Kellynch were merely the first step toward re-entering it at Bath; as if she had walked away from the Elliot egotism only to walk toward it here at Bath in a form that finally has caught her eye; as if her father's house has proved to have many mansions.

Thus it seems impossible not to see some bones growing brittle with allegory beneath Mr Elliot's spare flesh. He is not much more than the seductive appeal of that state of mind common to all Jane Austen's heroines when reduced to its most basic terms. He is the appeal of the self; and in this late, confident novel Jane Austen is not afraid to let him deliver his appeal in words that might be as suitable to a Vanity Fair as to a concert room at Bath: 'The name of Anne Elliot . . . has long had an interesting sound to me . . . and, if I dared, I would breathe my wishes that the name might never change' (p. 188).

4

Anne's attraction towards Mr Elliot is never strong or un-equivocal (see for instance p. 160).[10] But his romantic overtures at Bath put her in a dilemma, for her affections are now pulled two ways. Jane Austen's predilection for neat schemes and geo-metrical arrangements goes back as far as the Thorpes in *Northanger Abbey*; and she has done some fiddling with the plot here so that both sides of Anne's dilemma will be nicely balanced at this point in the novel. On the one hand there is Mr Elliot. He is being sponsored by Lady Russell, who up to now has made all Anne's significant decisions for her. It was Lady Russell's persuasion that long ago parted Anne from Wentworth; it has been Lady Russell's persuasion that has played such an im-portant part in guiding her through life since Lady Elliot died (p. 5); it is indeed Lady Russell who has brought Anne to Bath.

---

[10] But Wiesenfarth is in error when he says that before Mrs Smith reveals Mr Elliot's true character Anne 'has decided against' him, p. 139. She has almost decided against him, but not quite. See pp. 211–14 of the novel (discussed below, my p. 202).

On the other hand there is Captain Wentworth. To make him just as marriageable as Mr Elliot, Jane Austen suddenly engages Louisa Musgrove, with whom he had been carrying on a mild affair, to someone else. He is then brought to Bath and abruptly introduced into the plot (p. 174), perhaps to nobody's surprise quite so much as his own. It only remains to find a sponsor for him, to balance Lady Russell. Captains Harville and Benwick passed muster for this at the seaside, but it may be that no number of captains can counterbalance a titled Lady on her own firm footing in Bath; and Jane Austen has consequently enlisted as Wentworth's sponsors there no less than an admiral and his wife, who arrive in Bath a month after Anne does, ostensibly on account of the admiral's gout, but actually because they are needed to round out Jane Austen's design.

They are the Crofts. Anne has always liked them. They are 'people whom her heart turned to very naturally'. Whenever they appear together 'she always watched them as long as she could; delighted to fancy she understood what they might be talking of . . .' (pp. 162, 168). She has an instinctive rapport with them. They are suited to be her spiritual parents. They have indeed supplanted Sir Walter in his own house. Here then is the couple to lead her to a husband. Anne meets the Admiral on the street now in Bath. He asks her, 'where are you bound? Can I go any where for you, or with you? Can I be of any use?'; and his words seem to rise above Milsom Street to refer to matters nothing short of spiritual. He sounds like Mrs Gardiner when she undertakes to guide Elizabeth to Pemberley: 'My love, should not you like to see a place of which you have heard so much?' To the Admiral's question Anne answers, 'None, I thank you, unless you will give me the pleasure of your company the little way our road lies together' (p. 169). He takes her arm, and will be her guide.

Against the polished fascinations of Mr Elliot and Kellynch he reasserts the fascinations of Wentworth and the sea. He and his wife have come into the novel with a fund of salty romantic experience that can be Anne's. Mrs Croft tells the tight little landlocked society at Uppercross that she has crossed the Atlantic four times, and 'have been once to the East Indies. . . . But I never went beyond the Streights – and never was in the West Indies. We do not call Bermuda or Bahama, you know, the

West Indies'; to which Mrs Musgrove 'had not a word to say in dissent; she could not accuse herself of having ever called them anything in the whole course of her life' (p. 70). Admiral Croft himself has spent much of his life at sea, and seems to have returned for the providential purpose of taking Anne's arm on the street in Bath to try to lead her where she ought to go. This kind, hearty, experienced old man now does what he can to guide her to Wentworth. With the aid of a picture in a shop window he helps her understand what is a proper boat; by telling her what his life is like he helps her understand what is a proper sailor; in discussing Captain Benwick he helps her understand what is a proper man. 'There is something about Frederick,' he says, 'more to our taste' (pp. 169–72).

Anne is poised between alternatives, both of which have been charged with great significance. Jane Austen now sends her to a concert that lays out her dilemma in stark, graphic terms. Here is another scene that appears to exist primarily to further the heroine's psychological development by whatever fictional means are lying closest at hand. Mr Elliot sits near Anne; Captain Wentworth hovers near her side. As the scene closes Wentworth is on the verge of sitting next to her on the bench – an act that could not but have signalled the end of the novel. But a touch on her shoulder had turned her the other way, toward Mr Elliot (pp. 186–90). Which shall it be?

5

Anne Elliot has been carried along by natural circumstances, and by Lady Russell, to this one point in the novel where a decision is being asked of her. All the spiritual agonising of the previous heroines has been reduced in this last, mild novel to one decision; and it is typical that the decision is now made for her. Once more Jane Austen has laid out her plot so that the heroine, having succumbed just a little to the powers of the false hero, will be disenchanted by the apocalyptic appearance of some dark 'fact' from his former life.

In no other novel is the fact hurled down into the novel quite so much like a bolt from the blue as here. There is a cute juvenile piece in which a Lady Williams and Alice, the heroine, encounter a wounded damsel under a citron tree, and promptly ask,

'Will you favour us with your Life & adventures?' The damsel does, and in an intense and endless monologue reveals that she had once been in love with the same fascinating cad that Alice now loves, but has discovered his wickedness:

> With a heart elated by the expected happiness of beholding him I entered [the woods] & had proceeded thus far in my progress thro' it, when I found myself suddenly seized by the leg & on examining the cause of it, found that I was caught in one of the steel traps so common in gentlemen's grounds.

'Ah,' cries Lady Williams, 'how fortunate we are to meet with you; since we might otherwise perhaps have shared the like misfortune' ('Jack & Alice', *Minor Works*, pp. 16—22).[11] What the young Jane Austen is burlesquing here she has done without the trace of a smile in *Persuasion*! With no preparation whatever[12] she introduces an invalid, Mrs Smith, who favours Anne with her life and adventures; and in so doing conveys to Anne information concerning Mr Elliot that 'no one else could have done' (p. 212). The plot seems unprofessional here, to say the least, as generations of readers have pointed out.[13]

If there is a touchstone for the appreciation of Jane Austen's art, it is this. Mrs Smith is merely the most daring instance yet of what we have been seeing all along. Jane Austen has never

---

[11] Likewise in the 'Plan of a Novel' the heroine's father is 'induced, at his Daughter's earnest request, to relate to her the past events of his Life. This Narrative will reach through the greatest part of the 1st vol.', *Novels*, VI (*Minor Works*) p. 428.

[12] Yet she criticises other writers for this. Concerning Laetitia Hawkins's novel *Rosanne* (1814), she mentions the 'thousand improbabilities in the story. Do you remember the two Miss Ormesdens, introduced just at last? Very flat and unnatural', *Letters*, p. 422. Jane Austen made a similar criticism of her niece Anna Austen's novel: 'St Julian's History was quite a surprise to me; You had not very long known it yourself I suspect. . . . Had not you better give some hint . . . in the beginning of the story?', *Letters*, p. 421 (and cited by Firkins, p. 133).

[13] 'Mrs Smith is introduced . . . without the salve of an anticipatory reference in the early chapters', Firkins, p. 133; 'the one comparatively dull and lifeless part of the book', *Life and Letters*, p. 337; 'may be improvisation', Lascelles, p. 194; 'interruption', Thomson, p. 206; 'clumsily patched on', Q. D. Leavis, X 274; 'clumsy', Allott, p. 178; 'a clumsy piece of exposition', Gooneratne, p. 190.

been particularly interested in making every episode in her novels seem to follow the time-and-place logic of 'real life' or of a novel aiming at a very thoroughgoing representation of life. The strong governing 'plot' in the novels has always been the drama taking place in the heroine's mind as she becomes spiritually prepared to take her place in the world; and at certain crucial points Jane Austen has never hesitated to influence the heroine's development by interfering in the plot, in veiled or open defiance of the laws of probability.

Thus her art has always had, more or less faintly, a characteristic of allegory. It is just that now this is becoming very obvious. There is only a little more reason to be bothered by the adventitiousness of Mrs Smith's appearance now than by, say, Mr Worldly Wiseman's in *The Pilgrim's Progress*. Both appear when and where they do simply because their authors think the time is spiritually right for them to appear. Likewise Darcy and Elizabeth came together at Pemberley when they were spiritually ready to; Sir Thomas returned when Fanny was ready for him; and now Mrs Smith appears at Bath – for the same reason that Mr Elliot appeared on the shore at Lyme.

In the earlier novels there is at least a perfunctory attempt to root events like these in the time-and-place logic of the plot. Jane Austen has managed, for instance, to give a certain maritime plausibility even to Sir Thomas's sudden arrival home from Antigua (see *Mansfield Park*, pp. 178–9). But as her art progresses such busy plot business concerns her less and less. It seems in *Emma* and *Persuasion* to be dropping away in tatters. The young lady's entrance into the world is appearing closer and closer to that ideal state of naked spirituality where the makeshifts of a true-to-life plot would have disappeared altogether.

It is likely[14] that Jane Austen could have worked Mrs Smith convincingly into the plot of *Persuasion* if she had wanted to. But why should she want to? Mrs Smith is scarcely a character at

---

[14] The authors of the *Life and Letters* think she would have revised the episode before publication, p. 337. Southam points out that the revised ending of the novel links Mrs Smith 'more closely to the fortunes of Anne and Wentworth' – perhaps betraying Jane Austen's 'uneasiness about Mrs Smith's place in the story', *Literary Manuscripts*, p. 97.

all; she is an idea that is crucial in Jane Austen's scheme for the heroine's psychological development. Mrs Smith is merely the close-to-disembodied voice of the truth of the world,[15] a Mrs Worldly Wisewoman, who is made to appear when she does simply because Anne Elliot has now come to that point in her development where Mrs Smith's truth is at last relevant to her.

Mrs Smith has 'lived very much in the world' (p. 153). Like so many of the characters in this last novel, she has retired from the world injured, and wiser. She lives in a tiny room now, and can scarcely stir. In her employ is a creature whose grotesque epithet, 'nurse Rooke', suggests that she might be more at home next to a cauldron than a bed. Nurse Rooke goes out into the world every day and brings back to her employer the fundamental truths concerning humankind – truths that she seems somehow to have gathered from their sick bodies:

> Hers is a line for seeing human nature. . . . Call it gossip if you will; but when nurse Rooke has half an hour's leisure to bestow on me, she is sure to have something to relate that is entertaining and profitable, something that makes one know one's species better (p. 155).

Of all Jane Austen's characters Mrs Smith is the one who seems most qualified to speak of what she calls 'human nature' (p. 156). She seems in this last, mature novel to be a fund of knowledge that goes beyond any particular time and place. Indeed she declares, 'I have shewn you Mr Elliot, as he was a dozen years ago, and I will shew him as he is now'(p. 204) – as if there were a crystal ball before her. Into her eerie conversation are woven expressions suggesting that her eyes are focused on some world beyond Bath, beyond the novel itself: 'I know it all, I know it all'; 'Hear the truth, therefore'; 'I know it all perfectly' (pp. 200, 199, 205). Mrs Smith seems capable of giving Anne the truth concerning that species, man, gathered from all experience. 'When one lives in the world,' she says, a man or woman's marrying for money, as Mr Elliot did years ago, is 'too common' (p. 201). She can give the sharp statistic that places this man among all others: 'Ninety-nine out of a hundred would do the same' (p. 196). She

---

[15] Alistair Duckworth oddly concentrates on the cynicism in what Mrs Smith tells Anne, *The Improvement of the Estate*, p. 192.

seems at last to be the ultimate source of those precious facts on which Jane Austen's art has been founded. 'Facts', as she now says, 'shall speak' (p. 199).

And so she produces a small inlaid box, and from the box comes almost the last of those incontrovertible documents Jane Austen usually has recourse to when it is time for facts to speak – a letter. There is a weary and half-hearted attempt, on both Mrs Smith's part and her author's, to justify the existence of the letter (p. 203); but that is hardly important any more. The letter proves that this last false hero is indeed 'black at heart' (p. 199). Here is the crucial, symbolic fact that appears in every one of the novels. For Anne 'the charm was broken' (p. 214) – the same words that had signalled Edmund Bertram's disenchantment earlier (*Mansfield Park*, p. 456). She has been saved from what she now admits was at least the possibility 'that she might have been persuaded by Lady Russell' to marry Mr Elliot. It remains only for Anne 'to retrace . . . the few steps of unnecessary intimacy she had been gradually led along' (pp. 211, 214).

The truth Anne has been given seems to rest only fitfully on its nominal subject, Mr Elliot,[16] and then to plumb down much deeper into the novel. His perfidy is saying something unpleasant about Anne too, and about the world. Mr Elliot is after all an Elliot. A little of the revealed blackness of his heart must therefore run in the family, and be chronicled in the Book. The truth Anne has heard thus reflects faintly on herself. Here is a true glimpse in a mirror; here is something of the true nature of that Elliot self she might have loved enough to prefer for ever to any other name. And there is something more. The truth she has heard comes closer to reflecting on mankind in general than would ever have been tolerated in any of the earlier novels except *Mansfield Park*. Jane Austen is nearing the end of her career, and she seems personally intent on a profundity that would have brought a sly smile to Elizabeth Bennet. Mrs Smith has said that ninety-nine out of a hundred would act as Mr Elliot had done; and she has lived very much in the world. This seems the single, final fact at the centre of a nest of Chinese boxes

[16] Thomson sees no reason why Mr Elliot should have been made guilty of anything at all. The part Mr Elliot 'plays in embarrassing Anne and in arousing the jealousy of Wentworth might have been equally well acted by an entirely blameless lover', p. 217.

in Jane Austen's fiction. Here is the truth. Ninety-nine out of a hundred are like Mr Elliot. That is the truth of the world.

But not quite the whole truth. There is still that one other man out of a hundred. Mrs Smith has made Anne know the species better, but Anne does not yet know it completely. She needs another lecture on the nature of man to complement the foreboding one she has just heard, and so Wentworth's friend Captain Harville now gives her one in the Musgrove's rooms at the White Hart. He speaks to her of 'man's nature'; he tries to explain to her 'all that a man can bear and do' for the woman he loves (pp. 233, 235). Here is the rest of the truth. There are Mr Elliots in the world, but there are a few steady, faithful, selfless men also.

To prove this, the person who has been seated close to her side throughout her conversation with Harville now demonstrates that man is indeed capable of undying constancy to the woman he loves. The person is Captain Wentworth, who has conveniently been overhearing the conversation.[17] He now conveys to Anne a letter he has been writing as his contribution to the topic under discussion. Presumably there is a quiet corner where at this point the two could have carried on a soulful private conversation that would have rendered paper unnecessary. But Jane Austen is not so much interested in acoustics as she is in following her plan. She wants to establish that Captain Wentworth's constancy is a final incontrovertible fact in the novel; and letters have almost always been her means. Thus this final letter that seems so implausible to so many readers. Anne feels that 'On the contents of that letter depended all which this world could do for her!' (p. 237). She opens it and finds that Wentworth has loved her from the day they parted; and that he is now offering himself to her again. Jane Austen's final truth concerning man's nature seems to be in that letter – and Mr Elliot's.

Anne accepts Wentworth's proposal without hesitation, only a few paragraphs after receiving the letter. She had been ready to

---

[17] One would expect Firkins to cast a cold eye on such an awkward fictional contrivance, and he does. He refers disparagingly to Wentworth's being 'in the same room, at a distance so artfully planned that he can hear perfectly without being suspected of overhearing', p. 118.

marry him at the start, where she is described as having been 'forced into prudence in her youth', only to learn 'romance' as she 'grew older' (p. 30). She was ready for Wentworth then, but it seems that Jane Austen thought differently. Now, the truths Anne has learned in the course of the novel concerning man's nature, and Anne Elliot's, have made her ready in a way she was not then. That has always been Jane Austen's 'plot'. That has been the plot of *Persuasion*. The novel can be understood in no other way.[18] The two lovers are described at the moment of their reuniting as 'more fixed in a knowledge of each other's character' than when they parted years ago (pp. 240–1).

6

The course of the novel has prepared Wentworth for this moment, too. He too has undergone a change. Long ago Anne was prudent and subject to the cool persuasion of Lady Russell; and he in turn was headstrong and impetuous, 'full of life and ardour' (p. 27). The intervening years have tempered Anne's prudence with romance; and likewise the plot of the novel tempers Wentworth's ardour with prudence. This is important, and easily overlooked. Jane Austen has concentrated his entire process of change in one curious episode: his romance with Louisa Musgrove leading to her famous fall on the Cobb at Lyme.

The episode begins when Wentworth first visits Uppercross. Both Henrietta and Louisa Musgrove are immediately attracted to him. Eventually his attentions settle on Louisa; and on a walk to Winthrop he favours her with a playfully solemn lecture on a hazel-nut – a lecture that comes very close to unintentional bathos on Jane Austen's part (p. 88). His moral seems to be that ladies, like nuts, should be firm. This is a proposition destined to have consequences in the novel more dire than one might readily suspect. For he encourages the same forthright impulses in Louisa that had years ago led Wentworth himself to want to

---

[18] But, again, there are those critics who seem to think that Anne's career in the novel simply plays no significant part in bringing the lovers together. Thus Firkins refers to the 'failure of the Elliot courtship to exert any influence upon the relations between Anne Elliot and Captain Wentworth', p. 131.

marry Anne in spite of Lady Russell's objections. He encourages Louisa to be something of a fellow romantic. And she is willing. She is 'now armed with the idea of merit in maintaining her own way . . .' (p. 94).

On the excursion to Lyme Louisa's new firmness has its consequences. She insists on jumping down a steep flight of steps on the Cobb, in spite of Wentworth's own advice against it. She jumps, before he is quite ready to catch her, and she falls to the pavement, lifeless. This is the single most violent event in any of the novels.[19] It has been much criticised, both because it seems so artificially contrived,[20] and because Jane Austen has wrung more melodrama out of the event than any doctor would be likely to think it deserved.[21] It is not even clear what she meant to accomplish by such a remarkable incident. It is true that Wentworth is so impressed with Anne's usefulness after the fall that it could not have done his love for her any harm.[22] But this seems hardly very important; he loves her anyway. It is also true that Louisa's accident eventually brings her together with Captain Benwick (pp. 164, 182–3), thereby freeing Wentworth for Anne; but surely this could have been accomplished with something short of a contusion.

The chief significance of the accident seems to lie not in its effect on Louisa, but in its effect on Wentworth. And the effect is clear. When Anne sees him later in Bath she notes that 'Time had changed him, or Louisa had changed him' (p. 176). He in turn tells her that the day on the Cobb 'has produced some effects however – has had some consequences which must be considered as the very reverse of frightful' (p. 182). This of course

---

[19] As the *Encyclopaedia Britannica* article on Jane Austen points out (14th ed.).

[20] For the interesting suggestion that there is even a hint of parody in Louisa's accident, see Lascelles, pp. 72–8.

[21] Bailey for instance refers to the 'absurdly extravagant results of Louisa's fall on the Cobb', p. 94.

[22] In making such suggestions the critics seem a little desperate. One thinks the episode 'discloses' Wentworth's heart to him because he sees Anne's 'calmness and courage at the time of Louisa's accident' (Thomson, p. 205). Another says that 'Wentworth has to rely on her . . . in meeting the crisis, and . . . [her] virtues are fuel to a flame rekindled' (Kennedy, p. 87). And another says, 'It is here that Wentworth is struck by Anne's presence of mind into regarding her personally again' (Mudrick, p. 238).

is a courtly hint at the engagement that freed him for Anne, but he also seems to be referring to a painful lesson he himself has learned. He has passed through the agony of self-discovery that has made him spiritually fit for her. Only at Lyme, he tells her, 'had he begun to understand himself'. He tells her that Louisa's accident taught him 'to distinguish between the steadiness of principle and the obstinacy of self-will' (p. 242). He has there-fore learned what Anne already knows: that, 'like all other qualities of the mind', firmness of character 'should have its proportions and limits' (p. 116). He is now not quite so roman-tic as he was. He has learned to make a compromise between the romantic impulses of youthful ardour and the cool demands of prudence.

This compromise makes him ready for Anne. Jane Austen is always very sketchy and unsure when it comes to the true hero's character development; but her scheme requires that there be such development. Therefore she has brought Wentworth to this point. He and Anne have come from opposite directions to share the same mature, balanced knowledge. It is prudent to look before you leap, but there is romance in leaping then. Anne has been made to look for eight years.

The two now stand on common ground in that scene we have come to expect as Jane Austen's plot nears its close. We are in the Musgrove's rooms at Bath; and there Anne receives from Wentworth's hand the letter that finally reunites them. Just what has brought them together in these rooms, at this particu-lar time, so that the destined can take place? Such details are scarcely important any more. Does it really matter much what streets, what time, what doors? Anne and Wentworth are simply ready in their hearts. Jane Austen has brought this about. Her steady, inexorable purpose is complete.

In the Chapter x she eventually cancelled from Volume II, she had gone to the trouble of creating some very clumsy plot business to bring Anne and Wentworth physically together. It seems that Admiral Croft has heard that Anne and Mr Elliot are to be married. He wants to know whether he should surrender his lease on Kellynch so that the two can live there, and enlists Wentworth to ask her. When the two are alone together in the Admiral's lodgings, Wentworth learns from her that the rumours are false. After what is described as a 'silent but very powerful dialogue' he bursts out with an audible 'Anne, my own dear Anne!', and the two are instantly 'reunited' (p. 258).[23] According to the *Memoir*, Jane Austen later came to feel that the chapter was 'tame and flat'[24] – although these seem hardly the words for the passage above; and she substituted for it the two chapters that appear in the published novel.

It is revealing that in the new chapters the plot business which brings the two lovers together has all but disappeared.[25] There is no lease to be discussed, no contrived closing and opening of doors. Rather, Anne begins to walk home from the White Hart, escorted by Charles Musgrove. They simply encounter Wentworth in the street. Charles has an appointment at a gunsmith's, and would just as soon turn Anne over to some other gentleman. He asks Wentworth, 'which way are you going?'; to which Wentworth answers, 'I hardly know', and agrees to go her way. 'In half a minute, Charles was at the bottom of Union-street again, and the other two proceeding together. . . .'

That slight matter of firearms is all that remains in the new chapter to bring the lovers together in a plausible way. Jane Austen has let everything else drift toward what seems dreamy, motiveless coincidence. The whole scene is plainly the last, playful little makeshift of a plot that has come to the end of its usefulness. Standing in the street in the presence of Charles, the two had given an 'obliging compliance for public view' that they were indeed willing to continue on without him; but the true drama is no longer public. Their 'spirits' are 'dancing in private rapture'. For that, no outward show is adequate, on their part or Jane Austen's. What matters is within, and no fiction can quite embody it. The movement of the two now toward a quiet and retired gravel walk is a mere public, fictive ceremony, like Mr Knightley's leading Emma to the dance: a fine, delicate, slight outward show of an 'action' which has all but disappeared inward,[26] where spirits are dancing in private rapture.

---

[23] The cancelled chapter immediately follows the novel in Chapman's text.

[24] *Memoir* (1871) p. 166.

[25] Litz suggests another reason for the revision: in the original ending the 'climax comes so close on the heels of Anne's visit to Mrs Smith that we are taken by surprise; the two critical scenes are so close together that they detract from each other', p. 158.

[26] Bailey observes that 'Anne Elliot's marriage is . . . less of a social

This beautiful, dream-like scene seems so clearly to reveal what have always been the aspirations of Jane Austen's art. The cancelled version is still rooted rather firmly in the comings and goings of a plot suitable to Bath; in the final version Jane Austen has perhaps come as close to being free of such a plot as she has ever been. Her art seems always to have been moving in this direction. Hence the relative casualness of *Emma* and *Persuasion*. The spiritual development of her heroines has always been her real theme. The clothes to make this visible as fiction have been stylish and beautiful; but surely for Jane Austen more than for most novelists they have been only clothes. In *Persuasion* we seem to see them dropping away – spirits dancing in private rapture. There is such great beauty in this: what Jane Austen seems always to have been striving for and could never quite achieve. The authors of the *Life and Letters* felt that, had the author of *Persuasion* lived, 'we might have had later master-pieces of a different type from that of their predecessors'.[27] Who knows? But there must always be clothes, at least for anyone who chooses to live and write in this world rather than the next. There is something characteristic in an offhand comment Jane Austen made in a letter criticising Miss O'Neill's performance in *Isabella*: 'I fancy I want something more than can be' (*Letters*, p. 415).

7

To Mr Collins's disappointment, good fiction, unlike some good sermons, does not generally give direct answers to moral questions. But the mellowness of *Persuasion* is nevertheless due partly to its having brought to some sort of conclusion a moral issue that has been nervously alive in Jane Austen's fiction from the beginning. It is the issue put in *Sense and Sensibility* as the 'old, well established grievance of duty against will, parent against child . . .' (p. 102). Her first novel begins with the heroine leaving home; in the course of her entrance into the world she seeks from others an answer to what is right and wrong. In each of the novels there is a mentor who comes eventually to provide

---

and more of a private and emotional event than those of the heroines' of *Pride and Prejudice* and *Emma*, p. 95.
[27] *Life and Letters*, pp. 335–6.

at least some moral guidance. Catherine Morland is adopted by the wise and sober Henry Tilney who emerges awkwardly in the course of the novel. He is followed by Colonel Brandon, the Gardiners, the stupendous, if fallible, Sir Thomas Bertram, and Mr Knightley. But who is there in *Persuasion*?

Anne, like the other heroines, is 'glad to have any thing marked out as a duty' (p. 33). We are told that Lady Elliot once gave her daughters such instruction in 'good principles' (p. 5); but that is not so important as the fact that she is now dead, and cannot teach Anne her duty in the novel itself. Not much moral guidance is going to come from Wentworth either. He is guilty of the hazel-nut lecture, and indeed has as much to learn as she does. Mrs Smith is a source of facts, statistics, and even profound truths; but, oddly, she offers no practical guidance of any kind. That seems to leave Admiral Croft as Anne's mentor. But he is not alone. An important and ignored aspect of this final novel is that Jane Austen has set up competition for him in the rather remote personage of Lady Russell. It is she who stands in the place of a mother and moral guide for Anne at the beginning, and Jane Austen never quite deposes her in favour of Admiral Croft, even at the conclusion.

But a subtle change is taking place in Jane Austen's art. When Lady Russell is first introduced, her author's treatment of her is curiously qualified and shifty – even wary (p. 11). As the novel progresses one continues to get this sense; and near the end Anne is made finally to face up squarely to a question that may have been bothering Jane Austen all along: was Lady Russell right, wrong, or something else, in persuading Anne eight years ago 'to believe the engagement a wrong thing' (p. 27)? The very title of the novel has made this an issue (see pp. 61, 244).

Anne's answer is ambivalent, and has tended to be many things to many readers.[28] It is difficult, though not impossible, to

---

[28] According to Whately's famous review 'we are left in doubt whether it would have been better for [Anne] or not, to accept the first proposal' (p. 23 n. 3 above). Another of the early reviewers thinks on the other hand that Jane Austen is woefully clear on this point: *Persuasion*, he says, 'contains parts of very great merit; among them, however, we certainly should not number its *moral*, which seems to be, that young people should always marry according to their own inclinations' (review cited p. 25 n. 8 above). Among modern critics, Harding thinks that Anne's attitude

find anything quite like this in Jane Austen's treatment of the moral guides in any of the previous novels. For Anne now decides that Lady Russell's persuasion was laudable in that it was 'exerted on the side of safety, not of risk' (p. 244). But at the same time Anne makes clear to Wentworth that she is not saying that Lady Russell 'did not err in her advice'. 'It was, perhaps, one of those cases in which advice is good or bad only as the event decides.' Indeed, the final chapter declares that, in the matter of opposing Wentworth and supporting Mr Elliot, Lady Russell had 'to admit that she had been pretty completely wrong'. But Anne nevertheless feels 'that I was perfectly right' in being guided by her. A 'strong sense of duty' demanded it. Lady Russell was, after all, 'in the place of a parent' (pp. 246–9).

This is apt to strike one as muddleheaded on Anne's part, and Jane Austen's too. But there is a finely-balanced, mature sense in it. Anne's thought seems to be that it was right to obey Lady Russell; and that it was also right to wait patiently for eight years only to find that Lady Russell was wrong. Thus Anne and her author seem in this late work to be questioning the conventional demands of 'duty', but without ever quite forsaking that profound obligation to obey them when they come. Not to obey such demands has never been less than an act of serious moral delinquency in Jane Austen's novels. Frank Churchill's faintly unwholesome character is revealed in his very name: he has forsaken his father's, and along with it he has forsaken his 'duty' to his father, as Mr Knightley points out (*Emma*, p. 146). His returning to Highbury and begging 'to be shewn the house which his father had lived in so long, and which had been the home of his father's father . . .' (p. 197) is therefore political, insincere, and utterly reprehensible. Perhaps we know all we need to know about the mysterious Mr Elliot when we read that in his youth he said, ' I wish I had any name but Elliot' (p. 203).

---

toward Lady Russell is left 'curiously unresolved' (p. 361); Yasmine Gooneratne refers to 'Anne's regrets at having conformed at eighteen to a social code she sees clearly at twenty-seven to be worthless and shallow', p. 166; and Firkins, an American, thinks the novel 'is meant to show that in the disposition of their hearts young people are often wiser than their . . . seniors', p. 119.

But in *Persuasion* this reverence for figures of conventional moral authority has been gently qualified. An idea that has appeared more or less unobtrusively in the novels from the beginning is now emerging into prominence. It is the idea that experience, rather than books or guardians, is finally the best teacher. Jane Austen's first heroine prepares herself for life by reading books (*Northanger Abbey*, p. 15). She then returns home at the conclusion with a fund of experience from the real world never touched by her reading, or by the chaperone who took her to Bath; a fund of experience impossible to communicate to anyone else. Her family will never understand the bitter lessons she has learned in the world. For them, 'good-will' is always going to have to supply 'the place of experience'. Her mother, having attempted without success to comprehend what has happened to her daughter at Bath and the abbey, makes a feeble comment that comes to be one of the profoundest truths in Jane Austen's fiction: 'Well, we must live and learn.'

This remark in the first novel lies at the very heart of *Persuasion*. All the heroines live and learn, of course; but only in *Persuasion* has Anne's experience in the world begun to impinge noticeably on the authority of her moral guardian, and of books, too. When she and Captain Benwick are discussing the relative merits of poetry and prose in easing the pangs of grief, this still naïve young lady solemnly recommends to him 'such works of our best moralists . . . as occurred to her at the moment as calculated to rouse and fortify the mind by the highest precepts, and the strongest examples of moral and religious endurances'. This excellent advice is worthy of Mr Collins, who is keen on the moral 'instruction' to be got by young ladies from reading Fordyce's Sermons. But what effect has Anne's advice had on her own sorrows? Like 'many other great moralists . . . she had been eloquent on a point in which her own conduct would ill bear examination' (p. 101). Slowly she comes to understand how little can be learned from moralists. When she and Captain Harville later discuss whether men or women are more constant in love, she makes a wiser comment, one that, for all its coyness, seems to have a special significance in *Persuasion*: 'I will not allow books to prove any thing' (p. 234).

Surely there is never much abstract intellectualising or moralising in Jane Austen's novels. What could be more foreign to her intelligence? The little there is often comes from the heroine's moral guide, or from Mr Collins. In *Persuasion* there is perhaps least of all. The sheer fact of having lived through whatever experiences life offers seems to have greater redemptive powers in this novel than would any amount of moralising by Lady Russell, by Mrs Smith, by Fordyce, or even by Jane Austen. *Persuasion* begins eight years after Anne and Wentworth have endured a painful separation; and it is those eight years themselves which are the most powerful force at work in the novel to bring the two lovers back together. Jane Austen is not even much interested in what happened during that time. She tells us little more than that Anne at twenty-seven thought along more romantic lines than she had at nineteen; and that eight years have 'passed over' Wentworth, 'and in foreign climes and in active service too . . .' (p. 179).

But those years have gone a long way toward replacing Lady Russell as the moral force that insures the happy end. Perhaps that is the real subject of this last mellow novel. It is true that Anne and Wentworth both pass through experiences in the plot that make them more fit for each other than they were at the outset. Jane Austen's art is founded on that from beginning to end. But in *Persuasion*, unlike any of the other novels, the romantic attachment already existed at the beginning. There is simply nothing like the agonising destruction and reformation of the heroine's psychology that is the very stuff of Jane Austen's previous work. The action of *Persuasion* seems merely the destined final ripening of fruit that has been growing unseen for eight years; merely the final, perfecting phase of an action that lies mainly outside the novel in the misty region of general 'experience'.

It is therefore no longer the heroine's spiritual mentor who seems instrumental in guiding her aright; it is more the sheer redemptive power of experience itself. To Anne, Lady Russell's advice is good or bad merely 'as the event decides'. Eventually it seems her advice was bad. But not when she gave it. There is a little wry humour in the fact that Anne never does get around to telling this kind, well-meaning lady the revealed truth concerning Mr Elliot (see pp. 220, 229). Does it really matter much anymore whether Lady Russell knows? Let her think what she likes. She means well. But Anne – perhaps Anne has passed her by.[29] Perhaps Jane Austen has too. The dutiful faith in the authority of some fellow human being that has been characteristic of Jane Austen's fiction from the start has gently given way to the idea that finally it may not be Lady Russell at all who can tell Anne what she needs to know. It may simply be time itself. Time will tell. We live and learn.

Hence in *Persuasion* the premium on patience, that virtue of farmers like Robert Martin and Mr Knightley. Nature has its ways, which only time will reveal. In this last novel there is so little demand made on human volition, with all its attendant pain. Mr Knightley had wished Emma to be guided by nature. If this is an ideal, the two lovers in *Persuasion* come very close to it indeed. When Anne has been providentially released from Mr Elliot, she tries 'to be calm, and leave things to take their course' (p. 221); and they do. Nature is moving in her calm, beneficent way. After all those officious authorial intrusions into the plot, the ending of the novel does seem remarkably natural, and inevitable. The fruit has always been safely implied in the seed. A charming little scene in the first volume seems to contain the whole of this last novel, its beginning and its natural end. Anne is seen walking a little despondently through the fields in autumn, and she comes to an enclosure, where there are ploughs at work – ploughs that 'spoke the farmer', who is, of course, 'meaning to have spring again' (p. 85).

8

In the development of Jane Austen's art, *Persuasion* is both an end and a fascinating beginning. Something is happening to Sir Walter's old, established home, and to his author's 'home' as well: those novels concerned with '3 or 4 Families in a Country Village'. It is time now for Sir Walter to move, and Jane Austen too. The 'old, well established grievance of duty against will, parent against child' is dying away. Sir Walter's place in society is now unsettled. He has been forced to leave his ancestral

---

[29] Sheila Kaye-Smith makes the interesting comment that Lady Russell is 'almost the only important character' in the novels 'who does not *present herself* in speech'. She 'seems, in fact, imprisoned in the narrative – we get no personal escape in speech', pp. 194, 196.

home. A new society is growing up around him, with modern minds and manners. Sailors, those strange creatures willing to live unsettled lives on a fluid surface, are returning from the war, bringing chaos to the old social order. The future seems to be theirs. Admiral and Mrs Croft move into Sir Walter's old home, where they are seen taking an interest in their 'new possessions' (p. 73); and in a memorable and deeply moving passage in this last novel we find Admiral Croft calling Kellynch 'home' (p. 92). Surely that marks an end for Jane Austen, and a beginning.

Her art is moving now toward the sea. True, we have seen a few sailors before. In *Mansfield Park* there is Fanny's brother, and a fine episode set in Portsmouth. But Jane Austen's has characteristically been an inland art, of families in a gentle country village. Emma says she has never even seen the sea. But now *Persuasion* and the fragment 'Sanditon' that follows it seem to be surrendering to ropes, sea breezes and sailors. This last novel strikes out for Lyme; and the heroine marries, not a pro-pertied country gentleman like Colonel Brandon, Darcy or Mr Knightley, not a man of the cloth like Henry Tilney or Edmund Bertram, but the successful and rather cocksure one-time captain of a frigate.

He does indeed have a brother who is curate of Monkford; and perhaps in any of the previous novels it is the brother who would have been the object of the heroine's affections. But in *Persuasion* the clergy has been eclipsed by the military, just as Mary Crawford would have wished (see *Mansfield Park*, pp. 91–4). When Captain Wentworth arrives at Uppercross the Reverend Charles Hayter seems lucky to get Henrietta Musgrove even by default. In 'Sanditon' again the sea shows its deep power. The heroine's society has been 'long limitted to one small circle' surrounding her parents' country cottage (*Minor Works*, p. 373); and shortly after the piece begins she is whisked away by a stranger to the resort of Sanditon on the sea – a sea described as 'dancing & sparkling in Sunshine & Freshness' (p. 384). A matter-of-fact observation of Jane Austen's in a letter of 1801 thus makes a good enough motto for the course of her career: '. . . the prospect of spending future summers by the Sea or in Wales is very delightful. . . . It must not be generally known however that I am not sacrificing a great deal in quitting the Country . . .' (*Letters*, p. 103).

Her interest in the sea and sailors is but one indication of a new, wistful, and never quite fully developed romanticism in her work. We should be careful not to make too much of this, nor too little. The family biographers of her sailor brothers point out that she has always been romantic where sailors are concerned;[30] and now at the end of her career she is being romantic about sailors and a good deal else. In *Persuasion* she is thinking of Lyme and nearby 'Pinny, with its green chasms between romantic rocks' (p. 95). She is listening, with something less than unbounded sympathy it is true, to Captain Benwick, who is full of Byronic suffering and Byron's poetry; and to Sir Edward Denham, who rants of romantic novels that display 'the progress of strong Passion from the first Germ of incipient Susceptibility to the utmost Energies of Reason half-dethroned' ('Sanditon', *Minor Works*, p. 403).

Sir Edward seems to be all for cultivating the passions at the expense of reason, and Jane Austen is laughing at him, of course. He must have had his opposite number sixty-five years earlier in Charlotte Lennox's Doctor of Divinity, who announces that 'romances' 'give new Fire to the Passions of Revenge and Love; two Passions which . . . it is one of the severest Labours of Reason and Piety to suppress. . . .'[31] Jane Austen doubtless laughed at the Doctor too. At no time does she ever have a clear-cut allegiance either to 'passion' or 'reason' – to use that pair of counter-words bandied about so briskly in the quotations above. If she had ever had anything so uncomplicated to say concerning the opposition between the two, she would not have been Jane Austen. She would not have created double heroines who embody characteristics associated with both of those terms. Elinor would never have been made to hold out her hand to Willoughby; Elinor and Marianne would never have come to their final happiness on the same plot of ground; Elizabeth and Jane would never have settled so close to each other after marriage; Emma and her Harriet would never have ended sharing, undoubtedly, the same apples, if not the same table.

---

[30] *Jane Austen's Sailor Brothers*, p. 5.

[31] *The Female Quixote* (London: Oxford University Press, 1970) IX xi 380. For Jane Austen's mention of the novel see p. 13 n. 25 above.

But it is nevertheless true that in her last works Jane Austen is just a little more sympathetic to Sir Edward's general, if asyntactical, drift than she was when she began. She is just a little more receptive to the new century. In *Persuasion* there is that scene in which Anne takes shelter in a shop out of the rain. She is soon tempted to look out into the street, and wonders why. Is it to see whether the rain has stopped, or to look for Captain Wentworth? She muses that 'one half of her' seems always to have been 'so much wiser than the other half, or always suspecting the other of being worse than it was' (p. 175). These two halves have jostled their way through all Jane Austen's novels, as they must through all human activity. It is just that the wiser half is now giving a little ground; the wiser half is no longer quite so suspicious of the other.[32] Later there is a passage in which Anne is thinking affectionately of Wentworth; and her thoughts conclude with the short paragraph:

> Prettier musings of high-wrought love and eternal constancy, could never have passed along the streets of Bath, than Anne was sporting with from Camden-place to Westgate-buildings. It was almost enough to spread purification and perfume all the way (p. 192).

There is just a hint of self-mockery in this, as if Jane Austen were slightly embarrassed that she has abandoned her heroine, and herself, to such romantic sentiment. The mockery is there, but is Jane Austen's heart truly in it anymore? Surely in this passage she herself is being a little sentimental! That has not happened often before. She tended toward prudence in her youth; and she has learned a little about romance as she has grown older.

In *Persuasion* and 'Sanditon' she is indeed flirting coyly with romance; and we see the effect in the astonishing exuberance with which she treats her material. Until now her subject has usually been those three or four families in a country village; her medium has been a little bit of ivory. There has always been a prim, careful constraint in her art. Now she seems tempted

---

[32] '*Persuasion* tranquilly states Jane Austen's newly achieved ability to accept the coexistence of opposed characteristics in a single personality . . .', Yasmine Gooneratne, *Jane Austen*, p. 183.

to let her imagination range a little more freely, a little less rigidly under the control of the social and aesthetic proprieties. That favourite writer of her youth, William Gilpin, says that a painter may relax the rules of his art when his subject is a body of water, like the sea; and perhaps Jane Austen feels the same as she now moves toward Lyme and the Sussex coast: '. . . the painter may take great liberties . . . in his representation of water. It is, in many cases, under no rule, that we are acquainted with; or under rules so lax, that the imagination is left very much at large'.[33]

In *Persuasion* and 'Sanditon' there are indeed some signs of an imagination left pretty much at large. That constrained, efficient, careful following of a neat fictional plan – where is it now? The very style of 'Sanditon' is self-indulgently expansive, impatient of restraint. Jane Austen's sly, tight-lipped prose has given way to phrases like 'planned & built, & praised & puffed, & raised', 'made many a Gazer gaze again', and 'so many to share in the shame & the blame' (pp. 371, 422, 420).[34] There are also signs of something – shall we call it raucousness? – that is hardly characteristic of the earlier novels. What is it that the erratic Admiral Croft just misses while out driving in his gig? He just misses running 'foul of a dung-cart'! – a vehicle, and tenor, far from familiar in Jane Austen's prose before now. In 'Sanditon' Arthur Parker describes himself as 'very subject to Perspiration' (*Minor Works*, p. 416); and Miss Parker, on examining her brother's sprained ankle, declares, the 'play of your Sinews a *very* little affected: – barely perceptible' (p. 408) – a comment Willoughby would never have dreamed of while bending over Marianne even if he had been related to her.

There may be more open heartiness and unrepressed good health in these last two works than in all the rest of Jane Austen's fiction together. In *Sense and Sensibility* the heroine's true love is encased in the constitutional safeguard of a flannel waistcoat; and who could imagine the same on Captain

---

[33] *Observations, on Several Parts of England* . . . (1808), I 108 (see p. 17 n. 30 above).

[34] It is perhaps a little misleading to quote from the manuscript of 'Sanditon' as evidence of Jane Austen's changing 'style', for the work as we have it is an incomplete first draft, somewhat revised. On this matter see Southam, *Literary Manuscripts*, pp. 101–2.

Wentworth? In *Emma* the heroine's father is named Woodhouse, and he sits querulously in his house by a fire; his counterpart in 'Sanditon' is named Heywood, and he first appears in a hay field (*Minor Works*, pp. 364–5). And his daughter's attitude toward invalids is less than sympathetic, to put it mildly. In the presence of the delicate Miss Parker,

> Charlotte could perceive no symptoms of illness which she, in the boldness of her own good health, w^d not have undertaken to cure, by putting out the fire, opening the Window, & disposing of the Drops & the salts by means of one or the other (p. 413).[35]

It seems right that the heroine of this last, sprawling, robust, uninhibited work should be one of fourteen children.

It is as if Jane Austen's Pegasus had for all these years been tightly reined in, and now has begun to break out into a frisky canter. Elizabeth Bennet was content to trot around the grounds of Pemberley with her friend, Mrs Gardiner, in a pony cart: but now her author would rather ride with Admiral Croft, whose haphazard driving, Anne thinks affectionately, is 'no bad representation of the general guidance' of his family affairs (p. 92). Then again in the first sentence of 'Sanditon' a carriage which has been made to 'quit the high road, & attempt a very rough Lane' is upset.[36] Jane Austen is ready for something off the beaten track now, something a little romantically devil-may-care, a little dangerous.

And so as her career closes she leaves that well-known road Catherine walked in the first novel. Jane Austen is drawn to the trackless sea, and to those who have braved the sea. She is drawn to open-hearted and casual sailors; Colonel Brandon and Edward Ferrars were hardly that. She is drawn to a sailor's unsettled, irregular and fluid life; a life hardly like that at

---

[35] When Jane Austen wrote this passage her own illness was far advanced. See *Memoir* (1871) pp. 192–3.

[36] Jane Austen has come a long way indeed. In the second chapter of her first novel, she thus describes, with tongue in cheek, her heroine's first journey to Bath: 'It was performed with suitable quietness and uneventful safety. Neither robbers nor tempests befriended them, nor one lucky overturn to introduce them to the hero.'

Mansfield Park. She is drawn to a sailor's craving for raw, unpredictable experience. She seems now a little like Anne before the concert at Bath, 'wearied of such a state of stagnation, sick of knowing nothing, and fancying herself stronger because her strength was not tried' (p. 180). Like Anne, she displays now a true admiration for men who struggle with 'difficulties, and privations, and dangers'; men who 'are always labouring and toiling, exposed to every risk and hardship' (p. 233) – a description that just does not fit even Mr Knightley. She is drawn to the potential beauty there was in Wentworth's early, reckless ardour – an ardour that is never displayed by any other reputable male in the earlier novels. If Jane Austen had been able to go on, who knows who would have won Charlotte Heywood in 'Sanditon'? A widowed Willoughby might have reappeared off the Sussex coast.

Finally, Jane Austen is drawn to the beauty there is in having enriched one's life by passing through danger. Admiral Croft and his wife have been to the East Indies and back again. They are weather-beaten now, and deserve, as perhaps Mr Woodhouse never did, to draw in their chairs by the fire at last:

> We are always meeting with some old friend or other; the streets full of them every morning; sure to have plenty of chat; and then we get away from them all, and shut ourselves into our lodgings, and draw in our chairs . . . (p. 170).

Mrs Smith too has lived very much in the world, and has come from it crippled, but wise. In *Persuasion* and 'Sanditon' we see this again and again. Captain Benwick has had his sorrow, Louisa her fall. She is 'altered: there is no running or jumping about, no laughing or dancing. . . .' These two have been hurt by romance, but they are better for it. It has brought them together.[37] Benwick sits at her elbow now, whispering to her, all day long (p. 218). Captain Harville likewise has come back lame from the sea, and now lives content on the edge of it. 'He drew, he varnished, he carpentered, he glued; he made toys for the children . . . and if every thing else was done, sat down to his large fishing-net at one corner of the room' (p. 99).

---

[37] Perhaps not for Firkins. He writes that Jane Austen 'snatches Louisa from Captain Wentworth by the crude expedient of . . . [an] attachment between Louisa and another man', p. 117.

Working on his little bit of ivory means all the more for his having passed over the deeps to do it.

His little house is buffeted by winter storms. Indeed we seem always aware of the wind in these last two works. It blows through one of the Admiral's cupboards at Bath, just as it had at North Yarmouth (p. 170). In 'Sanditon' the house of Mr Parker's forefathers was built in a hollow sheltered from the wind and sea; but he has built a new one – Trafalgar House! – in an exposed place so close to the sea that the wind rocks him and his wife in their bed at night, and they can experience what he calls the 'Grandeur' of a storm (*Minor Works*, pp. 379–380).[38] The grandeur of a storm? What would Colonel Brandon think of that? How remarkable that the Jane Austen we know should have veered at the end of her career even slightly toward romantic weather. How remarkable that pervading her last works is an exhilaration in the face of impending storms, and impending danger. Look before you leap – but leap then. In *Persuasion* danger even has its place in the heroine's final happiness for the first time. Anne has married a sailor. She is at the mercy of the restless sea; and in the next-to-last sentence she is given the further prospect of living the rest of her life in the dread of a future war.

And so Jane Austen, who was at least a little prudent in her youth, now has begun to throw her emphasis on – we had better call it romance. Whatever it is that has thinly existed all along, since Elinor Dashwood held out her hand so long ago. Jane Austen has come overland from her country villages to begin

---

[38] Jane Austen may have had in mind the following lines from Cowper's *The Task*:

> . . . th' abode
> Of our forefathers – a grave whisker'd race,
> But tasteless. Springs a palace in its stead,
> But in a distant spot; where, more expos'd,
> It may enjoy th' advantage of the north,
> And aguish east, till time shall have transform'd
> Those naked acres to a shelt'ring grove (III, 767–73).

For Jane Austen's reading of Cowper, see *Letters*, p. 39 (18 Dec 1798); and the 'Biographical Notice', *Novels*, V (*Northanger Abbey, Persuasion*) p. 7. Lascelles quotes these lines in discussing 'Sanditon', p. 46 (see also Edward Malins, *English Landscaping and Literature, 1660–1840* (London: Oxford University Press, 1966) pp. 100–1).

a new home that is exposed to the weather on the edge of the sea. Keats and Byron are finding new, romantic inspiration there:

> O'er the glad waters of the dark blue sea,
> Our thoughts as boundless, and our souls as free,
> Far as the breeze can bear, the billows foam,
> Survey our empire, and behold our home!

Anne and Captain Benwick have read these lines (p. 109 and Index). They seem very far indeed from the general spirit of Jane Austen's art, that carefully conceived, prim intellectual plan – that little bit of ivory. But these lines are not that far from the spirit of her last, remarkable work. Around her has risen a hubbub of new voices, new enthusiasms, new threats to the old, settled values by which Sir Thomas, Mr Woodhouse, Sir Walter and their author have lived their settled indoor lives. Winds are blowing in, from the sea.

INDEX

CHATHAM HOUSE,
SCHOOL, RAMSGATE.
LIBRARY.